TWO
SECONDS
UNDER THE
WORLD

TWO

TERROR COMES TO AMERICA—

SECONDS

THE CONSPIRACY BEHIND THE

UNDER THE

WORLD TRADE CENTER BOMBING

WORLD

JIM DWYER
AND
DAVID KOCIENIEWSKI
DEIDRE MURPHY
PEG TYRE

Crown Publishers, Inc.
New York

Grateful acknowledgment is made to Simon & Schuster for permission to reprint an excerpt from "Remorse for Intemperate Speech" from *The Poems of W. B. Yeats: A New Edition,* edited by Richard J. Finneran, copyright 1933 by Macmillian Publishing Co., copyright renewed 1961 by Bertha Georgie Yeats.

Published by Crown Publishers, Inc., 201 East 50th Street, New York, New York, 10022.

CROWN is a trademark of Crown Publishers, Inc.

Book design by Mercedes Everett

Manufactured in the United States of America

Library of Congress Cataloging in Publication Data

Two seconds under the world: terror comes to America—the conspiracy
  behind the World Trade Center bombing / Jim Dwyer . . . [et al.]. —
  1st ed.
    1. World Trade Center bombing, New York, N.Y., 1993.
  2. Terrorism—New York (N.Y.)
  HV6432.T88   1994
  364.1'09747'1—dc20
  94-21576

ISBN 0-517-59767-5

10 9 8 7 6 5 4 3 2 1

First Edition

CONTENTS

CAST OF
CHARACTERS

THE SUSPECTS

Sheik Omar Abdel-Rahman, 55, an Islamic cleric and spiritual leader of Gama al-Islamiya, a Muslim fundamentalist group seeking to overthrow Egypt's secular government and install an Islamic state; accused head of a terrorist network in America.

El Sayyid Nosair, 37, an Egyptian acquitted of murdering militant Rabbi Meir Kahane in 1990 but imprisoned on related weapons and assault charges; a follower of Rahman, accused of being a top member of the terrorist cell.

Ibrahim El-Gabrowny, 42, Nosair's cousin; accused of being a core member of the cell; also a cousin of Mohammad Salameh, one of the World Trade Center bombers.

Siddig Ibrahim Siddig Ali, 32, a Sudanese computer and security specialist; aide and translator for the sheik; ringleader behind the plot to blow up the United Nations, the Lincoln and Holland tunnels, and the George Washington Bridge.

Mahmud Abouhalima, 33, the Egyptian-born New York City cabdriver accused of organizing the World Trade Center bombing. Former aide and driver for the sheik. Known as Mahmud the Red. Prosecutors called him the "Gentle Terrorist."

Mohammad A. Salameh, 25, the mostly unemployed Jordanian of Palestinian descent who drove the bomb-laden rental van into the World Trade Center parking garage. Later went back to the rental office for a refund.

Nidal A. Ayyad, 25, a naturalized American citizen, born in Kuwait to Palestinian parents; a chemical engineer and Rutgers University graduate who helped build the bomb.

Ahmad Ajaj, 27, a Palestinian with ties to Fatah and Hamas; arrested entering the country at Kennedy International Airport with a bogus passport and bomb-making books in his luggage. Was in prison when the bomb went off.

Ramzi Yousef, 25, explosives expert imported from Afghanistan to make the World Trade Center bomb; arrived on the same flight from Pakistan as Ajaj but escaped detection. Vanished on the night of the bombing.

Abdul "Aboud" Yasin, 33, American-born of Iraqi descent; an engineering student and Salameh's roommate; questioned by the FBI after the bombing and fled to Iraq the next day.

THE INFORMANT

Emad Salem, 43, a former Egyptian army colonel who posed as the sheik's security adviser while working as an informant for the FBI; star witness against a dozen men accused of plotting bombings and assassinations.

THE GOVERNMENT

J. Gilmore Childers, 38, the lead prosecutor in the World Trade Center bombing and deputy chief of the Manhattan U.S. Attorney's Criminal Division.

Henry J. DePippo, 33, Childers's co-prosecutor and also a deputy chief in the Criminal Division.

John Anticev, 35, FBI special agent assigned to the joint New York Police Department–FBI Anti-Terrorist Task Force.

Nancy Floyd, 32, FBI counterintelligence officer assigned to the New York City regional bureau.

THE DEAD

William Macko, 47, of Bayonne, New Jersey.
Stephen Knapp, 48, of Staten Island, New York.
Monica Smith, 35, of Seaford, New York.
Robert Kirkpatrick, 61, of Suffern, New York.
John DiGiovanni, 45, of Valley Stream, New York.
Wilfredo Mercado, 37, of Brooklyn, New York.

ACKNOWLEDGMENTS

Thousands of people were affected personally by the bombing and murders at the World Trade Center, and many of them spoke with the authors. We are particularly grateful to people who are associated with the Port Authority of New York and New Jersey, either as employees or as family members of people who were killed in the explosion: Robert DiChiara, William Lavin, Louise Knapp, Stephen Knapp, Jr., Denise Knapp, Timothy Lang, Carl Selinger, Edward Smith, Stanley Brezenoff, Tom Cancielleri, Vito DeLea, Mark Marchese, Allan Morrison, Charles Maikish, Leslie E. Robertson, Lloyd Schwab, and Peter Yerkes.

The participants in the investigation and trial of the men accused of the bombing often provided assistance in understanding the events around the conspiracy or the trial. If they were not able to help, they at least were unfailingly cordial. We thank J. Gilmore Childers, Henry DePippo, Lev Dassin, Kevin Duffy, Michael Garcia, Hassen Ibn Abdellah, Atiq Ahmed, Jesse Berman, Austin Campriello, Clarence Faines III, Ronald Kuby, William Kunstler, Imram Mirza, Hamed Newbawy, and Robert Precht.

Also, we are grateful to Pete Berry, John Boland, John Clifford, Timothy Dowling, James Fox, James Esposito, Ed Gabriel, Anthony Guagdano, Roger Hayes, Charles Hirsch, Ray Kelly, Paul Maniscalco, Robert Morgenthau, Sam Nordmark, John O'Brien, Pers Anders Persson, John Pritchard, Richard Sheirer, Paul Sokol, Gloria Sturzenacker, Barbara Thompson, and Bonita Zelman.

The authors leaned heavily on the work and insights of our colleagues at *New York Newsday* and *Newsday*. We especially thank Russell Ben-Ali, Patricia Cohen, Anthony DeStefano, Donna Dietrich, Don Forst, Rich Galant, Joseph Gambardello, Molly Gordy, Debbie Henley, Kirsten Hamilton, Wendell Jamieson, Julio Laboy, Bob Liff, Linda Lutzak, Tony Marro, Kevin McCoy, Michael Moss, Michele Parente, Shirley Perlman, Kate Phillips, William K. Rashbaum, Knut Royce, Ray Sanchez, Susan Sachs, Jeff Schamberry, and James Toedtman. In every reporting task, the staff of *New York Newsday* is fortunate to have the excellent assistance and insights of the *Newsday* librarians, Karen VanRossen, Christine Baird, Donna Mendes, Karen Magruder, and Caroline Brooks.

A number of colleagues from other organizations provided help and advice. We thank Richard Bernstein, Ralph Blumenthal, Jeanne King, Allison Mitchell, Mary Murphy, Deborah Pines, Charles Sennott, Mary B.W. Tabor, and Tim Weiner. We are particularly grateful to Larry Numeister of the Associated Press, who provided in-depth materials and perspective on the trial.

Among others who were personally helpful were Tom Curran, Kevin M. Doyle, Pauline Flanagan, David Groff, Kevin P. Hayes, Joseph Hurley, Flip Brophy, and Lisa "Wagner" Wager. We are grateful to them and to Cathy Dwyer, Phil and Mary Dwyer, Peter Blauner and Fran Tyre, Denise Barricklow, Theodora Martens, and Denise Lanchantim.

In addition, many people provided invaluble information for this book and we can thank them only by not naming them.

Out of Ireland have we come.
Great hatred, little room,
Maimed us at the start
I carry from my mother's womb
A fanatic heart.

From *Remorse for Intemperate Speech*,
W. B. Yeats

PROLOGUE

PARK ROW, NEW YORK CITY
FEBRUARY 26, 1993
12:17:35 P.M.

He was a stranger, same as anyone else, just a record shopper in a record shop, walking in a long, smooth stride that left no wake. He could not be forgotten because he had not been noticed. Odd, in a way, that such a man could pass unheeded. He was six feet two inches tall, with shoulders as broad and sturdy as a steel beam. Curly red hair and beard made a bushy wreath around his face, and his nose was splashed with tiny freckles. But the low-level clamor of even a normal day in New York makes shadows of millions. Mahmud Abouhalima could vanish with ease. No one would remember seeing the tall, muscular, redheaded Egyptian in J&R Music.

Of course, the classical-music annex of J&R is a peculiarly calming place—perhaps because it is two flights of vinyl steps up from a Manhattan sidewalk that rumbles with crowds. Inside the store, the room is carpeted with music that transports. Spilling from big stereo speakers might be a fugue composed at a harpsichord three centuries ago and half a world away, a symphony written in the salons of Vienna, perhaps a sonata that ripened in the mountains of Bavaria. It was a gray winter Friday in Manhattan, the raw air drilling into the bones, and snow showers prodded people on the streets at a faster pace than usual. But inside J&R, the music lapped warmly along the aisles. Every few yards, someone was bent over the display racks, fingering the compact discs, flipping forward and backward through the centuries.

The big redheaded man had strolled past the browsers to the picture window that overlooked Park Row and much of lower Manhattan. Mahmud Abouhalima lingered at the window, gazing at streets he knew well. After all, he had been the model of a New York taxi driver: a confident, breezy man who could yak it up with the customers about politics in the Middle East while spinning across town on two wheels. Of course, the ideal Hollywood cabbie talked with a gonging accent that to the more practiced ear would suggest a Jew from Brooklyn or the Bronx. Mahmud Abouhalima's English was accented, yes. With fragrances of Yiddish, absolutely not.

Everyone talked oddly in New York, or so it seemed—so much so that the city, babbling and quarreling and noisy, at times is barely recognized as part of the United States. But as Mahmud Abouhalima looked out the window, he saw America. Indeed, in one way or another, every important piece of the country's history had unfolded in a few acres in Manhattan, within view of that window. Directly ahead of him was City Hall Park, a cataract in the steel heights of vertical Manhattan. Once the park had been a public commons grazed by cattle for the colony founded by the Dutch. Later it was a prison yard. In the old days, people were hanged here. Now it was a trampled patch of grass, littered, undistinguished by shrub or care. A few pigeons airlifted tidbits of winter trash.

By turning to the right, Abouhalima could see City Hall—a delicate palace, startling in its grace for New York, where few structures age with dignity. The front steps were partially blocked by a platform set up for some ceremony. It was up those steps that the remains of Abraham Lincoln had been carried more than a century ago. New York had not been much of a Union town during the Civil War—the immigrant Irish raised bloody riots against the federal draft—but when Lincoln lay in state, a half-million people paraded through the City Hall rotunda to pay respects to the assassinated Emancipator. And colonial New York had not been overly zealous in opposition to the British crown, but twenty years before Lincoln's birth, George Washington took the oath of office as the nation's first president a few blocks away, on Wall Street. Even before Washington, at the same spot, a newspaperman named Zenger had been cleared of sedition for writing against the British throne, establishing the principle that truth may be spoken freely to power; and, there, too, the Bill of Rights was adopted by the first U.S. Congress. Few great moments in the life of the nation had gone unmarked on the southern tip of Manhattan.

In modern times, this tiny speck of land served as the great stage for the American Century. Today, Mahmud Abouhalima had a seat front and center. Directly across the park is Broadway and the finish line for the city's unmatched ticker-tape parades. Icons walk here, in the splendid loneliness of adulation. Charles Lindbergh, the great aviator, and his successor in outer space, astronaut John Glenn. The V-J Day Parade, led by General Douglas MacArthur. The 1969 world champion New York Mets baseball team. Here, too, Nelson Mandela received an enormous greeting in 1990, after twenty-seven years in South African prisons.

Even today, when New York City is frayed at the seams, lower Manhattan remains a place that dares to speak for a nation from which it has drifted into a cranky estrangement. True, the country's enemies are no longer cut from such bold marble as a Hitler, a Stalin, a Khrushchev. But if the New World Order provides foes mysterious in shape, strange in tone, New York provides familiar ground and ritual to celebrate the nation's triumphs. So it was here that the hostages taken by fundamentalists in Iran were given the classic New York ticker-tape welcome after they were freed in 1981; a decade later, it was here that the city honored the soldiers of all nations who fought in the Gulf War against Iraq.

And on this cold winter afternoon, as Mahmud Abouhalima looked into the great pond of American history, a new image was mirrored back. Mahmud could see a soldier's face, fixed for an instant in the plate glass when the light of the dull day bounced off the window at J&R. A proud guerrilla who had fought a holy war for Allah in Afghanistan, turning back the mighty army of the infidel Soviet Union—yes, with U.S. guns and money and know-how. But the first weapon had been Islamic bravery. He himself had searched the fields of Afghanistan for Soviet mines, armed only with a thin reed and nerves of steel. The United States thought the war was over, with the Soviet Union not only gone from Afghanistan, but an entire empire dissolved in a puddle of failure. Well, the Cold War could end. *Jihad,* the Holy War, does not. The Muslims still had the American weapons and know-how. They still had their mission. The FBI could chase him all over the world, and that would not change. They could subpoena every Egyptian living in New York or New Jersey. They'd tried that two months ago and got nothing. They listened to his telephone. He was still a step ahead, because his was a holy mission blessed by Allah, the merciful, the beneficent.

Anyway, if things were going according to social custom, no one in J&R even knew he was in the store. That soldier's face was a mere ghost, trapped for an instant in the window. For all anyone could know, he was just an ex-cabbie, now a chauffeur for a limousine service that carried passengers from the mighty banks that line Wall Street to airports, to homes in leafy suburbs. And he was about to take his place among those who, at this place, had made history in America.

For a clear view to the south, he had to stand in the far right corner of the window. His broad back was against the Mozart recordings, the biggest display in the store, comprising eight hundred CDs. Two big Advent stereo speakers were attached to the walls just over his head. A pale blue light glowed from a neon sign fixed outside the window. His own image still shimmered on the plate glass, but Abouhalima looked past it. There. To his left were thick steel stalks, the base of the Twin Towers of the World Trade Center. The walls of the store danced with music, but Abouhalima listened for something else, a sound then unknown to New York, an instrument never played in the country.

He was a cabdriver standing in a record store, at a pivotal point in twentieth-century American history: the settled certainties of the Cold War were about to give way to the supple shadows of the New World Order. Remarkably, Abouhalima and his comrades straddled both eras.

Just eleven days earlier, a man who had fought in the same war with Abouhalima had parked at a traffic light in Langley, Virginia. When cars had started pulling up to the headquarters of the Central Intelligence Agency, the soldier had emerged from his car with an AK-47 assault rifle and murdered two CIA employees. The killer fled to Afghanistan and vanished into the mountains and deserts of the only country in the world where CIA-sponsored freedom fighters had enjoyed victory during the Cold War. The assassinations at Langley had stirred tremendous interest in the media for all of two or three days, until the press sensed that the public's anger over the incident had abated. Live by the sword, and what can you expect?

Two and a half years earlier, Rabbi Meir Kahane had been assassinated in a Manhattan hotel. It had seemed, at the time, like an occupational hazard. Kahane was a zealot and hater of Arabs, a barred member of the Israeli parliament who was generally disliked by the American Jewish establishment. The contempt was mutual.

Kahane's murder was a two-day outrage that had no legs. The police quickly announced that it was the work of a lone psychotic gunman, although boxes of evidence collected from his house suggested otherwise. But the lone-gunman scenario concorded nicely with the foreign-policy interests of the U.S. government. The Kahane killing occurred just as Operation Desert Shield was being transformed into Operation Desert Storm. The United States was marshaling its resources for war in the Persian Gulf, the first utterance by the world's only superpower in the post–Cold War era. And the United States desperately wanted the backing of the major Arab nations and petro-states—so the State Department did not need the killing of a rabbi despised by the Arab world to be transformed into an international political incident.

Abouhalima knew all about the Kahane killing. He told people that he had been waiting outside the hotel as the wheel man for the shooter. The getaway was foiled when the gunman jumped into the wrong taxi. The getaway had been botched, but the police and the FBI so bungled the investigation—conveniently, as history would have it—that there was no chance that they could or would implicate Abouhalima or anyone other than the gunman in the murder of Kahane.

And so, low farce was the overture to the high drama that Abouhalima and his colleagues had planned for today. This action would be different; no one would write it off as the sort of expected casualties—the CIA workers killed mysteriously, the radical Zionist rabbi assassinated after a speech. A new epoch in American history was opening, and everyone would have to pay attention.

Mahmud Abouhalima stared out the window of J&R. That view of the Twin Towers yields a startling piece of geometry: from the prospect of J&R, the Towers appear to form a V. And rising between the two legs of the V is the steeple of St. Paul's Chapel— the oldest building in New York and George Washington's own church. The steeple, eloquent and ancient, ascends just high enough between the two towers to make a center line.

Two towers and one steeple, a perfect gunsight.

Beneath Abouhalima, the people on the street, buried in coats, shrouded by speed and hustle, passed by, indistinct, unknown. Any second now.

PART
THE BOMB
ONE

1

FEBRUARY 26, 1993:
TWO SECONDS

THE WORLD TRADE CENTER
NEW YORK CITY
12:17:35 P.M.

The World Trade Center sways in the breeze and buzzes in cyberspace. The Center covers sixteen acres and comprises seven buildings, but everyone sees just two. The Twin Towers are a quarter-mile high; to keep them from budging, they are bolted to a vein of rock one billion years old. Young bond traders, eight hundred feet up and invisible to the world, finger a few keys at a computer, firing electrons across the globe; an instant later, a fortune of money washes ashore in a computer on another continent. All the buildings of the Trade Center were built to shelter people who swap and finagle and barter and bargain and deal and gamble and hedge and bluff. Beneath those giant stalks are the world commodity exchanges. From the foot of Manhattan come deals and contracts that shape lives. A rice farmer in Louisiana will make money or not, depending on how the contracts for rice futures are moving at the Trade Center. A miner in South Africa will have work this summer or not, depending on how the commodities traders eye the stockpile of precious metals.

To say the Trade Center is, by population, a small city on the order of Dearborn, Michigan, is a good start, but does not begin to describe the place and its reach. Yes, fifty thousand tenants work there, and another eighty thousand people visit, heaving in and out on the rhythms of the day. All these souls are collected on a campus higher than it is wide.

At the bottom is a jail, and at this moment on February 26, 1993, Calvin Dudley sits sullenly in the police precinct at 1 World Trade Center, having been caught in a Woolworth's on the shopping concourse, supposedly stuffing housewares into his pockets. The Port Authority police who hover around the concourse were called. They cuffed him, led him down a staircase to their offices, then parked him in a cell. He is about to be booked.

Eighty floors above them, in the same building, a clerk makes account entries on a $5 billion sale of U.S. Treasury notes, executed by the Cantor Fitzgerald Company on behalf of the United States government. Every minute of every day, the United States government spends $6 million more than it receives in revenue. It manages this trick by borrowing vast, vast piles of money. By virtue of its dominance in the treasuries market, Cantor Fitzgerald arranges sixty to seventy percent of the loans to the government.

The Trade Center is home to the bookmakers of the world, the touts of the rice market, a place where the maximum altitude is the debt ceilings of nations. The government of Thailand has an office here; so do the official representatives of France, Tokyo, the Republic of China, the Ivory Coast, and Chile. On the roof of 1 World Trade Center, the northern tower of the twins, is an antenna mast 360 feet high, the equivalent of thirty-six additional stories. The mast throbs with the stuff and nonsense of news and TV; the signals pulse hundreds of miles into the electronic hearths of four states and 30 million people. New York is said to be the media center of the country, and the Trade Center most surely is New York's technical pulse, for twenty-two broadcasting companies lease space in the complex to beam their signals into every home of every consumer. The noon news shows are halfway over; "Days of Our Lives" is about to come on; "All My Children" is on deck.

Besides the Port Authority police, a small paramilitary force is quartered at the Trade Center. The United Nations is but three miles away, and virtually every world leader passes through town at some stage. So, to protect them, the United States Secret Service has a regional office at 6 World Trade Center. A flotilla of armored limousines and chase vehicles are parked in the garage below. Behind a gate, the Secret Service also has an ammunition depot on the B-2 level of the basement. Foreign leaders can expect to leave town safely. Even the Bureau of Alcohol, Tobacco and Firearms—the federal agency that investigates illegal weaponry, booze, and explosives—has offices in the Trade Center complex.

More than a dozen branches of state, city, and federal government hold space in the Trade Center, including, of course, the owner of the project, the Port Authority of New York and New

Jersey. Carl Selinger, an engineer for the Port, has just picked up a salad from the cafeteria on the forty-third floor. He has one of the ninety-nine elevators in Tower One all to himself.

If every visitor to New York has heard of the Twin Towers, it is not because of the tenants or the elevators. The Observatory on the 107th floor of Tower Two opened in December 1975. Today, a class from P.S. 95 in Brooklyn has just finished its morning tour of the Observatory. They were, to tell the truth, more excited about the fast, ear-popping elevator rides than they were about the view. Yet no vista in any American city comes close. All of the city's waterways are visible, the great bridges, the urgent sprawl of New York spreading out for miles. It would be churlish, but true, to mention that while the rest of the city's Beaux Arts skyline is visible from the Observatory, the sightseer does not have to endure the Twin Towers themselves—which, as one writer put it, "look like the box the building came in."

With twin towers, there was no need to build twin observatories. In 1 World Trade Center, the space on the 107th floor was turned into the Windows on the World Restaurant. In its early years, the push for seats at a Windows table was fierce. But the novelty of high-rise, high-price dining began to wear thin, and the food itself was not worth the elevator ride. In fact, the elevator may have helped to cool off the ardor for the food, since very little cooking is done on the 107th floor. The towers were built without gas lines—a safety decision, not a culinary one. So much of the building was devoted to commercial office space that a kitchen gas line was not a high-priority item. All the food preparation is done in the basement, where a small amount of natural gas is supplied. Even so, the glamour of eating in the sky, with so fabulous a view, attracts hundreds of diners every day.

Today, at this moment, Yasyuka Shibata is fielding a plate from the luncheon buffet. He has arrived on a flight from Japan this morning, representing Nippon Express, one of the dozens of freight-forwarding companies resident in the Trade Center.

To those possessed of a certain kind of imagination, the height of the buildings is a taunting triple-dare. A young athlete named George Willig once scaled the side of the tower, using rock-climbing gear. When he was arrested, the judge fined him $107—a dollar for every story he climbed. But the daredevil who made the world gasp was Philippe Petit, a wiry young Frenchman. One August morning, Petit fired a crossbow from Tower One to Tower Two, stringing a strong wire cable between the two buildings. Then he and some confederates—including a few steelworkers doing finishing touches on the construction—secretly anchored the cable on the deck of each roof. For nearly an hour during the morning rush hour, he walked across and back, 1,350 feet up, thrilling the morning commuters. He came down safely onto one of the roofs, into the arms of the Port Authority police. Later, clues to his plan were found scattered in odd places. For instance, in a stairwell on the eighty-seventh floor, Petit had drawn a picture of the Cathedral of Notre Dame—a French landmark to augur a French daredevil, the eighty-seventh floor presaging a stunt that would be performed on 8/7, or August 7. A steelworker cut out the picture and took it home.

The buildings are filled with mysteries and intrigues. One day the body of a construction-company owner named Louis DiBono was found in a car parked in the basement; in time, DiBono's murder would be laid decisively at the feet of Mafia boss John Gotti, who had swaggered past all earlier engagements with law enforcement. DiBono's murder finally sent him away for keeps.

Behind an unmarked door in one of the towers is an office that is used by the New York City Police Commissioner for his most sensitive meetings. Even though, just a few blocks away, the commissioner has his own office—in fact, the entire headquarters building—the "white room" at the Trade Center is the spot used when a top secret informant is to be debriefed or dealt with. It is away from the all-seeing eyes of the Police Headquarters permanent curiate. On another floor, behind another unmarked door, NYNEX has installed a multimillion-telephone switch for the region: it handles telecommunications not only for the thousands of phones in the Trade Center, but also for the Federal Aeronautics Administration, making the switch a vital link for air traffic through the three regional airports, John F. Kennedy, LaGuardia, and Newark. If the air traffic controllers at those airports lost their ability to guide planes, an entire country of airliners would be jammed up behind them.

The unseen Trade Center is a place of jails and secret rooms and ammunition depots; of bank vaults and train lines hidden belowground; and also a place in which ambition and ego have been writ large. It is high-octane human ego that raised the towers and kept them there against the great powers of the lunar tides that drag air currents across the globe. The tall buildings move constantly in the wind, like great sailing ships. The biggest displacement took place in March 1980, when the tops of the towers moved four feet in either direction off center, for a total of eight feet. They are built to move. If they were not, they would move anyway, in ways that no one would like to think about. The wind is relentless and powerful, stronger the higher up you go. For this reason, most buildings are tapered toward the top. But the Twin Towers are squares from top to bottom, built not only to take anything nature can bring, but to defy nature—to defy the inevitability of decay. They are proof that at least some people believe mankind is smarter and stronger than the wind.

One of the more remarkable features of the buildings' design involved the tests on humans. It was one thing to build two huge steel tubes. They were strong and flexible and those qualities could be measured. But humans were another story. How much wind could they take? To test people's tolerance of oscillation, the engineers went to Eugene, Oregon, and offered people a free eye exam inside an old car dealership. The people walked from the dealership into a trailer that was set up on giant springs. The investigators rocked and shook the trailer, measuring how long it took the subjects to start hollering that the ground was moving. Back in New York, an office was built inside a giant airshaft for the Lincoln Tunnel, then dangled from a cable. People were invited to sit inside the office and be pushed back and forth. Each tower has 5,500 dampers in the walls—devices that slowed the sway of the buildings in the wind.

Perhaps the greatest act of hubris in the building of the Trade Center was not its height, but its location. The credit for New York's skyscrapers has always gone to the powerful bedrock of Manhattan Island, the rock known as schist. For most of the island, the schist runs close to the surface, meaning foundations for tall buildings did not have to be dug too deep. Strangely, though, the Trade Center is built not above bedrock, but above colonial-era landfill. If nature had its way, the Twin Towers would be sitting in the Hudson River. To reach bedrock meant that the foundation had to be sunk seventy feet through muck and grime, old garbage, sunken ships, and spongy river soil. Inside that hole, a giant dry bathtub was built, eight square blocks, a 3,100-foot perimeter—all to keep out the Hudson and the waters of New York Harbor. The walls are three feet thick and seventy feet deep. In this bathtub is the basement of the Trade Center. Giant pipes carry Hudson River water for the cooling systems, pipes so big that a live elephant could be swept away through them. Here, too, are the great core columns of the Towers, sunk into the bedrock. Thousands of sensors all over the buildings are tied into a computer in the basement that regulates heating, cooling, and ventilation. A parking garage accommodates two thousand cars, making it a popular facility with people from the cramped streets of the financial district. One familiar yardstick of the Trade Center's total size is that it has seven times the office space of the Empire State Building. Here is another: underground, unseen, the *basement* of the World Trade Center encloses twice as much space as all of the Empire State Building, in all its height and glory.

THE LUNCHROOM
B-2 LEVEL
WORLD TRADE CENTER
12:17:35 P.M.

The place was quiet—payday quiet. Most of the basement crowd used lunch hour to scramble up to the banks. The phones were ringing, because they never stop in a place like the World Trade Center, but Monica Smith was at her desk and fielding them. Her pregnancy had left Monica as close to serene as the people downstairs had ever seen her.

"I need some of that good eggplant parmigiana," she had announced a few days before to Steve Knapp, the de facto mayor of the basement.

"Don't we all," Knapp said.

"When you gonna bring some in, Steve?" she asked.

"You like our eggplant?" said Knapp.

"I love it and now there's two of us to love it," said Monica, rubbing her belly.

"Two at least," said Knapp. "You got it."

He had gone home to Staten Island and announced to Louise, "Monica wants eggplant." Louise Knapp was a sharp and capable woman, plenty busy with her own job and household. But Louise was Brooklyn Italian, a proud cook. And she was fond of Monica. She went out to the markets, fixed the dish, wrapped it in foil. Steve carried it to the B-2 level.

"I personally," announced Knapp, "have made you"—he paused to fold back the foil—"a delicious tray of eggplant parmigiana."

"Oh," said Monica. "That's too bad. You better take it back."

"How come?" Steve demanded.

"Because I wanted Louise's eggplant, not yours."

They laughed. In all of the basement, where three hundred people work, maybe four or five of those are women. The basement was guy country. Mechanics for a small city, they fixed the air conditioning, the heating, the plumbing. They kept the place alive. At times the basement could be empty, which made people nervous about leaving the few women by themselves. Monica, whose official job was to check the time sheets submitted by the building's cleaning contractors, was the basement population's special favorite. She was from Ecuador, and was a chatty, sunny presence in the windowless offices beneath the Trade Center. She bantered playfully with the men, laughing and listening to them. Her husband, Eddie, was a salesman of big machines. They had met when he made a sales call to the Trade Center. Everyone downstairs knew when Monica and Eddie bought their first house in the Long Island suburbs. And everyone knew that she was expecting their first child.

To fortify security when the B-2 level emptied out, the electricians had set up a video monitor so that Monica could watch whoever was coming and going in the hallways. The cameras eyed the corridors in front of her. On the other side of her office was a solid concrete block wall; no one was coming through there.

Next door was Steve Knapp's lunchroom and conference area. The entire area was the Cathedral of the Routine, and Knapp was its laid-back high priest. On Thursdays they sent out for Chinese food, and crowds swarmed in. On Fridays, Knapp and company were in the room by noon, religiously. Today, though, a meeting in the lunchroom had run late, with an intense discussion about services to the fifty thousand tenants of the Trade Center. It seemed as if the meeting was going to last through lunch hour, when the door suddenly swung open. In walked Bob Kirkpatrick, the chief locksmith for the Trade Center. He was a man on a mission.

"Ed, you're sitting in my chair," said Kirkpatrick. "Get up. It's lunchtime."

Ed Monteverde stood up with exaggerated formality. "Why, certainly, Bob," he said, sweeping his hand to the big oak chair. Everyone laughed, relieved that Kirkpatrick's arrival had given them a graceful ending. The group broke up and headed for the elevators. Kirkpatrick pulled up his chair, set it against the back wall of the office, and opened his bag from the Coffee Express station.

Bill Macko followed him into the room, smiling about Kirkpatrick's technique in adjourning the meeting.

"Efficiency!" he said.

Kirkpatrick chuckled. Macko pulled up his chair, spread a newspaper across the table, and drew a knife from his pocket. He laid an orange on the table and began to peel, slowly. Macko was the kielbasa king of the basement, often bringing a bag of the Polish sausage from a shop in Bayonne, his hometown in New Jersey. The treats brought scavengers from all corners. Today he was sticking to his fruit and sandwich. Last Friday he hadn't been around the Trade Center for any lunch; he had taken the afternoon off to ride down to the Jersey shore, a working-class Riviera, to check on his family's beloved summer beach house. This week was payday, and he had cashed his check. He segmented the orange. Then the boss came in. Steve Knapp wore big-framed glasses, and was a tall and lean man with a head of floppy brown hair and a beard.

At one end of the room was a small kitchenette. Knapp kept the refrigerator stashed with beer. The beer was against the rules of the Port Authority of New York and New Jersey, which owns the World Trade Center, and no doubt there were good reasons for the rule prohibiting consumption of alcohol on the premises by employees during their hours of service. And good reasons to break it. Beer at lunch is a custom among those who work with their hands and backs. It is not likely to die out, "total quality management" teams notwithstanding. Knapp also happened to be one of the few executives among the nine thousand employees of the Port Authority to have received the top rating in his annual job review. Just yesterday, his boss had sent the review along to the personnel department.

Knapp liked the good grades—he had come up through the ranks of the air-conditioning and ventilation department, and had never worked upstairs with the suits—but he was hardly torn apart with ambition. Now that promotion and custom dictated that he wear a tie and jacket, he would pull just about anything out of the closet as he dressed at six in the morning. He left an all-purpose sport jacket at the office in case he had to go to a meeting. Naturally, he was regarded as a hopeless case by his sixteen-year-old daughter, Denise. She intervened in the wardrobe catastrophe by trying to lay out a matching shirt and tie the night before. This morning, though, he had escaped the house with brown slacks, brown tie, and a blue oxford shirt. Knapp didn't work too many Fridays because the Freehold Racetrack in New Jersey had free admission in the afternoon. He would dismember blocks of his vacation so that he could make "Freebie Fridays" at Freehold, often taking along his son Stephen. The track happened to be closed today on the threat of snow. The Knapps loved the horses; for his first date with Louise, twenty-two years ago, he had taken her to the Liberty Bell track, near Philadelphia.

That and all family matters were the subject of brutal ribbing in the lunchroom.

Sitting across from Steve was Bill Lavin, who ran the operations for the Port Authority's chief maintenance contractor. Knapp was his boss.

"I'm taking the kids camping in the state park when the weather gets better," said Lavin.

"Oh, yeah?" said Knapp. "I'm taking Steve Junior to the racetrack."

"What are you—the Bundy Family?" asked Lavin, referring to the dysfunctional clan of the sitcom "Married With Children."

"Who do you think you are?" retorted Knapp. "The Brady Bunch?"

"Boys, boys," said Bill Macko, laughing.

Macko and Knapp and Kirkpatrick were military veterans. Macko had been a marine, and Kirkpatrick had served during the Korean War. Knapp had been in Vietnam. They had come to work at the Port Authority immediately afterwards, finding secure and comfortable jobs with the massive agency. All were good at their work, so they ended up taking care of the Trade Center when it opened in 1970. Over their heads every day were about 200,000 tenants, visitors, and people just passing through the shopping mall and rail lines—that city the size of Dearborn, Michigan.

Knapp's lunchroom was a vault against the psychic pressures from the city that leaned on them. But the room also gave Knapp and the men who worked under him a few quiet minutes to go over the business of the day: a leaking pipe, a ventilator that wasn't putting out fresh air, a corner office that was too cold or too hot. It didn't take the 200,000 people upstairs long to figure out ways to occupy the maintenance department.

Today, though, things were quiet. Just on the other side of the wall from the lunchroom was a ramp for a big public parking lot. The ramp was a no-parking zone, but the maintenance people often used it to leave one of their vans while making a fast pickup or delivery. A yellow Port Authority van was sitting there when Kirkpatrick broke up the meeting. A purchasing agent grabbed the keys and took the van out to buy a salad.

A moment later, another yellow van pulled into the space vacated by the Port Authority van. It parked against the south wall of Tower One, the second-tallest building in the world.

The driver and his passenger did not emerge for some minutes. When they did, no one saw them.

On the other side of that wall, Steve Knapp was popping the top on a can of beer, and he pulled over an extra chair so that he could lean back and put his feet up. He opened the paper and started noodling over the crossword puzzle.

"I'll be back in a few minutes," Bill Lavin suddenly announced. "This mole has to get some light."

"See you later," said Knapp.

Lavin went down the corridor to the elevators. He rarely left the basement. Today he decided to see about the weather outside. Snow had been forecast. For all he knew, it could be monsooning or showering meteorites outside. Down on the B-2 level, people would never know. Around the Trade Center, the basement is called "the bathtub" from its construction as a huge basin. Knapp had his seat on the far side of the table, away from the door. Kirkpatrick was on the other, and Macko was next to him. Everyone in his regular place. Monica Smith was in the office next door, chatting with someone. As Bill Lavin boarded the elevator, things were one hundred percent normal in the Bathtub Cathedral of the Routine.

WINDOWS ON THE WORLD
THE RECEIVING AREA
B-1 LEVEL
WORLD TRADE CENTER
12:17:36 P.M.

Wilfredo Mercado was among the most important workers at Windows on the World, the famous dining room a quarter-mile up in the World Trade Center. Now, Mercado knew, the restaurant was minutes away from the most frantic time of day. Tourists from every continent would swarm by the hundreds to lunch in the sky, wrist-to-cuff with expense-account executives. The daily nervous breakdown, one waiter called it. And as dishes flew and the staff four-stepped from table to table, as the managers peered around corners, at the peak moment of the Windows day, Wilfredo Mercado had a ritual. He went to sleep.

A quarter-mile below the frenzy, Mercado propped his chair into place. He had earned a few minutes of shut-eye. He arrived every morning, faithful as the dawn, to supervise the food deliveries: huge panel trucks from the city's fruit and vegetable market, their brakes squealing as they backed into the loading dock at the foot of the tower. Under Mercado's eye, they heaved crates of produce onto hand trucks and wheeled them into the receiving zone. By 9:00 A.M., he had checked in six thousand pounds of potatoes and onions, oranges and bananas, kiwis and cucumbers. Virtually all of the food preparation is done in the basement and then hustled 107 stories up on a freight elevator dedicated to the use of Windows. The restaurant is operated by the Inhilco Corporation, a branch of Hilton International. Mercado haggled with the suppliers on price, quantity, and quality. He worked for an enormous multinational corporation, but he treated the business as if he were the owner, frowning at a tray of tomatoes, squinting between the rails of a crate to make sure that the truckers had not slipped in a box of rotten fruit. By eleven in the morning, the crush of vendors had eased; the line of trucks at the loading dock was down to one or two with quick packages.

Mercado, a round-faced man with a pleasant manner, was an American success story who made his way in a path cut by footsteps that had fallen a billion times before him on the sidewalks of New York.

As a young man in Peru, he studied engineering, then immigrated to the United States in 1981, where he met and married Olga Mercado. They had two daughters—Yvette, ten, and Heidi, three. He took up accounting at Hostos Community College, a two-year school that is a branch of the City University of New York. The Mercados bought a house in East New York, a tough Brooklyn neighborhood, but not too tough for people as determined as Wilfredo and Olga. Yvette went to the Catholic parochial school, St. John Neumann, the tuition an expense that the Mercados considered mandatory. Olga stayed home with the baby. And Willie actually worked seven days at the Trade Center. Monday through Friday, he checked in the produce for Windows on the World. On the weekends he worked as a security guard.

At eleven-thirty, one of his friends, Joaquin Fernando Villafuerta, took a break from running an elevator the entire height of the building.

"I bought the lottery this morning," said Willie.

"How are you going to spend the money?" asked Villafuerta.

"My mother in Peru is getting old," he said. "I'll go to see her."

The thought between them was that for all his work, for all his seven-day weeks, Willie Mercado could not afford the price of plane tickets home for his family. Villafuerta looked at his friend and read his weariness.

"I think we should take a vacation. I will come with you," said Villafuerta.

"Where would we go?" asked Mercado.

"I think Orlando, Florida," said Villafuerta. "It is a fantastic place. Warm. You don't have the snow to freeze you there."

"I don't know, I'm so tired, I work all the time," said Mercado.

"The kids will be fine, we will take them to see Disney World," said Villafuerta. "They'll love it."

"I will speak with Olga," he said.

Villafuerta returned to the elevator. Willie finished his rounds. Upstairs, at Windows on the World, the vegetables that Wilfredo Mercado had counted this morning were laid in big platters, ready for serving. Mercado sat in his chair with his arms across his chest. His eyes were closed. He breathed slowly and deeply.

THE PARKING RAMP
B-2 LEVEL
WORLD TRADE CENTER
12:17:36 P.M.

The Ford Econoline van, built by the hundreds of thousands, is the most popular commercial van in the country, next to the Dodge Ram. They are bought by the thousands by small businesses and government agencies. The Port Authority of New York and New Jersey owns hundreds of Dodge Rams. The Ryder Truck and Van Rental Company buys thousands of its cousin, the Ford Econoline, every year for its short-haul customers.

The Ford Econoline parked on the ramp of the B-2 level today was owned by Ryder. It had been rented three days earlier at a

Ryder outpost across the Hudson River in Jersey City, not four miles from the Trade Center.

This van was not the largest of the Econolines sold by Ford, but it could carry about 2,000 pounds of cargo, which was plenty for this job. All of Ryder's trucks are painted yellow, just like the Port Authority's. This one was built at a Ford plant in 1990. It had 295 cubic yards of cargo space. A long, cushioned bench extended from the driver's window to the passenger side. This was the only seating in the van.

Behind the driver's seat was a metal grid that separated the cargo from the passenger and driver, to prevent the stuff in the back from sliding forward and hitting anyone seated in the front. That was a particularly useful feature, considering the cargo. It consisted of 1,500 pounds of explosives, mixed in a vat in a storage locker in Jersey City. The explosives were connected to four twenty-foot fuses threaded through surgical tubing. The tubing suppressed smoke and slowed the rate of burn, extending it from ten minutes to maybe twenty. The bulk of the bomb was a gooey paste that lay in four cardboard boxes. Stacked alongside the boxes were three red metal cylinders of compressed hydrogen, each four feet long. In addition, four containers of nitroglycerin were loaded next to the goo in the boxes. A blasting packet of gunpowder was attached to each of the nitroglycerin containers. The fuses in the surgical tubing ran into the gunpowder, which would ignite the nitro. This, in turn, would detonate both the hydrogen gas and the gooey paste, which consisted primarily of urea, nitric acid, old newspapers, and paper bags.

The fuses had been burning for about fifteen minutes, or ever since the purchasing agent had pulled the yellow Port Authority van out of this parking space on a ramp that led from the garage. The Ryder van had then pulled in and taken the same space. It was not a legal spot, but the rented yellow van had the look and color of a Port Authority vehicle, and it wouldn't matter for very long, anyway. The two men in the Ryder van had flicked a cheap lighter and laid the flame against the fuses. Then they had stepped into a red car that had trailed them. Since they had not used a legal parking space, they had not passed through any of the toll gates, and they were able to loop out of the area without paying. The fuses they left behind smoldered. Thanks to the surgical tubing, the smoke was minimal. No one saw anything.

THE GARAGE
B-2 LEVEL
WORLD TRADE CENTER
12:17:36 P.M.

Timothy Lang sat in the front seat of the Toyota Four-Runner and tried to follow the words on the page. He was having a hard time concentrating. Of course, he kept pulling his nose out of the book, to see if any parking spots had opened up. He had driven into the garage at the Trade Center less than ten minutes earlier. Ahead of him in the line was a silver Ford Taurus, and the parking attendant was consulting with that driver. Lang hopped out of his car, but the attendant had gone back to the booth. He leaned over the silver car and leaned down to the driver's window.

"What are our chances of a spot here?" asked Lang.

The driver had not seen Lang approach, and was startled to hear someone talking in his ear.

"The guy said five or ten minutes, maybe more, we might have some luck," said the driver.

"Okay," said Lang.

The man in the first car, a dark-haired, olive-skinned man, looked away from Lang. He's just as distracted as I am, Lang thought. Maybe he's embarrassed about cutting me off on the way to the tollbooth. The guy had seemed to be in an almighty hurry. Lang coasted in behind him and waited it out.

Timothy Lang, who was not yet thirty-nine years old, had traded hundreds of millions in stock on Wall Street. He was tall and slim, handsome, with pepper-gray hair and cobalt blue eyes. Lang had married young. He already had four children, unusual for a man so young and prosperous. But he himself was one of twelve kids in an Irish-American family from Brooklyn. His father had been a subway conductor. It seemed to everyone that Tim was one of the sons who had made it big. He had been trading since he was twenty-five, and had made senior partner a few years later. A year ago he wouldn't have doubted his own success. But six months ago his life had begun collapsing. He and his wife had separated. He couldn't keep his head in the business, and he left his job. A man who had never taken more than a few days off in his adult life— a week was his longest break since high school—dropped out completely.

But he was drawn back to the game. A few weeks earlier some

partners in his old company had invited him to join a new firm. With equilibrium restored on the home front, he had agreed to return. He was easing back into work, going two or three days a week while the communications and high-tech links for his work were installed.

He hadn't planned on working today, but one of the new partners had urged him to, so he decided to come in for the afternoon. He lived in an affluent town on the coast of New Jersey, and when he came to work at the normal time for Wall Street, he took a high-speed ferry to a pier on the East River. Today, though, he was too late for the ferries and drove himself. That meant he had to cope with parking.

Now he found himself, almost by habit, gnawing his insides over a little detail like a parking spot. What if a space in the garage didn't open up? It was almost impossible to get a spot around Wall Street. The streets were as narrow today as they had been when Peter Stuyvesant built a wall as a fortification against Indian raids from northern Manhattan and named a street forever. The lanes were still wide enough for a couple of wagons, maybe, to squeeze by. So no one could park at any curbs. Every commercial space was filled by young masters of the universe like himself, who thought little of springing twenty or twenty-five dollars for a spot. The Trade Center garage was the last resort. It was set up as a do-it-yourself lot. The top level was a yellow zone, at B-1. That was completely jammed with cars. Lang, who had parked here for years, knew that level was a hopeless cause. He would wait for the next one down, the red zone in the B-2 area. The silver car went in first, and Lang was waved in right behind him. The first driver went off to the far end. Lang spotted something nearer to the exit he was headed for, and he pulled into a space. His coat and papers were in the backseat, and he opened the door to get them.

ROOM 107
B-2 LEVEL
WORLD TRADE CENTER
12:17:36 P.M.

Monica Smith had the time sheets out and was again running through how to keep track of the contractors' time. Helen Boyce—everyone called her LaToya—was going to replace her in a few weeks, when Monica went on her maternity leave. It was a complicated system, and everyone was up in arms recently over an audit that had revealed that the cleaning contractor had overcharged tenants. It had nothing to do with Monica, but it had hit the papers—*New York Newsday,* the only city newspaper to cover the Port Authority aggressively—and now auditors were riding shotgun on every detail of the operation. Monica was a sure and steady hand at the job, and she was passing that along to LaToya.

It was getting past time for lunch.

"Why don't you go now?" said Monica. "I'll take mine when you get back."

"That's fine," said LaToya. She turned to leave.

2

FEBRUARY 26, 1993: CRESCENDO

J&R MUSIC WORLD
PARK ROW
NEW YORK CITY
12:17:37 P.M.

The time galloped along, but the buildings stood tall. Look at the time. How long does a twenty-foot fuse burn? Ten minutes, fifteen? Mahmud Abouhalima brooded in the window. Later he would remember that the moment was filled with worries of failure, but a man may not know what is on his own mind at any moment. Perhaps they were given to the events in his public life. For two years the FBI and police had been tracking and chasing the tall, redheaded Arab, because they were treating as ordinary homicide what Abouhalima regarded as casualties of war. That thieving traitor near Coney Island in Brooklyn, who had argued about the money for the holy war in Afghanistan. The glorious assassination of the Jew, Kahane. The FBI had come close a few times. After all, the Egyptian expatriate community was crawling with informers. They could not stop the action now—that was close to certain. The fuse could only have a millimeter or two to burn. Would they catch him now? A few months ago they had broken into his house when no one was home, looking for the blasting caps.

What was happening? The snow was heavier now. In the park, the flakes landed and coated the ground. But they were boiled on sidewalks that lay over hot-blooded subways and steam pipes, and devoured by the big, heat-heaving skyscrapers. On the biggest ones, the Twin Towers of the World Trade Center, the snow melted seventy-five floors up, never made it to the ground. The Towers were indifferent to weather. But surely not a bomb. After all this trouble, maybe it had gone wrong. Mahmud Abouhalima checked his watch again. The moment was charged with tension for

Abouhalima and his handful of confederates. But a nice fall of snow would promise to throw a shroud of peace and calm over lower Manhattan. The J&R stores are spread all across Park Row, in buildings that were old vaudeville houses and home to the city's newspaper industry before World War II. The main J&R shop is at 15 Park Row, which was the world's tallest building at the beginning of the twentieth century. At thirty-nine stories, it was the wonder of its day. Soon the technology of making a tall building was seen as the manifest destiny of a small, congested island: pump it upward. The tallest building in the dawn-of-the-twentieth-century world was followed in lower Manhattan by dozens of tall and then taller buildings. Within the first decade of the twentieth century, 15 Park Row had been surpassed by a half-dozen other tall buildings. People were working in the air once owned by the birds. A new word was coined for the landscape first breached by what became the main J&R store: skyline.

All those buildings were nothing now. Any of the early skyscrapers could fit 150 times over into the World Trade Center. Mahmud Abouhalima stood in the window, watching the great tower. The classical music selections of the week played in the background. He watched a skyline that did not seem to move. Had something gone wrong?

B-2 LEVEL
WORLD TRADE CENTER
12:17:37 P.M.

The flames raced across the four fuses, an inch every two and a half seconds. Each fuse fed into a different blasting cap. All four fuses had the same rating: ten-minute fuses, twenty feet long. But one fuse would burn to zero inches first and touch off its blasting cap before anything else. Then all the other fuses would become immaterial, because the laws of thermodynamics would take over. Explosives are called energetic materials, because they release great bursts of energy when a solid or liquid is converted to a gas. When the first spark from the first fuse licked into the gunpowder, it would ignite the total explosion.

The gunpowder was packed in Atlas Rockmaster blasting caps, devices used probably hundreds of times a day in the United States to excavate building sites and in mining. The purpose of such a cap is to increase the pressure on the minute flakes that make up gunpowder. The same quantity of gunpowder, sprinkled in a line along the ground, would ignite and burn at a relatively slow rate, but it would not explode. It is the pressure of being confined in a cap that accelerates the rate of burn. The ignition of the powder began and finished within a single millisecond. At the instant when the powder was fully consumed, the pressure inside the cap rose to one thousand atmospheres, about 15,000 pounds per square inch. The gunpowder turned into a gas, carbon dioxide, and water, in the form of a high pressure vapor. The gas demanded more space than the powder did, and it expanded rapidly, bursting open the container of the cap. With that explosion—probably not audible more than a few yards away from the truck—the starting impulse of the entire 1,500-pound bomb had been generated, in the form of a concussion wave. The wave smacked into the first container of nitroglycerin, a liquid compound that decomposes and explodes upon impact.

The detonation of the nitroglycerin—that is, the speed at which the reaction moved through the bottle—was about 275,000 feet per second. In the time a person needs to read and recognize the word *time*, the nitroglycerin no longer existed. It had chemically changed into gas under immense pressure—about ten thousand atmospheres, or 150,000 pounds per square inch—and heat, in the area of 1,250 degrees centigrade. From the detonation triggered by the first bottle came an enormous concussion that detonated the unexploded nitroglycerin in the other three bottles in the truck. Three of the four fuses could have failed, and the bomb would have gone off.

The final phase of the explosion took place in the cardboard boxes. All explosions consist of fuel and a source of oxygen, known as the oxidizer. Here the urea pellets were the fuel; the oxidizer was the sulfuric acid. The mixture was not considered a "sensitive explosive," so the bomb makers devised the nitroglycerin cocktail to get them started. The ball of high-pressure gas from the nitroglycerin expanded, and its great pressure brought into reaction the sulfuric acid and the urea pellets. With a terrible, crawling rumble, like the roll of thunder across an August sky, the whole mass was transformed from a sodden paste into hot gas. Each kilogram of explosive created ten cubic yards of hot gas. The gas devoured the cardboard boxes that had contained the paste and moved outward until it hit the metal walls of the truck. Everything was moving under pressures of thousands of atmospheres. The walls of the van were torn into pieces moving faster than bullets. The concussion wave of expanding gas created a tornado-level wind, ripping through the underground garage. It hit the wall of the tower with a force of 1,500 pounds of pressure per square centimeter. This turned the cinder block wall into dust, and ripped a steel diagonal beam, weighing 14,000 pounds from its welds. Masonry walls collapsed.

Technically, the bomb had failed in its goal, which was to topple the 107-story building into its twin a few yards away. After the initial explosion of nitroglycerin and the paste in the boxes, the apparent intention of the bombers was that a secondary explosion would be fired from the hydrogen tanks. (Liquid hydrogen is used as rocket fuel.) The theory behind two, phased explosions was to first stretch the structure of the building—the atomic bonds of the steel columns and structural members. Then, they would be hit with a second blast while they were still distorted from the first explosion, and before they had contracted to their normal shape, hit them with a second explosion. But the timing was difficult to calibrate, and explosions of the tanks in the Ryder truck, near the end of the detonation of the urea bomb, served only to intensify the heat and pressure.

Because the truck had been parked at the base of the north tower, the effect of the explosion was roughly doubled. Just as the containment of the blasting cap increased the power of the initial explosion, the structural steel along the bottom of the tower also increased the pressure. While all the concrete walls collapsed, the vertical steel did not flinch. The bulk of the explosion was reflected away from the tower building. In effect, 1 World Trade Center had been turned into the world's largest blasting cap. A "mirror" effect was created by the strength of the tower base, roughly doubling the explosive forces and deflecting them into the garage.

The van had been sitting on an eleven-inch concrete slab, reinforced by steel. The concrete disintegrated into tiny rocks. The explosion went upward, blowing through another eleven inches of concrete overhead, then up another story, through another concrete roof, where it picked up a woman sitting at an airline ticket counter three stories above, and flung her thirty feet. Inside the garage, the gas concussion tore through cars and cinder blocks and found a ramp that allowed it to vent. A man waiting in a car at a light on West Street, three hundred feet from ground zero, felt a wind roar through his car. That made no sense, because all the windows were rolled up. He turned around and found his rear windshield blown open. Much of the floor of the B-2 level collapsed.

Wilfredo Mercado, the receiving agent for Windows on the World who was napping one floor above, was ejected from the room and landed headfirst five floors down, still seated in his chair. He was buried under twelve feet of concrete.

ROOM 107
B-2 LEVEL
WORLD TRADE CENTER
12:17:37 P.M.

The explosion seared the pattern lines of Monica Smith's green sweater into her shoulder and back. All time values now vanish. Yet an instant unfolded and swallowed six lives, aged thirty-five and sixty-one and fifty-eight and thirty-seven and forty-five and forty-seven: 282 years of living. The greatest force of the explosion had been deflected away from the base of the tower, where the Port Authority workers were having their lunch. Yet there was more than enough to kill. Monica, seven months pregnant, was hit with the concussive blast and cement blocks. She suffered immediate "acoustic injuries" that killed her instantly by tearing apart her lungs and arteries. The blocks crashed across her head, ripping at her scalp. Had she not already died from the hurricane of air, the rubble would have finished her. Her shoulders and ribs were broken. Her other internal organs were torn. Her pelvis was fractured and her leg was broken. Her seven-month-old male fetus died from injuries that were very similar to his mother's. The Smiths had planned to call him Eddie.

The blast continued across the hall, into the next room, Steve Knapp's lunchroom. Nearest the wall and the bomb was Bob Kirkpatrick, the chief locksmith and genius handyman. He was leaning against the wall, having finished his lunch, a man six months away from retirement. His skull was fractured by a tremendous blow from a pipe that had been propelled from a ceiling over his head faster than any bullet. The great mechanical mind was dead. The left side of his chest was flattened when he was hurled against cinder blocks, then crushed by them.

Bill Macko was seated next to Kirkpatrick. When he'd left home that morning, he'd stopped at a candy store in Bayonne to buy a lottery ticket. "Give me a winner," Macko had said. "I don't want to work anymore." Funny, Wilfredo Mercado, almost directly over his head, had bought a lottery ticket, too. The explosion fired concrete pellets into the left side of his face. His left shoulder was separated and all his vertebrae were broken. His spleen and kidney were torn; so were the arteries that fed them. These, too, were acoustic injuries, the gases filling his body so quickly that no blood vessel or lung could survive the pressure. His intestines were ripped from the wall of his abdomen. Like everyone else caught in the blast, he appeared to have fallen from a twenty-story building.

Stephen Knapp, Vietnam veteran, who fished at sunset in the Great Kill waters, who brought eggplant parmigiana from home to his pregnant friend Monica Smith, and who took the great love of his life on their first date to Liberty Bell racetrack, probably was the last person in the room to die. Monica had been the first. The blast killed serially: Smith, then Kirkpatrick, then Macko, then Knapp. It started by imprinting Monica Smith's green sweater onto her skin. It finished by firing particles of concrete into the white of Steve Knapp's left eye at a thousand miles per second. The fastest reflex in the human body shuts the eyelid. But Knapp's eyes did not close. From Monica Smith to Steve Knapp, death ran faster than the blink of an eye.

CONSOLIDATED EDISON ELECTRIC UTILITY
NEW YORK CITY
12:17:37 P.M.

A light blinked on a control panel at the Con Edison command center. The World Trade Center was fed by eight high-voltage lines. One was out of service for routine maintenance. At 12:17:37, four of the remaining seven feeders shut down. The remaining three were still operating without any overloads.

J&R MUSIC WORLD
PARK ROW
NEW YORK CITY
12:17:38 P.M.

The snow was twisted by the wind into crazy coils. In J&R, more people drifted in to pass a few minutes of their lunch hour. For Mahmud Abouhalima, failure was blowing in gusts. Where was the explosion? He had known a colossal failure once before. He had, he told friends, been the man in charge of driving the getaway car at the assassination of the radical Jewish rabbi, Meir Kahane. He had steered his cab to the entrance of the Marriott Hotel in midtown, but had realized that the parking regulations would not allow him to sit there indefinitely. His story was that he'd had to move the cab around the block. Then the shooting happened. When the gunman came running out of the hotel, he leaped into the first cab he saw, and rode three blocks before he realized that it was a Puerto Rican from the Bronx, not the tall redheaded Egyptian getaway driver. The gunman screamed, jumped from the cab, and ran wildly across Lexington Avenue, where he grappled with and shot a postal policeman. He was arrested and tried. His cohorts blamed Abouhalima for botching the getaway. He had to beg for his life. No matter how much he had done in Afghanistan, he had to redeem himself.

The Ryder van had been parked against the south wall of the north tower. They had packed enough explosives to send it to outer space, or at least to send it hurtling into the Hudson River, or crashing into the tower next to it. Had he failed again? Why was it still standing?

Across City Hall Park, he could see a fire engine racing down Broadway. Traffic was light, almost Sunday-light. Abouhalima watched for a moment and paid no attention, barely knowing what he saw. Then another truck appeared behind it, then an ambulance, and soon the slow currents of music in the second floor of J&R were penetrated by the harsh whine of a siren, another siren, another siren, all joining together in one loud scream. Oh joy.

FIRE ENGINE 10
12:17:38 P.M.
LIBERTY STREET, MANHATTAN

Lieutenant Matt Donachie stood on Liberty Street, watching the two young firemen on Ladder 10 as they backed the truck into quarters. From the corner of his eye, he could see all the lights in 4 World Trade Center. He did not know what he knew, that the lights were on or that he could see them until the nine-story building went dark for a bare instant. Then the lights came back on. The flicker fell weightlessly on his eyes. Not so the tremendous thud that followed and hammered into the street. Pieces of the Vista Hotel seemed to go hurtling into space, but that was an illusion caused by pigeons and sparrows, the winter air force, scrambling from ledges and windowsills into the security of the snowy sky.

Donachie saw the blinking lights and heard the bang, the birds taking flight, and when he'd processed these facts through the screen of a dozen years in the New York City Fire Department, he felt sure he knew what had happened. It was a transformer explosion in a Con Edison substation. They were very common in lower Manhattan. A dictionary definition of New York might read, "a city where things inexplicably boom." In the field of noises, Donachie, thirty-six, knew the sounds of New York, could read them from far away. He had heard dozens of transformer explosions over the years, and knew without waiting for an alarm that his outfit would roll on this. It was not a big deal.

He signaled the men on the truck to put the truck in reverse. Then Donachie hollered in to the dispatcher and told him to enter an alarm from the box at the corner of West and Liberty streets. At eighteen minutes and ten seconds past noon, the first emergency response to the World Trade Center explosion had started.

It would be thirty days before the Fire Department left the scene, but as Matt Donachie swung into the front seat, he was sure it would be a dull, short job. His truck pulled up to the corner of West Street and turned right. As they drove past the Vista Hotel, he saw a doorman standing outside. The doorman looked as though he were hailing a cab. Donachie's gaze ran along the pavement in the street. He expected to see a steel plate over a vault that had been knocked asunder by the burnt-out cable beneath. In his mind, he could see the whole job unfolding: the firemen would locate the site of the transformer explosion and call Con Edison, then stand by until the utility's trucks arrived for the repair. They drove along West Street, until he saw a thin line of smoke rolling up a ramp from the underground garage.

About the same amount of smoke that you'd get from a steak on a grill, Donachie thought. It must be an indoor transformer. He didn't want to send for more trucks—why waste resources?—but the smoke could curl into the hotel lobby. Better to be safe. He radioed a 10-75 to the dispatcher. That would bring more units.

3

FEBRUARY 26, 1993: AFTERMATH

911 TAPE
CALL 1, RECEIVED ON RADIO POSITION
96, CHANNEL 50. CALL COMMENCES
AT 12:17:42 P.M.

The first call of 648 to report trouble at the World Trade Center "incident" came some four seconds after the explosion. It reached into a system where doubt is the operating theology, and the opening words were straight from the catechism.

"Police operator 5. Is this an emergency?"

New York City's 911 system receives 9.3 million calls a year, and the Police Department estimates that close to half are nonemergencies—stray dogs, handbags left on the subway, cranks, criminals, and people with too much time on their hands. A few years ago, the city tried to cut down on the calls to the system by advertising against its use except for emergencies. And now, as the explosion first resounded outside the Trade Center, the operators, by custom, challenged the caller to prove that urgent action truly was needed.

"Yes, there is an emergency," said the caller, a male. "Something just blew up underneath the parking-garage tunnel between World Trade Center Tower One and the World Financial Center, across the street."

"Okay, it's in the World Trade Center?"

"No, it's an underground parking garage, the entranceway down there."

"Hold on a minute. What street is it on?"

"On West Street."

"And what?"

"Ah, West, near Vesey, just toward the FDR from Vesey."

"Okay, hold on for the Fire Department, you're in Manhattan, right?"

The 911 operator actually has no ability to dispatch anything; instead, he or she patches the call through by dialing the Fire Department or the Emergency Medical Service.

"Hello, sir, hold it for the Fire Department."

"Fire Department, Fletcher, 191."

Now the caller must explain his story again.

"Hi, there was a big explosion in the underground entranceway to the parking lot on West Street between World Trade Center Tower One and the World Financial Center across the street on West."

"Okay, would that be, like, by the Vista Hotel?"

"Exactly."

"Okay, and it's what number are you calling from?"

"I'm calling from 298-6020."

"Okay, Fire Department is on our way, sir."

911 Tape
Call 5, received on Radio Position 95,
channel 49. Call commences at
12:29:02 p.m.

"Police operator, hello."

"Oh, hello, there's been an explosion in the garage underneath the Vista Hotel."

"Okay, ma'am, what's the address?"

"The Vista Hotel on West Street, in the World Trade Center. I'm the only one here, I'm bleeding, I can't find anybody."

The caller begins to cough.

"And it's getting smokier in here, and I'm scared to death."

"Okay, ma'am. That's Vesey Street and Church or something like that?"

"Yes." There are sounds of retching.

"You need an ambulance too, right?"

"Probably."

"Okay, ma'am, hold on, 'cause we have units close enough for that. You're at the hotel?"

"I'm in the parking garage *under* the hotel. I'm the only one *down* here, and I'm trapped."

"Okay, ma'am—ma'am, I need you to stay calm because I'm

going to help you, we have help on the way, but it's important that you stay calm."

"Okay, I'll try."

"You're in the parking lot?"

"I'm in the parking lot, underneath the hotel."

"And you probably have a concussion? Okay?"

There is silence on the line. The 911 operator asks another question:

"Okay, ma'am, listen, can you like give me something that can pinpoint where you are, like a trademark or a . . . you know . . ."

More coughing, then the woman calling from the garage answers:

"Where they return the Hertz rental cars to."

"Okay, ma'am," says the operator. "And your last name is?"

"Nash. N-A-S-H."

"Okay, ma'am, listen, the police and ambulance and the Fire Department will be there as soon as possible. I know they're on the job, that you're in the parking lot, under the hotel, and you're bleeding and you're near the Hertz Rent-a-Car."

"Yes, and I'm the only one here, I don't know where everybody else is."

"Okay, miss, and you said you're trapped."

"I'm trapped. I can't get out of here. The emergency exit is blocked, it won't open."

"Okay, they'll be there as soon as possible. I just need you, you know, have some patience, okay? We'll be there as soon as possible."

"Okay. I'm glad I got you."

"Okay, ma'am. Bye-bye."

THE GARAGE
B-2 LEVEL
WORLD TRADE CENTER
12:35 P.M.

Timothy Lang felt the pavement under his head. So he was not dead. He had opened the back door and was reaching for his coat when the explosion went off. His car had blown up, or maybe it was the car next to his. All the air in his lungs had been sucked out by the blast, and he had been hurled into the air. Now he lay on his back and put his hand in front of his face, but he could not see it. Blind? Would he be blind in the month of March? He knew a blind man—Joe Stokes, another piper. They played the bagpipes together in a band, and now they were coming up to the busiest time of year, when parties around Saint Patrick's Day seemed incomplete without the pipes calling. Now the band would have two blind pipers. An awful wailing sound rose from the car alarms. His ears were working.

What about the rest of his body? He reached down to his legs, felt his knees, his hands taking inventory of his body. Everything was still there. He ran his hands up his body, to his neck. It was wet. On the back of his head was a long, deep gash. He tried to stand, but made it just halfway to his feet. He started to crawl. The ground was a course of glass shards and tiny, punishing rocks. Then he glimpsed a faint light.

By God, he was not blind after all. He could see, he was all in one piece, and so Lang dragged himself toward the light. It was the dome bulb inside his car that went on when the door opened. He reached inside, switched the headlights on. Around him, the smoke was rising—not too badly. Now that he could see, he knew where he was. But the car—the front looked as though it had been in a head-on collision. The hood was buckled in a V toward the driver's seat. He'd had his keys and coat in his hand at the moment of the explosion. Where were they now? He looked around on the ground. That was a ridiculous idea. Just get the hell out of there.

He turned off the headlights, closed the door. Everything was fine. Lock up, can't leave the car open. This is New York. He could head for the elevator bank. A stairway could be not far. They usually were in the same area as the elevators. Now the smoke was thickening. He saw a light from an exit sign, and beneath it was an opening. It had been a door to a stairwell, but now the door was gone. He poked his head into the opening. Huge rocks filled the shaft. The stairs were covered with rubble. That was a dead end.

He turned around, and now was groping in the dark smoke. His foot kicked into something—a low wall, maybe two feet high. He crawled over that. A step, two steps. The dimness held shapes that looked like an office—file cabinets, he wasn't sure what. He really could not see anything. Then he pitched forward, falling over a chair. He threw his hands ahead of himself, and caught himself before he hit the ground on something soft and yielding. Flesh. An arm. A person. A woman. The person did not move or speak when Timothy Lang, five feet eleven inches tall, fell with his full weight on the arm. A scream died in his throat. Death was this way. Lang turned back. He scuttled over the wall. He crawled forward, away from the office. His hands were tearing through glass and metal, but the fear had put calluses on his pain. Then he stopped.

Directly ahead of him, the floor seemed to disappear. He looked down into a huge, glowing pit, smoke and hot particles rising within it. He could nearly taste them. He lurched away from the abyss. Someone was screaming over the wail of the car alarms. It might have been his own voice, but he listened long enough to know that he was not screaming himself. The sound came from somewhere in the smoke. He did not know how to reach that person. Behind him had been the dead person. Ahead of him was the pit. Years before, in high school, Timmy Lang had studied to become a member of the Xaverian Brothers, an order of Catholic monks. The school had closed and Tim had dropped the idea of a religious life. He had abandoned the notion of an evil force called the devil, and had hedged on God, taking a position as if faith were the stock market; he didn't want to be left alone if it turned out there really was a God. He faced left. Went a few steps. Turned right. Then left again. He spun around. He had been parking in this garage for ten years and now he didn't know which way to look, and he began to breathe faster, and faster, and with every breath his chest heaved with pain. The dead body, the roaring pit, the destroyed cars, the pitch-blackness at midday, the air that was one poisonous wind, the car alarms: it was a celebration of evil, Lang thought. He was killing himself by breathing. He could not save himself. He was going to die. Someone else had to rescue him. He curled into a fetal position. He was going to die on the floor and he was afraid and he wished he could pray, just so that he would not tremble in the face of death.

Yesterday, wandering around his home in Sea Bright, he had flipped open a calendar that had a biblical saying for each day. Someone had given it to him for Christmas. On an impulse, he had torn off the sheet for February 25 and stuck it in his wallet. That day's meditation was from the Book of Genesis, the story of Creation. He could not reach it now, and if he could, it was too dark to see. But as the car alarms screamed, the words from the calendar ran in a low drum roll across his mind.

His marriage had been difficult, but he knew his children had a good and loving mother. They would be sad, but kids could carry on, and they had the great unlined pages of life ahead of them. They would be financially secure and loved. Lang felt his own breathing slow down. He was surprised to find himself calmed. To sleep would be delightful; he could escape the horrible noise and air. The firehouse down the street would get the call, he realized. This was a big one. Lots of people upstairs had to be rescued. Hundreds could be dead, maybe thousands. It would be a long time before they got down to the basement. He might die here. He didn't want that, but he had run out of ideas, and he thought it might be good to die with some dignity. Every time he moved, another scorching breath would billow through his lungs. No sense in budging. He could go to sleep, but those words from Genesis looped through his mind, again and again.

I am with you and will protect you wherever you go. . . . I will be with you constantly until I have finished giving you all I am promising.

Timothy Lang was at peace.

911 Tape
Call 83, received on Radio Position
8, channel 9. Call commences at
12:36:00 p.m.

Only in a high-rise tower could car fires a quarter-mile away cause people to fear for their lives. The Trade Center's entire communication system was destroyed by the explosion. People one thousand feet above were drawing breaths of smoke within minutes of the explosion in the basement. They found their elevators motionless, and headed for the stairwells by the thousands. But the stairwells served as flues for the smoke that was shooting from the basement, as if this were nothing more than the world's tallest chimney.

"Police 1258, where is your emergency?"

"Listen, this is a person in the World Trade Center building, okay? One World Trade Center, there's smoke in the building, and we went into the hallways, and we're stuck in the hallways. There's so many people in the hallways, and we're stuck."

"What, are you in the smoke condition—hold on, let me connect you with the Fire Department, all right?"

"All right, well, I didn't know what to do."

"Hold on, let me connect you with the Fire Department."

. . . . .

"Fire Rescue."

"Yes, hello, this is somebody from the World Trade Center building. One World Trade Center."

"What building are you in, sir?"

"One World Trade Center."

"What floor are you on?"

"I'm on the forty-ninth floor now. Forty-eighth floor."

"What are the conditions there, sir?"

"There's smoke all around us, there's people in the hallway, there's people in the hallway, we don't know, we went down four floors, we can't go anywhere. We went up four floors."

"Why can't you go down any further?"

"There's so many people. We can't—"

"You've got to stay on your floor, okay?"

"Stay on our floor?"

"Stay on your floor. Is there smoke coming out of the vents?"

"Yes, there is."

"Get something to cram into the vents, okay, sir?"

"Cram into the vents? On the floor, you mean?"

"Yes, your air vents where the smoke is coming from. You know where the smoke is entering your floor?"

"Well, I'll tell you the truth, the vents I think are in the ceiling."

"They're in the ceiling?"

"Yeah."

"Put something around it, sir."

"Well, this guy's trying to break the window."

"Sir, you're not going to break the window, it's not going to go out. All right? If you've got your jacket, anything like that, you put it into the vent. Jam it up. Okay? We're controlling the fire now, we're fighting the fire right now. Stay where you're at."

"The people in the hallway, should they go on to the floors?"

"Bring them in to your floor if you can get them in there, okay?"

"Okay, because the people on the stairwells are breathing a lot of smoke in."

"There's a lot of smoke, sir, sorry. What's your phone number there?"

"It's 432-6679."

"Okay, stay on your floor though, sir, okay?"

"Okay."

Elevator 66, near the 50th floor
1 World Trade Center
12:40 p.m.

After ten minutes by himself in the stalled elevator, Carl Selinger sniffed an acrid odor. The motor in the car must have burned out, he decided. He was due at a meeting at two-thirty with the director of the building. He could break chops, but good. Selinger was an engineer who had spent his entire professional career at the Port Authority. He enjoyed full-court basketball and, in the bureaucracy of the Port Authority, wouldn't mind throwing an elbow, in fun, at the director of the building. The smoke got thicker, and it wasn't so funny. His nose started to run, and he ran a finger over his lip. He stared at the finger. It was black.

The children are teenagers, nearly grown, they can get on, Selinger thought. Barbara will manage without me. My mother is ten years dead; maybe I will see her again. The Port Authority life insurance will be multiplied because this would qualify as job-related, line-of-duty death. Just when I was able to make a baseline move on the basketball court. I have a few things to say to them.

He reached into a pocket and found a pen and a piece of loose-leaf paper.

> To my family—from Dad
> 12:40 PM, smoky elevator 66, 2/26/93
> A few thoughts if I am fated to leave you now—
> I love you very much. Be good people.
> Do wonderful things in your life.
> Barbara—I've always loved you, and showed you as
> much as I could.
> Debbie—my beautiful girl, with wonderful bear hugs &
> kisses. Do good.
> Jeff—what a terrific person, stay well, make good deci-
> sions, help people.
> Doug—My boy. Discover secrets to cure lots of the
> world's problems.
> I'm so proud of my children—they're each so wonderful.
> Things I love & cherish—ideas, people, Cooper Union

(alumnus of the year!!!), my work, my family, doing the
best I could. Nothing more to say.

(12:59 very smoky)

Love,

Dad

(Carl Selinger)

Bloomfield, N.J.

He stood in the elevator and read it over. Did it have the right
words, enough of them? Should he include the Port Authority, having worked there for twenty-four years, his entire career? He decided that he didn't love the Port Authority, but he did love his
work. Should he tell people that he was not in any pain or discom-
fort? No. It would upset them. They would be able to see by the
letter that he was in a calm state of mind.

Where to put it? Somewhere it wouldn't get lost or overlooked,
thrown out as just some notes, but somewhere safe, where it
wouldn't go astray. He folded it and stuck it in the breast pocket of
his suit jacket, so part of it was showing. Like a fancy handkerchief.

ALLIED SIGNAL RESEARCH OFFICES
MORRISTOWN, N.J.
FEBRUARY 26, 1993
12:45 P.M.

The man with the glasses walked into the secretary's office. He
was agitated.

"Did you hear on the radio about the World Trade Center?"
he asked.

"No, what happened?" asked the secretary.

"They had a big explosion there," he said. "They aren't sure
if it was a transformer or a bomb. It was just on the news, on
the radio."

"My God, was anyone hurt?" she asked.

"They don't know yet," he said. "Why would someone do something like this? It must be some kind of group, what do they want?"

The first news of the explosion had just been broadcast on the
city's two all-news radio stations, WINS and WCBS, and neither

had identified the cause as anything other than a transformer fire. But the slight, thin man with glasses seemed certain that it had been a bomb.

"We're very fortunate to be living in this country," he said. "We have freedom. We don't have any radical leaders."

"That's true," she said.

"In the Middle East, the leaders are so strong, they do mind control on the people," he said. "They do so much mind control, in their religion and in their beliefs, that if they tell them to do something to kill themselves, in whatever they are doing, it wouldn't bother the people. They would do it."

The man often stopped at the secretary's desk to talk about the politics of the Middle East. She mostly listened. His name was Nidal Ayyad. Of all the research chemists who worked at Allied, he was among the most animated. He had just gotten married a few months ago, and had moved into a home in a nice suburban town. She had helped him with the paperwork so that the company's records showed his new address. He seemed eager to talk, then and now.

"When I was at Rutgers, I told the other students that they were fortunate that they could go to school and do whatever they wanted in their leisure time," he said. "In the Middle East, it's not like that. I was a young boy in school, we couldn't carry bookbags, or backpacks. We had to carry the book out in the open, so anyone could see, and we had to have the lunch, so they could see that, too."

"That's very interesting," she said. Another of his harangues.

"A terrible thing to happen at the World Trade Center," he said. "What kind of people would do that?"

THE GARAGE
B-2 LEVEL
WORLD TRADE CENTER
12:55 P.M.

Although Tim Lang had considered that he might die and decided that he wouldn't fight too much, there was no sense in ignoring things that might work. He pulled himself off the ground and crawled into a car blown open by the blast. He pulled the headlight switch on, and then went back around to the front of the car and lay in the headlights' beams. Nothing happened. Maybe no one would find him, but at least he wouldn't die without trying something.

Time collapsed and accordioned. He didn't know how long he had been lying on the ground in the headlight beams when he heard a banging noise.

"Help me!" yelled Lang.

"Where are you?" came a voice.

"Parking level red, by the lights," shouted Lang.

Lang moved to one elbow. He could see nothing. The headlights were smothered by the thick smoke.

"Where are you?" the voice called.

"Parking level red, by the lights," Lang screamed, and realized his voice had also been smothered in the dark, rolling hell.

"Where are you?" the call came again.

The words sat on his tongue, but he had nothing to blow them out with. He could not speak. They could not see him, they could not hear him. He was going to die.

"Where are you?" said the voice, and it was very loud now.

In front of Lang's face was a strong light, and in the light was a boot. A policeman named Cory Cuneo walking in the smoke had pointed his light straight down because the beam was swallowed by the haze. The boot was a step away from Lang's face. The man in the boots could not see him. Lang reached up, toward the light, and grabbed the boot.

Two police officers lifted him onto their shoulders. Lang began to choke in the smoke, which was much thicker five or six feet off the ground. They walked into a wall, smacking Lang in the face. Then they walked into another wall. Again, Lang was belted. Finally they reached a safety line and followed it out to a stairwell, where Lang drank in the clear air. A few minutes went by.

"Is there anyone else down there?" asked one of the cops.

"A guy in a silver car," Lang gasped. "The parking attendant. Someone was screaming in an office." He didn't know what to say about the dead arm that he had fallen upon.

GARAGE RAMP, WEST STREET
1:35 P.M.

The man in the silver car was John DiGiovanni, a dental products salesman. He had pulled into the garage just ahead of Tim Lang. DiGiovanni found a spot near a ramp leading out to West Street. His exact movements are not known. When the bomb went off and the expanding ball of gas was searching for a place to vent itself, it blew through the ramp, carrying everything and everyone in its path. DiGiovanni was thrown perhaps thirty feet. He landed just up the ramp, far enough for people on the street to see him. Sal Ciniglia, a Port Authority electrician who was outside when the bomb went off, ran to the ramp and, looking over the side, saw DiGiovanni on his back. The injured man waved his fingers in the air. Ciniglia hailed a police officer on a scooter, who went down the ramp to check on the injured man. Another man saw Secret Service agents also helping DiGiovanni in the moments after the explosion.

At that time, DiGiovanni was conscious, although badly injured. In any event, there is no official record of what happened to him next. One fire company reported that it had helped rescue him from the garage, although this appears to be incorrect by all other accounts. All that is certain is that the Emergency Medical Service technicians were summoned to the ramp at approximately 1:35 P.M. He had been sprawled on the concrete for more than an hour, inhaling the smoke from the burning car fires. The EMS workers found him in a condition called traumatic cardiac arrest, which results from violent injuries. As he was wheeled up the ramp, a volunteer fireman from Long Island was performing CPR. The paramedics inserted tubes into his chest and throat. They raced off to St. Vincent's Hospital and arrived there at 1:59 P.M.

RYDER TRUCK LEASING
KENNEDY BOULEVARD, JERSEY CITY
FEBRUARY 26, 1993
2:00 P.M.

Him again.

Pat Galasso, the owner of the Ryder truck franchise in Jersey City, watched the skinny Arab push open the door and come in from the snowy afternoon, as excited and confused now as he had been three days ago. When he'd rented the van, you would have thought he was building it from scratch: How big? How much? How long? Then he makes a call to someone else to find out if the van was the right size. The guy made a federal case out of renting a van, and now he was back.

"Ryder truck was stolen," said the man, Mohammad Salameh.

"Is that right?" said Galasso. "Where did that happen?"

"I park in the Pathmark at 440," said Salameh.

Galasso knew the store—just a half mile or so away, on Route 440, in Jersey City. It was not a city famous for its consumer amenities. No one made special trips to shop there. It was just a neighborhood place, an old industrial town with the industry scooped out.

Galasso knew that the supermarket security guards and the police towed away cars in the Pathmark lot that were parked in the handicapped parking zone without a permit. This dopy bastard just parked it there and got it towed, Galasso guessed.

"Were you legally parked?" asked Galasso.

"Legal? Yes, yes, everything legal," said Salameh. "I am coming out of Pathmark with the parcels, my arms are all with bundles, and I cannot find the truck, it is gone from where I parked it."

Salameh displayed the key to the van, hooked onto an acrylic tag that included the van's license plate number.

"I want refund," said Salameh.

"You can't have your deposit back just yet," said Galasso.

"I pay for one week, I have the truck two days, it is stolen," said Salameh. "I want the refund procedure to get back the deposit."

"You said the van was stolen Thursday," said Galasso.

"This is truth," said Salameh.

"So why didn't you call me on Thursday?"

"I don't know what to do—I am carrying so many packages and the van is stolen," said Salameh, excitedly. "It is very confused to me. I didn't call. I am sorry, my English is not good. I need refund, please."

He could say *refund* with no problems. "Do you have the police report with you?" asked Galasso.

"Oh, yes, I call the police," said Salameh.

"They gave you a report?"

"Yes, I reported it."

"Where's the report?"

"What?"

"The report. Where is the police report? Do you have it?"

"No, no. I tell the police, but they do not give me a report," said Salameh. "I need to have a report, like a paper?"

"Yes, the police should give you a report," said Galasso.

"Okay, I bring," said Salameh. "You give me refund."

"I'll give you the deposit when you bring the report," said Galasso.

"You can't give me refund now?"

"I can't close out your contract until you bring me the police report. It's for insurance purposes."

"Yes, the insurance. I bring the paper from the police. Then you give me deposit refund."

"We'll take care of all the paperwork," agreed Galasso.

Salameh left the office. Galasso switched on the radio and listened to the news reports about the big explosion across the Hudson River.

EMERGENCY ROOM
ST. VINCENT'S HOSPITAL
2:20 P.M.

John DiGiovanni is pronounced dead at St. Vincent's Hospital. The causes of death are deep smoke inhalation and traumatic cardiac arrest.

WEST STREET
LOWER MANHATTAN
FEBRUARY 26, 1993
2:30 P.M.

Fire Lieutenant Matt Donachie stood patiently with a group of reporters, explaining how he had gone down to the garage under the Trade Center but could not see a thing. Then, as they played their hoses on the fire, the smoke rose, "like a curtain," he said, and it was the unveiling of a horror show of destruction.

"So it was a transformer that exploded?" someone asked.

"I wouldn't say that was a transformer explosion," said Donachie. "We never get that kind of damage."

"What was it? Gas?"

He paused. Donachie knew it must have been a bomb. He glanced at the Police Department brass floating around. He looked at his own bosses. "I don't know. Maybe gas."

As the fireman spoke to the reporters, a million dramas were piling out of the building. A woman in a wheelchair was carried down sixty flights by her colleagues at the Port Authority, in her chair. The governor's secretary, Drew Zambelli, started walking down the stairs, then abruptly stopped and went into an office, where he stayed for hours, calming people who could not negotiate the stairs. He opened lines to the state police and to Albany, filling in the governor, receiving instructions from the Fire Department. A Port Authority worker on the B-5 basement level, Fred Ferby, slung two of his barely conscious co-workers over his shoulders and carried them up a flight of stairs. He knocked a coffee cart away from a possessive waiter in the hotel, laid the men on it, wheeled them out to the ambulances and rode to the hospital with them. Then he came back to the basement to search for other missing friends. The head of the Special Operations Division of the city's Emergency Medical Service, Paul Maniscalco, was organizing a triage unit for a thousand people, the largest in the history of any medical service in the country. As he bent over a patient, he heard a voice screaming his name.

"Paul! Paul!"

He turned around. His cousin's pregnant wife was hidden by an oxygen mask. "All right," he said. "We got you covered." She was loaded onto an ambulance and taken to a hospital.

Stan Brezenoff, the executive director of the Port Authority, wandered out to speak to his secretary. "Has this building ever been hit by lightning?" he asked. He was on the sixty-seventh floor; people from floors above started piling down the stairs, and Brezenoff assumed they knew something that he didn't. With no one answering in the command center, he started the trek down. But the line halted on the forty-ninth floor, and as far as he could see, up and down, people had stopped. A disaster was on the horizon, he was sure. He urged people to go inside the floors. At the forty-ninth floor, he took over a Japanese bank's space. "I'm probably the last person you want to hear from," said Brezenoff, "but I'm your landlord." The Port Authority executive director was one of the most powerful people in metropolitan New York. But Brezenoff quickly was discovering how meaningless that was in a world with little ability to communicate—even a person like himself who knew the gears of government as well as anyone. He called Port Authority offices outside the building, becoming increasingly furious that no one could give him good information. By evening, he would help carry a man in a motorized wheelchair down the stairs. Until he evacuated the ghost tower, it was about all he could do.

Yasyuka Shibata, the Japanese man who had been sitting down to lunch at Windows on the World when the explosion shook the china on his table, arrived coughing at a side stairway on Vesey Street. He had walked down 107 flights in thick smoke. His face was covered with soot. His handkerchief wiped blackness from his nose.

"I went from Windows on the World," said Shibata, "to a window on hell."

THE GRANGER CO.
BOSTON, MASS.
3:00 P.M.

When they all decided to take a break from the meeting, a guy Ed Smith didn't know joined them. He was making small talk out of bits of news he had just heard on the radio.

"Hey, didja hear about the fire at the World Trade Center down in New York?"

Ed Smith shook his head, but said nothing. If he had wanted, he could have made a phone call to his wife's office in the basement of the Trade Center and gotten the whole rundown. Monica and the gang probably were working on it. They didn't need to be disturbed by him. As it was, Ed had his hands full. He was one month on a new job and a big sales meeting was under way. Of course they had fires in the Trade Center. But they always were minor affairs, really, with no injuries to speak of.

The meeting started up again, and a few minutes later, they were joined by the man who had been listening to the radio.

"Apparently, it wasn't a fire in the Trade Center—they had some kind of huge explosion," said the man, sitting down at the desk.

"Excuse me a minute," said Ed. "My wife works there. Let me make a call and see that everything's okay."

He stepped into the reception area and dialed Monica's office. The phone rang and rang. They're all tied up, he thought. They've gone crazy, trying to take care of things. He turned back for the meeting, then stopped. He dialed the police emergency number. No one answered.

He tried a Port Authority office in Newark.

"Yeah, there was an explosion," said the cop on the phone.

"My wife works in the basement," said Smith.

"It was pretty bad," said the cop. "We don't have much information yet on injuries."

Smith thanked the cop. Then he went inside and explained that he had to get home, to make sure things were all right, and they could wrap up without him. Then he went downstairs to his car and headed for New York.

1 WORLD TRADE CENTER
LOWER MANHATTAN
FEBRUARY 26, 1993
3:30 P.M.

At bottom, the engineering mind, so famous for its bloodless calculations, is filled with fantasies of violence. Load ratios and square footage, tensile stress factors and shearing-strength measurement are the polite cover for the brooding imagination of catastrophe. And no one had dreamed more of disaster and the World Trade Center than Leslie E. Robertson, the original structural engineer of the Twin Towers. When a police car roared up to his office building on East 46th Street, lights and sirens flashing, it seemed as if the day had been ordained before the first spade of soil had been turned.

Robertson had first come to New York nearly thirty years before the bombing, to work on the structural design of the Trade Center. It was a fluke. His tallest building, up to that point, had been twenty-two stories, but he had impressed the architect, Minoru Yamasaki, with some government work he'd done in the Pacific Northwest. Robertson, at age thirty-four, set to studying the idea of very tall buildings.

He began his research by moving into an apartment near 38th Street on the East Side of Manhattan, so he could stare out the window at the mast of the Empire State Building. It was not a romantic idyll. He knew how to measure the weights of humans and their furniture and the concrete, and knew how much steel to put beneath them. But in tall buildings, the most vital force in design is invisible. The wind passes unseen but not unfelt. The measurements of winds at a weather station in Central Park, or at LaGuardia Airport, were irrelevant to the winds that would lap against the tower a quarter-mile up, night and day, as long as the sun and moon moved across the skies. The forces of the wind at the one-hundredth floor would be four times higher than at the fiftieth floor, he calculated. But how would it move? His apartment became an observation deck for him to watch the hidden hand of the wind. Around the mast of the Empire State Building he could see the fog swirling, obedient to the whim of every draft, rushing around one side of the building, then bunching up on the other side.

Now, as Robertson and his staff climbed around the debris in the basement, the engineer had been told that an explosion had occurred, and officially no one knew what had caused it. One look at the basement and Robertson realized that it had been a bomb. The Port Authority's director of the Trade Center, Charles Maikish, had come to the same conclusion: nothing that was normally in the building—no electrical lines, no natural gas—could cause that level of damage. It was centered in an area with public parking, which meant someone could have carried in an explosive device.

With a slight chill, Robertson realized that it had been a bomb, and that the intention had been to knock down Tower One. It was a moment, in a sense, that the Trade Center had been waiting for.

The design of the towers included unusual steps because they would be the world's tallest, and therefore the world's biggest, sitting ducks. The word *terrorism* was not in general use at the time of the Trade Center's design. But as Robertson would later write: "Sabotage of perimeter columns was considered to be an expected event in the life of the building." The Empire State Building had been rammed accidentally by a twin-engine bomber during World War II. The Twin Towers would be built to withstand the impact of a fully fueled Boeing 707 jet—at the time, the largest and heaviest plane in the air.

These were fantasy items, though, compared to the effect of the wind. The buildings had been constructed to withstand a sustained hurricane. And it was this design criterion that shielded the Twin Towers from a bomb that the FBI would later say was the "largest by weight and by damage of any improvised explosive device that we've seen since the inception of forensic explosive identification—and that's since 1925."

It was one thing to build against the chance of a bomb on a column, or a plane crash. The wind was altogether more powerful. As Robertson would later point out, "The energy input from hurricane winds, acting over 110 stories, far exceeds the energy from aircraft impact or from the bomb."

The load of the wind was greater even than this huge explosion.

The bombers may have thought that with their bomb alone, they could knock down the tower. They were wrong in their assumptions. But they came closer to getting their way than anyone could have expected—with help from New York Harbor.

The bathtub-like, seven-story basement of the Trade Center's seven buildings keeps out the waters of New York Harbor, where the Hudson River meets the Atlantic Ocean. The lateral support for the bathtub comes from the two thick slabs of concrete known as B-1 and B-2—the floors of the basement. The walls of the bathtub are pressed in by the harbor water and tides; this force is counteracted by the outward pressure exerted by the B-1 and B-2 basement floors.

When the bomb exploded, its impact bounced off the base of Tower One and then gouged a huge crater in B-2, where the van had been parked, and extended up through the B-1 level.

Mahmud Abouhalima's bomb had been placed, unwittingly, in a sensitive position.

The loss of the two basement floors meant that the support of the bathtub walls was in question. In fact, although the concrete floors near the perimeter walls were intact, one of the slabs had dropped three feet.

This led Robertson's imagination to another disaster scenario. His towers would not topple in a single blast, but the bathtub would be penetrated. The Hudson River and the Atlantic Ocean would rush into the seven-stories-deep basement. At whatever level the water reached, the structural columns of the towers would begin to rust. All the wind load was carried to these columns, and if they rusted, in time they would no longer be able to stand against the millions of pounds of force that would be spread over the walls on a breezy spring day.

Not just one of the towers, but both, would be compromised. "Eventually, you would find that the wind would make them hinge at the water line in the basement—where the rust had cut into the strength of the columns," Robertson mused later.

The engineers inspected the slabs nearest the perimeter walls and found that they were intact, despite the huge craters in their center. The slab that dropped three feet was given additional bracing. It was, in some ways, the most frightening possible consequence of the bomb—and one that got the least attention from the press and the public in the days afterwards.

The more obvious damage was compelling enough. The van was

parked against a wall behind which were a quarter of all the columns that held up Tower One, the north building. The wall separated the garage from Monica Smith's office, which was directly next to the van, and also from the Port Authority lunchroom where Steve Knapp, Robert Kirkpatrick, and Bill Macko were eating.

But the wall that fell on them did not hold up the tower. Each side of the tower is supported by twenty-one steel columns, spaced ten feet apart. Every column is connected to its neighbor by a massive diagonal brace.

How powerful was the bomb? One answer is given by the diagonal brace inside the wall where the Ryder van was parked. When the bomb exploded, it first tore through the seven-and-a-half-inch masonry wall. Then the impact ripped away the nearest diagonal steel brace. The brace propellered across the lunchroom, destroying everything in its path, landing seventy-five feet away. The brace had become a spear twelve feet long and weighing fourteen thousand pounds.

The blast then continued deeper into the core of the building, another one hundred feet, and ripped down the masonry blocks around an elevator shaft.

Nearly thirty years before, Les Robertson had thought long about how to keep the towers airtight. The air that enters a skyscraper at the ground level drones through the building, disrupting elevators, wearing on the internal structure. The entire building becomes a flue. At the time, the tower with the most notorious airlock problem was the Pan Am Building, which straddles Grand Central Station. (Today, it's called the MetLife Building, although most New Yorkers remember it by the older name.) To explore the source of the Pan Am structural problems, Robertson actually rode up and down on top of an elevator car—a ride that gave him a look at the interior skin of a building that did not work. It also changed high-rise construction forever. Instead of joining floors and ceilings with gypsum blocks, Robertson ordered that sheets of gypsum be used in the Twin Towers, and that they be connected to the floors with studs. This allowed the floors and walls to move slightly, instead of cracking at solid connections. It became a standard technique.

A big piece of the plan to eliminate the towers' "stack" effect was to seal the service cores, where the elevators run. This would keep the air from whistling up to the roofs and stealing heat, especially during the winter.

All that planning was shattered by the explosion, not only at the base of Tower One, nearest the bomb, but also in Tower Two. The masonry around the freight elevators was blown in the elevator pits. In what seemed like an instant, the smoke from the car fires in the basement rose a quarter-mile through the elevator shafts, then spread along the floors. The heating system was buried in the basement, and with the building now ventilated by cold air from the basement, the temperature of the walls went below freezing. The Twin Towers shrunk: 200,000 linear feet of plaster cracked.

But for all that damage, the energy of the explosion was deflected by the main vertical columns of Tower One. In fact, an instrumentation package at the top of the towers measures every shift in the load on the building. Although people from the top to bottom felt the blast in their shoes, the meters in the building did not blink. A few days later a windstorm with gusts of fifty-five miles per hour would hit the city, and then the instruments read the shifts in the steel. But the "measured stiffness" of the structure was not decreased.

The explosion essentially bounced against the base of the tower and then tore backwards into the open basement parking area. Above this was the Vista Hotel, a twenty-two-story building. Each floor of the basement consisted of eleven-inch-thick concrete slabs. The floor of B-2—outside the tower walls—was gouged open into a ragged crater, 200 feet by 150 feet. The blast moved in all directions; overhead, the eleven-inch concrete ceiling of the B-2 level— that is, the floor of the B-1 level—was opened to a smaller size than the floor of B-2, about eighty by fifty feet. The force of the bomb still was not spent. It continued to the ceiling of B-1, ripping through the concrete ceiling that was the floor of the Vista Hotel.

The explosion was no doubt as vicious hammering down below the B-2 level as it had been in the uppercut. It so happens that the B-2 floor serves as the ceiling of a huge underground vault. Inside this three-story chamber are the giant chillers that make it possible for people to work in the towers during the hot New York summers. The shattered concrete collapsed by the ton into and around the chillers.

The smallest details speak as loudly as the largest. The cars nearest to the explosion were pulverized, their metal opened up like petals on a flower. The paint was blasted off some sides, the rubber melted in the tires, the hoods and sides of the cars looking as though a deranged giant had beaten them for hours with a baseball bat. All energy seeks to dissipate. The concussion moved at five thousand miles per second through the garage, pushing down floors and walls.

It found a vent in the two ramps that led from the garage to the street.

INTERSTATE 95
CONNECTICUT
4:15 P.M.

Ed Smith had worked the car phone until he ran out of people to call. His father, Monica's friends. The obstetrician. The doctor had told him to get someone over to his house, in case anyone was trying to locate him, so Ed had called his father and sent him there to sit by the phone. The highway spun beneath him. He had worked it out in his head that so many people were calling down to the basement that getting through was impossible. When Monica caught her breath, she'd call one of her brothers, or her girlfriend.

He turned off the car phone and switched on the radio. The lead news story was the explosion at the World Trade Center. At the top of the hour, a broadcast from New York came on with interviews of people lurching out of the Trade Center.

"I work on the B-2 level," said one man. "It's destroyed down there."

The voice was familiar. Smith thought about it for a minute, his hands gripping the wheel tighter.

"My whole area is wiped out," said the man.

It was Vito. Vito DeLea. He worked with Monica. Now Ed could not hold back his sense of dread. It spilled over the dam of excuses and explanations he had made for the silence in all the offices on the B-2 level, and he felt it rising. She must be hurt. God, no. The baby—is the baby hurt, too?

He could see the B-2 level, could see the offices, he knew where Vito worked. He knew that whole place down there—he knew it even before he knew Monica. Their romance had started in the basement of the Trade Center.

"So when are you coming on a date with me?" Ed had asked her.

"You're like every other salesman," said Monica Rodriguez, black hair, smooth coffee-colored skin. "You keep talking, you keep moving."

"How could you say I'm like every other salesman?" said Ed in mock anguish.

That day in 1982, young Eddie Smith was flirting with Monica again. He was tall and apple-cheeked, just two years out of high school, making money and spilling the high exuberance of the young and strong. She was a secretary for the building management of the Trade Center, famous for her cheerful energy. He made sales calls to the B-2 level of the Trade Center. He had been working on Monica for some time.

"Anyway, I can't go on a date with you," she said. "I'm going to Hawaii on a vacation."

"Bring me back some pineapple," he pleaded.

She rolled her big, beautiful eyes. A few weeks later, he was back in the Trade Center. Monica reached for something and produced a fresh pineapple.

"Hey," said Eddie, delighted. "Now I owe you. You have to let me take you out." She consented to a movie. Then they stopped at JT's Alehouse on Jamaica Avenue in Queens. A guy Ed knew from the bar came charging over. It turned out to be Monica's brother, Ernie. The Rodriguez family had immigrated to New York from Ecuador when Monica was a girl of twelve, and the family thrived in the city. Monica and Ed became an item. They loved to make trips to Atlantic City, or work the bars in Queens, roaring up at the New York night.

He was wild and five years younger. She was full of fun, but ready for marriage. They broke up.

"Someday," Ed promised. "I'll give you a call if I can ever settle down."

One day in 1989, he walked through the concourse of the Trade Center and saw a florist near the subway station. Flowers of the World was the shop's name. In the window was a dog fashioned from push-in pom-poms and mums. He had brought one to Monica years ago. Now, the little floral dog hit him in the eye. He changed directions and found a pay phone. He felt his palms sweaty. He took a deep breath and dialed.

"You want to meet me for lunch?" asked Smith.

"I don't think so," she said.

"C'mon," said Smith. "You want to go to Atlantic City?"

She paused to think of her response. "I have a boyfriend," she fibbed. "Call me tomorrow."

He did. "I'll go back to you, but you know, this is serious," she said.

"Absolutely, I wouldn't have called you unless I was," promised Ed.

On the ride down to Atlantic City, she wouldn't let him near her. He tried to kiss her, she turned her face. He wanted to hold her hand, she slipped them under her arms. They were engaged three months later. They married in the Church of the Nativity in Queens on August 31, 1990. At the party afterward, Rodriguez relatives arrived from Ecuador, Smiths came from Queens and Long Island. It was a hot, muggy night, but Monica stayed on the floor all night.

The world had been impossibly fresh and young that night. Monica danced and laughed with her bosses and friends from the Trade Center, Steve Knapp and Bill Macko.

Ed and Monica bought the house in Seaford where Ed grew up. On weekends, they stopped at the Cherrywood Tavern for a drink. During the day, they tore apart the house and made it new. They put seven coats of polyurethane on the wood floors, painting their way out the door in the morning as they left for work. Each wanted bragging rights for the glow on their house.

Ed was going to night school at Queensborough Community College. When he got home after ten, Monica would get out of bed to make sure his dinner was warm. Sometimes, they argued about moving out of New York.

"I love my job, I don't want to leave," she told Ed. "The people are the best."

He had to agree. Many nights, he'd stop in at the B-2 level of the Trade Center and grab one of the fellows for a beer, even if Monica wasn't around.

One evening, just after they'd finished the last touches on the house renovations, Monica called him at school to rush him home. She had bought a pregnancy test. He held the tube while she dipped the stick. Together, they watched the color swell from a blank white to a soft, sure pink. That night, they slept entangled in each other's bliss.

Monica bought Winnie the Pooh books for Ed to read to her belly, to the boy growing inside. They had decided to call him Eddie, Jr. They moved Ed's office out of their bedroom to make space for the crib. Just last week, they shopped for baby furniture.

How badly hurt was Monica? Was the baby okay? He picked up the phone and started dialing numbers again.

43RD FLOOR
ONE WORLD TRADE CENTER
5:45 P.M.

Carl Selinger put his feet up on a chair in the cafeteria he had left more than five hours ago. As the afternoon had crept on, he had heard the rescuers in the elevator shaft, but they had not heard him. He had heard the people walking in the staircases, but they couldn't hear him. When the public had emptied out of the building, he'd begun to consider in the silence the possibility of a nuclear attack. He'd thought of a movie, *On the Beach,* in which a submarine surfaces and its crew contemplates a city silenced and darkened by a nuclear bomb. The elevator had finally moved at around five-thirty. He'd shouted out, and the rescuers had been shocked to find him inside.

"We were just about wrapping it up here," said one.

They'd brought him to a medical staging area in the cafeteria. He'd sat there, not wanting to talk or eat or even go to the bathroom. The police offered to carry him down the forty-four floors, but he declined, preferring to make the journey under his own power. About halfway down, he thought of his daughter Debbie and broke down in tears. The police escorts patted him on the back. He pulled himself together, and expected to be greeted by a throng of news cameras.

But they all had gone off chasing the kindergarten kids who had been trapped on an even higher floor. They were brought home to wild cheers and klieg lights. Selinger chuckled when he got downstairs and realized how bored the press seemed. He went to a hospital for a sip of oxygen, then took a cab to the bus terminal and rode home.

He pressed his face against the window of the bus and watched the dark streets of New Jersey, the shapes and dimness. He walked two blocks from the bus stop to his door. He found his key in his coat pocket, brought it as far as the lock, and stopped. He wept.

I hope the neighbors don't see me, he thought.

He unlocked the door and fell into the arms of his wife and kids.

Diana Limousine Office
Woodbridge Sheraton
Woodbridge, N.J.
6:30 P.M.

The big redheaded man burst in the door of the limousine office, wringing his hands.

"What happened?" asked Wahed Moharam, the owner of the car service.

Mahmud Abouhalima turned his head away. He raced through the Muslim *Rakat* prayer twice. The boss, Moharam, was not a fervent Muslim—it was the month of Ramadan, when the devout fast during the day, and Moharam often excused himself from its rigors on the grounds that his stomach hurt—but he knew that it was not the time for the evening prayers. Not only that, Abouhalima did not have any scheduled limo jobs. So what was he doing here in the office?

"Mahmud, what happened?" Moharam asked.

"An accident happened," said Abouhalima.

"Oh, my God," said Moharam. "Anybody get hurt?"

Abouhalima nodded.

Wahed Moharam was not happy. He began to think about insurance. He did not like any official questions about his business operations. He was not a bomber, but he had landed himself a nice stall in the lobby of the Woodbridge Sheraton for his limousine company, where he cleared a few thousand dollars a week—much of it cash and impossible to tax. He did weddings, funerals, and prom nights, and carried executives staying at the Sheraton. Also, he had the added profit of being located in the near suburbs of New York City. Many people visiting from out of town hated to drive anywhere near the city. That was money in the bank for Moharam, who had three or four men available as chauffeurs. The big redheaded man had introduced himself to Moharam a few months earlier in Woodbridge Gardens, the apartment complex where Moharam lived. He'd said he was a taxi driver in the city and had a nice limousine, and was available for any extra work. He was also a neighbor, so Moharam was happy to give Abouhalima the business. But he had never seen him so upset. It must have been a tremendous accident. The insurance agents would be crawling all over his operation, asking questions. No good.

"Are my cars okay?" asked Moharam.

"Don't worry," said Abouhalima, shaking his head. "Your car is okay."

Moharam went to see for himself. He walked into the lobby and out to the front door. The limousine was parked a few yards away, and he walked around it once. No dents that he could see. Back in the office, he drew a cup of water for Abouhalima, who pushed it away. Then Abouhalima stood facing a wall and prayed the *Rakat*.

"I don't see anything wrong with the car," said Moharam. "What kind of accident was this?"

"I can't tell you," said Abouhalima.

The tall redhead walked out of the office. He seemed as though he were about to explode. Moharam shrugged.

WOODHAVEN BOULEVARD, QUEENS
7:00 P.M.

They had gone through a list of hospitals once and were starting over again. They couldn't find Monica. Ed's father sat in the house in Seaford, dialing everyone he could think of. Ed had come straight from Boston to Queens, where Monica's brothers lived. Some of Monica's friends were calling.

"She has to be in a hospital somewhere," Ed said. "She would have called us otherwise. She must be hurt badly."

The phone rang. Ed grabbed it and heard the rattle of overseas lines. It was a call from Ecuador. Monica's parents had recently retired back to their native land and the news of the Trade Center explosion had been flashed around the world.

"Eddie," said Monica's mother.

"Hiya, Momma," said Ed.

"Where's my daughter?"

"I don't know," said Ed.

"What do you mean, you don't know? You're her husband. You should know where she is."

Ed handed off the phone to one of the brothers. He had to agree with the mother. He wished, with all his heart, that he knew where she was.

BALLROOM, THE VISTA HOTEL
WORLD TRADE CENTER, N.Y.
9:00 P.M.

"Mark, you have to help me," said Gene Fasullo, coughing. "We have to get out of here. We have to get these people out of here."

"What's the matter?" asked Mark Marchese.

Marchese, the public affairs director for the Port Authority, was exhausted and exhilarated. He had climbed down the stairs late in the day. At one point, he had called WCBS, an all-news radio station, to see if he could get some information. To his shock, he was switched immediately into the studio and put on the air. He politely explained that the people inside had no idea what was going on.

Now, all the bosses had made their ways out of the building, and were gathered in the ballroom of the Vista Hotel, which seemed to be undamaged. And just about every rescue agency between Manhattan and Boston had staked out space in the ballroom.

"The ballroom is in danger of collapsing," whispered Fasullo, the chief engineer for the Port Authority. He was a slim man, retching in a distinguished way, and not so often that he could not be heard. Fasullo had spent most of the afternoon in a dark, smoky elevator. A few other mechanically inclined people were with him, and when their car stopped between floors, they had pried open the doors and cut a hole in gypsum walls with their keys. They had used the tiny lights on their beepers to guide them. Fasullo probably should have been in a hospital, sipping oxygen for his smoky lungs. But as soon as he made it to the street, he went down to the basement to inspect the damage. Now he was frightened.

The columns in the basement supporting the hotel and the plaza between the towers normally were twelve feet long, distributing their weight onto the floors. But with the collapse of the concrete slab floors, the columns now ran nearly five stories—long, spindly structures, much weaker than the short stubby ones that they had been at the start of the day.

"They're like spaghetti," Fasullo told Marchesi. "Stand a piece of dry spaghetti on end. Put your finger on top of a short piece and it's rather strong. Press the top of a long piece and it will bend."

Consulting Engineer Les Robertson had calculated the safety factor of the columns and determined it to be less than one—meaning they were subject to collapse at any time. Only the hotel would have fallen—but it was twenty-two stories tall. The top officials from the FBI and two or three hundred people were inside the ballroom.

"You've got to help me move them out," said Fasullo. "Tell them to move to the other side of the ballroom." He passed the same word to Charles Maikish, the director of the Trade Center, who got up on a chair.

"May I have your attention please," he said. No one stopped chatting.

A children's athletic league had been scheduled to hold its awards dinner that night. All the trophies were parked on tables, and the agencies had staked out space by planting their agency signs in the arms of the figurines. They were distributing heavy duty bureaucratic toys: cellular phones and beepers, hats, walkie-talkies, and any other gadgetry that had been lying around. Down the hall, in the Tall Ships Bar, a temporary morgue had been set up in anticipation that massive casualties might result, but by now, the remains of the four workers who had been in the lunchroom—Monica Smith, Steve Knapp, Bob Kirkpatrick, and Bill Macko—had been moved to the medical examiner's office.

"This is extremely serious," said Maikish. The quiet spread in patches across the room. "We will all be fine if we immediately move out of this end of the room. It is in danger of collapse."

That made an impression. Maikish had enough to do without worrying about the death of every top bureaucrat in New York. He had thousands of tenants who wanted to go back into their offices on Monday. They had to be relocated. The executives of Cantor Fitzgerald had a $5 billion bond trade that they had not been able to enter into their books when the bomb went off, and they spoke in specific terms of the entire market for the debt of the United States being affected. Someone from the White House, in fact, was trying to reach the head of the Port Authority to impress the importance of accommodating Cantor Fitzgerald.

Later, someone from the commodities markets was saying how important it was that they be able to get back into their trading floors by Monday morning. Otherwise, commodity trading everywhere would be fouled up.

"The entire world oil market, for instance, would be disrupted," said the commodities man.

"Okay," said Maikish.

Then he had the phone company yelling at him. They had a major switch in an unmarked room in one of the towers that only had eight hours of backup battery power. They needed power restored by 8 P.M. or else they would lose the ability to transmit millions of calls.

"Okay," Maikish had said. "Okay."

They might not have liked the sound of his "okay."

"And the switch carries the FAA's air traffic," continued the man from the phone company. "We lose that, we have to shut down the airports. We shut down the airports, the entire country will get backed up."

Maikish nodded. The next domino to fall back would be international traffic coming through the major airports of the city. The Port Authority ran JFK, LaGuardia, and Newark airports. No one had to tell him twice what it would mean to shut them down. He grabbed someone from Con Ed, and they had been able to restore partial power in time to keep the switch humming. The airports were moving.

In all the confusion, no one had gotten around to notifying the families of the dead workers.

ROYAL JORDANIAN AIRLINES
PASSENGER LOUNGE
JFK INTERNATIONAL AIRPORT
QUEENS, N.Y.
11:00 P.M.

A good thing for "Abdul Basit" that the airports had not been shut down. Forget about being blamed for delaying air traffic. He would have missed his flight to Jordan. He had a first-class seat. His real name was Ramzi Yousef, if a man with a dozen aliases can have anything like a real name. Now they were calling for people to board. His time in New York was coming to an end. He had arrived six months earlier, traveling with a man who had been carrying bomb manuals but was arrested for holding a blatantly fake passport. The man had stayed in touch with Ramzi from prison. And Ramzi had been very busy in Jersey City. People who saw him around a mysterious garage on Pamrapo Avenue, where the Arab men had been lugging big loads, called him "Horse Face." Some Arabs called him "Rashed." The FBI called him "Mastermind."

Horse Face–Rashed–Abdul Basit–Ramzi Yousef stepped into the cabin and vanished from the United States. His work was done.

WOODHAVEN BOULEVARD, QUEENS
11:30 P.M.

As midnight reached toward the Rodriguez home, Ed Smith had few illusions left. He was heartened that no one from the Port Authority had called the house in Long Island. He stayed with the brothers to be closer to the city. The phone rang. It was the mother of Monica's best girlfriend.

"Eddie, honey. You better call the morgue."

He took a breath. "Do you have the number?"

He made the next call in a haze, knowing that no one would tell him it was a mistake, hoping that was all that they would say.

"Medical examiners office, good evening."

"I'm Monica Smith's husband, I heard that she's there," said Ed.

"I can't give any information out," said the man at the morgue.

"Well, you just told somebody she was there."

"That's her mother."

"That's not her mother, her mother's in Ecuador. I promise you, she didn't call you."

"Who was that?" asked the man at the morgue.

"I guess it's a friend of the family trying to find out where she is. Is she there?"

"All I can say is, if I was you, I would come down here."

Ed and one of the brothers went out to the car. He dialed his home phone in Long Island to tell his father they were going to First Avenue, to the medical examiners office.

"Hold on a minute, there's some people here to talk to you," said his father. It was the police from Nassau County. They told him to call a detective in New York.

"Yes, hi, Mr. Smith," said the cop. "Very sorry. Can you come down tomorrow morning? We're just about ready to go home and wrap things up."

"What about the baby?" asked Smith.

"Sir," said the detective. "Do you know how bad it was?"

4

FEBRUARY 27, 1993:
SATURDAY MORNING

The rope hung lifelessly, dropped from somewhere out of the darkness above. Malcolm Brady looked up through the heavy air, thick with dust and oil particles. He could make out the outline of a hole above him, about twelve feet wide. The rope was suspended from its center.

His eyes followed the plumb line down, out of the gaping rupture in the floor of the Vista Hotel's lobby. It passed through empty space, into the crater blown through the sixteen-inch concrete floors, down into the pit below him. He raised his eyes, struggling to see by the dim glow of work lights, and leveled his gaze across the two-hundred-foot void. About twenty-four hours ago, the void had been the B-2 level of the garage. The rope, floating in the empty center, marked ground zero. It was here that the bomb had been placed.

Brady stood as close to the crater as he could, and scanned the damage. For twenty-four years he had worked bomb sites for the Bureau of Alcohol, Tobacco and Firearms. But he had never seen anything like this. With his usual penchant for understatement, he remarked, "It was kind of scary at first."

The crater extended before and below him, devastation for another five hundred feet in every direction. Around him, people in protective clothing were moving slowly, delicately, looking like astronauts exploring a dead planet. Some were scanning the area with thermal imaging cameras—heat detectors that could spot a body trapped under rubble. Others were bent or kneeling at the perimeter of the wreckage, examining, drawing lines in the dust with cotton-tipped swabs and dropping them into plastic bags.

Overhead, six tons of concrete clung precariously to warped rebars. Chunks of concrete plunged around them. The fractured floor near the crater crumbled away beneath their feet. Four floors down, at the bottom of the crater, pumps tried to clear away a flood of water and sewage from broken pipes. Brady knew the crews would have to be pulled back soon, and the investigation would be delayed until the floors and ceilings could be shored up.

All morning, investigators had been walking through the scene, drawing what conclusions they could, while three hundred workers sifted through debris. Leslie Robertson, the structural engineer who had designed the towers, had been first in the hole. Just after dawn, he'd gone in alone, not wanting to risk any of his staff in the unstable underworld. He spotted ground zero by looking at the way the floors and walls were blown away. He knew it had to be a car bomb.

"It was parked right next to the outside wall of the north tower," Robertson concluded, just the other side of the building services room. "It just blew the cinder-block wall out," moaned the assistant engineer director, Robert DiChiara. The thought of his colleagues, having lunch while a bomb fuse burned nearby, made him nearly sob. "They should have gone to lunch," he managed to say.

Officially, the disaster at the World Trade Center had not yet been declared a bombing, although no one in New York City seemed to have any doubt.

Overnight, security details were put on alert at airports and public buildings. The Empire State Building was evacuated after a bomb threat. City detectives and Port Authority police fanned out through lower Manhattan, looking for anyone who might have seen anything. As the sun came up that Saturday morning, the frenzy of the bomb scene was gone. The barricaded streets were quiet. The Trade Center was closed. Reporters wandered back and forth outside blue sawhorses, trying to get comments from whoever went in or came out. Underground, it was still dark and oddly silent.

It was into this deadened scene that the Governor of the State of New York stepped that morning after his limousine maneuvered through the barricades. Mario Cuomo, the patriarch of the state for more than a decade, glowered at the abandoned towers and at Port Authority director Charles Maikish, who met him inside the command center set up at the Vista.

"How could you let this happen?" Cuomo shouted, and let loose in precise words his impression of the psychic as well as monetary damage wrought on the citizens of his state. "This must return to normalcy as soon as possible. How long until the towers can reopen?"

"Six months," Maikish quietly estimated.

Cuomo was enraged even more. "Six months? In six weeks you're going to lose all your tenants. These will be ghost towers. Ghost towers!"

"Governor, the damage . . ." Maikish began to explain as the governor raged on. Finally he wedged in a suggestion: "Perhaps you should see for yourself."

Cuomo warily eyed others who had emerged from underground, dressed in boots and slickers. "Is there water down there?" he asked.

Water and just about everything else, Maikish thought as he nodded. Cuomo suited up and followed Maikish and their guides down the roundabout path of staircases and ramps into the former B-2 parking level.

Cuomo stood and stared at the hole from hell. "Charlie, what used to be there?" he asked several times, pointing around the debris.

"The general services room . . . the building maintenance room," Maikish replied. He pointed to a collection of cinder blocks. "This was our command center, where all the information for the entire building was collected."

Then law-enforcement officials put on rubber boots and hard hats and carefully climbed through the twisted site with FBI and ATF agents. Acting U.S. Attorney Roger Hayes stared at the wreckage in disbelief, hardly able to breathe in the cold, dank air. FBI chemical expert Dave Williams, appropriately clad in rain slicker and army fatigues, gave him a quick rundown of what investigators had deduced thus far: it was a bomb, a lot of explosives. It must have come in a van or a delivery truck. No one knew yet what kind of bomb it was. Chemists were taking samples, trying to determine that now.

Hayes watched the agents dusting through the rubble. "How are we ever going to find the people responsible?" he said into his face mask.

*   *   *

Moharam could not understand. He had Mahmud Abouhalima down for a job at seven this morning at the Edison station, and he did not answer the beep. Never before. What is with him?

He decided to walk next door to the Abouhalima apartment. He banged on his door. There was no answer from inside, but then he saw a curtain moving. Someone had checked him out. The door opened, and Mahmud stood there.

"What's the matter, I beep you, you don't answer?" asked Moharam.

"Listen, Wahed, I have problem," said Abouhalima.

"So you cannot do the job?" asked Moharam.

"No. I can't do any work today."

Moharam stalked off angrily. He would have to do the job himself. It would be many months before he again came face to face with Mahmud Abouhalima.

*　　*　　*

Roger Hayes walked the few blocks from the World Trade Center to the federal office building at 26 Federal Plaza. The first of a series of meetings was scheduled there for 10:00 A.M. A briefing room had been set up. Coffee was brewed. Pads and pencils were set out. Bottles of Bufferin and Excedrin were lined up next to the Cremora.

The governor was there, as were Police Commissioner Ray Kelly and the FBI's regional director, Jim Fox; also present were the FBI's chief counsel from Washington, the Manhattan district attorney's staff, ATF and PA officials, the Secret Service, emergency services staff, the bomb squad—officials from more than a dozen agencies.

Hayes was the interim federal prosecutor in Manhattan until President Clinton appointed a replacement. Of all the people to keep a seat warm in the U.S. Attorney's office, it happened that Hayes was the best suited to handle vicious murders. Many federal prosecutors have no experience with street crimes. The crimes brought in the federal courts usually are of the white-collar variety—swindles and violations of federal laws that rarely excite much attention or bloodshed. This was especially true in the Manhattan federal prosecutor's office, which was known officially as the U.S. Attorney for the Southern District of New York. The office was packed with young men and women from the top law schools in the country, people whose blood boiled—well, *simmered,* perhaps—over criminal cases that most people couldn't fathom. Imelda Marcos had been tried and acquitted on tax charges in the Southern District. It was in the Southern District courthouse that Mike Milken, the billionaire junk-bond expert, had been brought to the bar—again, for violations of little-known securities laws. But Roger Hayes had cut his teeth a few blocks away, in the state court system, as an assistant district attorney in the office of Manhattan District Attorney Robert Morgenthau. His most famous case had come a decade earlier, when he prosecuted a stagehand at the Metropolitan Opera who, during an intermission, had raped and murdered a member of the orchestra and then dumped her body down an airshaft. Back then, he had worn his hair over his shoulders. Now he is a curly-haired man bearing a strong resemblance to Stuart Markowitz, the television lawyer on "L.A. Law."

Hayes had moved into the number-two job in the federal prosecutor's office when an old friend became the headman. Now the friend had stepped down, and Hayes was holding the chair for a few months. He knew all about the sharp-elbowed competition and rivalry among the law-enforcement agencies. Another federal prosecutor's office—the one for the Eastern District of New York—was located just across the East River in Brooklyn, a five-minute subway ride away. In fact, one of the most ambitious Brooklyn prosecutors had showed up this morning, sniffing around to see if his office had any jurisdiction.

"Unless you can move the Trade Center across the East River," Hayes had advised him, "take a hike."

In fact, not even Hayes was calling the shots just yet. Until the explosion was officially declared a bombing, it was still under the jurisdiction of the New York Police Department. But Hayes knew that this case would be in the hands of the FBI before the weekend was over. That meant the case would end up being tried in the federal courts, so he called an assistant to this meeting. His pick for the case was J. Gilmore Childers.

Tall, skinny, and balding at thirty-seven, Childers on the surface seemed the stereotype of a bloodless, passion-free federal prosecutor. He was a methodical lawyer, cool under pressure, and was strictly business in the courtroom. He didn't resort to drama or histrionics before a judge or jury. He relied on the facts.

Hayes knew Childers had another side as well. He had street smarts. He'd been an assistant DA in Brooklyn, prosecuting transit crimes, before he joined the U.S. Attorney's office in 1988. He had pulled off a conspiracy prosecution against mobsters accused of killing a New York City cop. The state had twice lost murder trials against the killers, but Childers had nailed them. The conspiracy case had been the last chance to bring them to justice.

Childers also had the ability to work with very little sleep, a talent he was going to need.

And Childers had at least one more credential: he had worked with the Anti-Terrorist Task Force before. When a Prozac-popping Muslim militant was arrested for the assassination of Rabbi Meir Kahane, Childers had been involved in the FBI's investigation of the alleged killer's friends. As recently as six weeks ago, Childers had overseen another investigation of the same circle of Muslim fundamentalists. Childers was definitely the guy for the case, especially if these Islamic militants had anything to do with it.

Hayes and his assistant sat quietly as Fox and his assistant began the briefing. First the discussion focused on coordinating the various agencies, with Fox and Kelly outlining what little they knew so far. Then they talked about the upcoming press conference and what the public should be told.

All the morning newspapers had quoted law-enforcement sources saying the explosion had been caused by a bomb.

But Fox and Kelly were adamant that they should not confirm it. Air tests had found traces of nitrates at the site, an indication of explosives, but the samples had been flown to a special lab, and they wanted those results back first.

"It was in a public parking area," said Maikish. "It was parked at the base of the towers. Nothing that is part of the mechanical systems of the Trade Center has the strength to cause that kind of damage."

Cuomo was in favor of stating the obvious as well, but conceded to the law-enforcement authorities.

Little else had emerged from the investigation so far. A nervous search overnight for a second device hidden somewhere at the site had convinced the bomb squad that there wasn't one. There had been no prior warning, with the usual parade of anonymous calls afterwards, all claiming responsibility. The only call given any credibility was the first. A man with a foreign accent had called the First Precinct at 1:35 P.M. and said the bombing was the work of the Serbian Liberation Front.

That call—a little more than an hour after the explosion—had come when emergency service radio calls were still broadcasting the blast as a transformer fire. And the Trade Center is within the First Precinct. All the other calls were made to 911.

Four members of the joint NYPD-FBI Anti-Terrorist Task Force were dispatched to spend the night in upstate Rockland County, surveilling the homes of known Bosnian activists. But neither Croatian nor Serbian nationalist groups had been active in the United States for more than ten years. The deadliest terrorist attack on American soil had been a bombing at LaGuardia Airport in which eleven people were killed, and no one had ever taken responsibility. Later, investigators had concluded it was the work of Croatian nationalists. But that attack had happened eighteen years before.

By the time Kelly walked into the 10:00 A.M. session, twenty-seven callers had claimed to know something about the blast. After the 1:35 P.M. call to the First Precinct, others didn't start flooding 911 until after 4:00 P.M. By midnight, Colombian drug cartels had the most votes: three calls claimed the drug lords were responsible. The Black Liberation Front, Chinese Militants, and Arab terrorists each had one call. So did the New World Revolution, whatever that was. The rest of the calls were too disjointed to be understood.

But shortly after midnight, Serbians took credit again. At 1:29 A.M., Iraq weighed in, followed by another vote for Yugoslavia at 2:31 and Iraq again, twelve minutes later. More disjointed, rambling accusations came in throughout the morning.

A freewheeling speculation session began, and a litany of possible motives were tossed around. "Could this really be over Yugoslavia?" someone asked. President Clinton had just announced that the United States was airlifting food and supplies to Bosnia. The timing made the motive plausible.

The Bank of Kuwait had been damaged in the blast, its vaults blown open. Friday the twenty-sixth had been the second anniversary of the start of the ground war in Kuwait. Another plausible motive. Several months earlier, Hamas had promised reprisals in the Middle East in the tug-of-war over displaced Palestinians. Could the bombing be some kind of delayed reaction?

The last previous car-bombing attempt in New York City had been twenty years earlier, when the Palestinian group Black September tried to blow up Israeli Prime Minister Golda Meir with three car bombs. The plot failed, but one of the bombers had finally been caught in Italy. His trial in Brooklyn federal court was scheduled to begin on Monday. Could the timing be more than coincidence?

If any Middle Eastern country had a motive, it was Iraq. But the State Department believed the Persian Gulf War had shattered Iraq's terrorist network. Still, the Palestinian Liberation Front and the terrorist group Fatah both had bases in Baghdad. They couldn't be ruled out.

Drug cartels couldn't be totally dismissed, either. They had put contracts out on the lives of New York judges and law-enforcement heads before. In 1989, one thousand pounds of dynamite stuffed into a car blew up Colombia's secret police headquarters in Bogotá, killing fifty-two people.

Even poor Wilfredo Mercado, the employee of Windows on the World, didn't escape suspicion. That Saturday morning, he was still missing. He was from Peru—could the Shining Path somehow be involved? His battered body wouldn't be found for weeks.

The meeting adjourned as the morning ended. Cuomo, Kelly, and Fox were expected back at police headquarters for the noontime press conference to reassure the shell-shocked city. Brady went to ATF headquarters to meet the rest of his team. Hayes and Childers went to their office to watch the news on television.

As the TV cameras began to roll, an NYPD detective picked up his home phone and called an FBI agent he'd worked with on the joint Anti-Terrorist Task Force. "You sure as shit better hope it's not those guys who did it," he said into the phone. He didn't need to explain who "those guys" were. The agent knew. "Anybody seen Salem around lately?" the detective asked.

Emad Salem, spy and former informant, was watching television too, waiting for his phone to ring.

*　　*　　*

The cast on the stage at 1 Police Plaza was an all-star lineup. Only the mayor was missing. David N. Dinkins was on a return flight from Japan. Just moments before the speeches began, someone called 911 and threatened to bomb the United Nations. No one mentioned the threat at the press conference.

Police Commissioner Raymond Kelly, whose NYPD was still officially in charge, made the first statement, and he immediately addressed a question that, at least by the official line, was based on conjecture: If it had been a bomb, who had done it? "It is impossible to speculate at this point why any person should have committed such a horrible crime. Nevertheless, the fear it may engender among New Yorkers, and others in our nation for that matter, is very real. We must remember that fear is a type of weapon as well, one to which we must not submit."

First Deputy Mayor Norman Steisel described the damage and

dropped names. "I should also point out that I've been in constant touch with the mayor, advising him of what has been going on. At several occasions, he has been in consultation with state officials and also had a conversation with the President. . . ."

Stanley Brezenoff, executive director of the Port Authority, explained why the explosion was able to screw up the entire complex. "The major problems we faced as a consequence of both our systems . . . primary and backup systems being out, was that we could not communicate with the people who were stranded on the floors and in the stairwells, and there was no light, particularly on the stairwells." He didn't mention that, six years earlier, the PA's own terrorism task force had warned that the World Trade Center's public parking garage made it a likely target for a car bomb.

Cuomo gave a buck-up-and-be-brave speech: "Fear is another weapon that's used against you. And that's what terrorists are all about, if these were terrorists. And what they're trying to do is deny you normalcy and what we must do in this safest and greatest city and state and nation in the world is return as quickly as we can to normalcy."

Even the governor of New Jersey, James Florio, whose state operates the Port Authority jointly with New York, came for a tour and issued a statement connecting the bombing with his own legislative battle for gun control: "If we are entering into a new chapter in American society . . . as a society, we're going to have to start thinking about things like access to weapons and explosives and guns . . . with a more focused attention than perhaps we did in the past."

Reporters shouted questions: "It wasn't a bomb?" "Are you saying you don't know what caused the explosion?" "If it wasn't a bomb, what was it?"

FBI director Fox dodged: "We have not, of course, formally declared this a terrorist-related bombing or even a bombing. Our best guess is there's a high probability it is a bombing. It may be terrorist-related."

Cuomo pushed the point. "There's an immense crater," he said. "It looks like a bomb. It smells like a bomb. It's probably a bomb." As Cuomo left the microphone and passed by Fox, he whispered, "Well, I didn't say it *was* a bomb."

Kelly, with nowhere to duck, added that the amount of damage, the intense heat, and the traces of nitrates found at the scene all suggested a bomb, probably a plastic explosive like Composition 4, a "standard military explosive widely available in the U.S."

Back at the explosion site, Lieutenant Walter Boser, the NYPD bomb squad commander, snorted. "A lot of people who don't know anything about this are talking," he told a reporter. "And those who do know aren't talking."

*   *   *

Malcolm Brady would have been surprised if nitrates hadn't been found; everything else had spewed into the dank hole. Sewage pipes had burst; food and meat lockers had been blasted open; gasoline, oil, and rubber from the 1,200 cars parked there had blown everywhere. Even the compound they were using to melt the frozen flooded water contained nitrates.

Brady, the supervisor of the ATF's National Response Team in the Northeast, had flown in from his base in Miami that morning, and another twenty members arrived at the NRT New York City office by noon.

Brady had spent most of the morning in the standing-room-only crowd of law-enforcement supervisors for their first interagency coordinating meeting. Afterwards, Brady met with the incoming members of his team, then grabbed a hard hat and mask and went underground.

The NRT is a unique concept in federal law enforcement. Four teams are set up around the country, composed of veteran ATF specialists from the region. Within twenty-four hours the team members—investigators, chemists, explosives experts—can mobilize and rendezvous at a fire or bomb scene.

New York City's request for the Response Team was approved by the ATF less than four hours after the blast. Brady already had his bag packed. In fact, he had gone home from the office when he heard about the explosion because he knew his team would be called in.

But underground, even a veteran like Brady was slightly overwhelmed by the task. "How do you approach something this size?" he asked as he stared at the sheer size of the blast's damage. The NRT had never seen such devastation before.

Brady wasn't a chemist or an explosives expert; he was the team supervisor. But he had learned to read a bomb scene. He'd leave determining exactly what the bomb was to the laboratories. That afternoon, Brady began looking for something entirely different. He was searching for the car.

"Find the vehicle, and you find the suspects," he said. Something had brought the bomb into the garage, and it hadn't been a suitcase. It had been something big, and pieces of it were out there somewhere. That's the problem with a bomb: it leaves clues.

So he stood as close to ground zero as he could, and simply looked around. He'd get a good view of the site and apply what investigators call the "best evidence rule." He knew how explosives blew debris through the air. Find the likeliest path the exploding metal of a vehicle would take, and that's where first to look for clues in the massive destruction.

Once he got into the site, he didn't need a test tube to make some deductions about the bomb's composition. It had caused massive destruction, and had left a lot of soot. On the surface, that gave the impression of a plastic explosive like C-4. Its main component—a compound called RDX—generates a lot of heat and leaves a lot of carbon residue. But C-4 doesn't leave nitrates. Still, the presence of nitrates alone can't rule out plastics. Another RDX-based plastic explosive, called Semtex, leaves very distinguishable nitrate traces. But Semtex is hard to come by, even for terrorists.

The damage itself made Brady doubt that fast-moving plastic explosives were responsible. Cars, blocks of cement, columns, floors—the wreckage had been pushed and shoved and thrown as the concussion wave moved through the area. It had been twisted, broken, blown all about—but not shattered. The force of a fast-moving explosive—speeding through the area at about 2,400 feet per second—would have blasted debris into smithereens. Slow-moving explosives, such as TNT, travel half that fast, doing the same amount of damage but in a different way.

If C-4 had been packed in the bomb-laden vehicle, agents would be digging its embedded pieces out of the concrete walls. C-4 would rip the metal into thin, threadlike shards and hurl them against the objects left standing. But a slower, TNT-type explosion would tear metal into large fragments and shove them along the path of the detonation wave. For now, Brady and his team would concentrate on the path of the wave.

From the spot where the plumb line showed ground zero, Brady's team knew the blast would have sent material flying into the general services room, and under the escalator behind it. They would even dismantle the escalator in the search for some metal fragment that could be critical evidence. In the coming days, the team would decide to focus on four more hot spots. Sifting by hand through rubble four feet deep, they would examine each piece in all six spots. When they finally reached the floor, they would sweep it and remove every particle.

As Brady climbed out of the garage and headed for another late-afternoon meeting, a reporter called out to him, "Will you solve it?"

"I have no doubt about it," he replied, without missing a step.

5

FEBRUARY 28, 1993: SUNDAY

Donald Sadowy completely forgot how much his feet hurt. Sadowy, a detective in the New York Police Department's bomb squad, was preparing himself for another mission into the pulverized scrap heap that had once supported Manhattan's tallest building. Two days ago he had been sitting in his office in Greenwich Village, working on old case files and waiting to go to a 2:00 P.M. appointment with the podiatrist. Now he was one of thirty investigators sent into the bomb crater to hunt for clues to New York's biggest mystery in a generation. There's no time to worry about your aching feet when you're searching for a needle in the apocalypse.

Somewhere, buried beneath a seething refuse pile the size of a city block, was evidence that could lead detectives to the bombers—maybe before they set off another killer blast. It would probably be something minute and seemingly insignificant: a shred of cloth, a scrap of paper, a wallet, a shard of metal, an unusually scarred piece of concrete. All Sadowy and the evidence team had to do was to figure out where the hell it might be hidden among the galactic mounds of rubble, then get to it, recognize it, and haul it out without being crushed to death.

At the insistence of their superiors, Sadowy, his partner Joe Hanlin, and the other searchers were forced to put on special protective gear before entering the hole. The explosion had literally ripped open the Trade Center's entrails—breaking plumbing and sewage lines, sending streams of untreated human waste cascading into the cavern. That stink had mingled with the acrid chemical mist left behind by the bomb, searing the lungs and stinging the eyes of anyone unfortunate enough to be inside. Scientists from the Occupational Safety and Health Administration advised that the searchers wear masks to guard against respiratory infection or asbestos contamination. Sadowy slipped the respirator over his construction helmet, and tried to adjust to the stuffiness, heat, and humidity. The mask added a surreal distance to the world outside, making people and things resemble objects from some underwater documentary. But it was better than choking on the toxic atmosphere.

Hanlin, meanwhile, was taping up his wrists. He wore special work gloves and ATF coveralls. To seal out any harmful chemicals or microorganisms, he was also covered with a two-piece jumpsuit made of a high-tech plastic known as Tivex. The bureau was proud of the top-of-the-line equipment; Hanlin and the other investigators called the ridiculous looking getup, with its puffy white hood, a "bunny suit."

Hanlin was what investigators called a "bomb guy," one of the ATF's team of explosives experts who flew to every major explosion and arson fire in the country. He'd done twenty years in the military, dismantling ordnance on some of the great battlefields of his generation. He'd crawled under a hooch at an army base at Quan Tren, Vietnam, to disengage a hand grenade planted by the Viet Cong. After the Six-Day War in 1967, he'd helped the Egyptian Army dismantle the unexploded Israeli artillery shells left beneath the desert sands. He'd disarmed air bombs in Lebanon, and had built hundreds of explosive devices himself to instruct trainees at the Army Explosives School. Hanlin had even taught an ominous-sounding course in "Nuclear Ordnance Disposal." Yet, after taking a quick tour Sunday morning, and inspecting the B-6 level—the "chiller floor," where the refrigeration and air-conditioning units were located—even Hanlin was overwhelmed by the devastation. "I've never seen damage like this in my life," he said.

"None of us have," Sadowy replied.

Although some of the wreckage piles were still smoldering, there was already intense pressure coming down the chain of command, heading straight for Sadowy, Hanlin, and the other detectives in the hole. The public was terrified and wanted speedy assurance that the city wasn't under siege. Everyone from Wall Street to the most godforsaken Bronx housing project wanted the bombers arrested before they struck again. The media were relentless. Jim Fox, head of the FBI's New York office, had complicated matters by releasing bad information, claiming that the explosion had been caused by dynamite and that the prime suspects were Bosnians. At this point, two days after the blast, only the bombers knew the answers to those questions. But when the White House, the Pentagon, and the State Department start grilling the local police brass for updates, the brass starts squeezing the field supervisors. And when the field supervisors start getting pressured, police protocol virtually assures that they begin leaning on the worker ants.

The cops had spent most of Friday assisting trapped office workers and searching for additional explosives. On Saturday they'd made a few preliminary forays into the eerie moonscape, trying to get some sense of the damage. But the wreckage was still too unstable for a full-scale search. By Sunday afternoon, though, the FBI had moved in and announced that they were taking control. At an informal meeting in the rubble-strewn ballroom of the Vista Hotel, which was located on the ground floor of the Trade Center complex, the FBI declared its jurisdiction over the case. That meant the local cops could assist in the search, but all evidence, reports, decisions, and credit would be the property of the Feds. Dave Williams, head of the FBI's explosives team, told the searchers to brace themselves because the operations would take weeks.

But right now they needed leads, Williams stressed.

He was assigning all the investigators to do surveillance of the crater, make sketches and notes of the scene, and take swabs of residue from anything that looked unusual. The samples would be shipped back to the lab, where chemists could then analyze the type of chemicals used and figure out where the heaviest concentration of residue was located. The heavier the residue, the closer to ground zero.

"Whatever you do," Williams stressed, "don't move any evidence. Just take your swabs and leave it where it is."

Williams was a no-nonsense guy in the best of times, and the urgency now ringing through his voice was compounded by the haunting Vista ballroom. The hotel had been scheduled to host a youth sports awards banquet at 1:00 P.M. the day of the bombing. The ballroom had already been set up with linens and china, banners and bunting, even a dais and podium for the prize-winning young jocks. But the explosion below had blown the room into disarray, knocking over tables and chairs, burying furniture in piles of concrete. Huge chunks of ceiling had crushed a tableful of trophies, breaking the tiny brass heads, arms, basketballs, and baseball bats off of the brittle metal figures. Hanlin, a father of two, shuddered to think that hundreds of bright-eyed young athletes had come within forty-two minutes of being showered with concrete and plaster.

The investigators were divided into teams of ten. Hanlin was paired with the NYPD bomb detective, Sadowy, and assigned a chemist, a sketch artist, a photographer, and several evidence technicians. When the last searcher had finished suiting up, each of them grabbed a flashlight and set off to read the rubble.

"Excuse me," said a chemist, as they made their way down the ramp. "Can anyone tell me exactly what we're looking for?"

"I don't know," Sadowy said. "But we'll know it when we see it."

All bomb investigations are the art of doing physics in reverse. With an explosion moving outward from its center in all directions, as this one had done, it must vent directly above ground zero. The day before, Malcolm Brady had figured that a plumb line dropped through the spot where the bomb vented would intersect the point of the greatest horizontal damage. The line coming down would cross the line going across, and that would be ground zero.

Those calculations may all sound plausible on paper or in a classroom. Down in a concrete Acropolis they're not quite as easy to follow. Sadowy suggested they head for the B-2 level, a barely accessible patch of concrete near the lip of the crater. The reasoning was simple: it was heavily damaged and no one had been there yet.

As they moved off the ramp and into the cavern, the friendly chatter ceased. The searchers had put their respirators in place, and were busily scanning the wreckage as they walked. Each piece of concrete, battered auto, and exposed steel reinforcing rod became a possible clue in the biggest investigation any of them had ever handled.

After advancing into the wreckage for five minutes, they could see the B-2 level, and the foreboding piles of debris standing between them and their destination. "It looks pretty bad up there," Hanlin said, the reverse psychology of bomb investigations making the statement sound optimistic.

Sadowy had trained all his career for a case like this. He was a city kid, a Polish-American born and raised in Flatbush, Brooklyn. He was a graduate of a technical high school, and had done a four-year tour in the marines. Except for his lack of Irish lineage, Sadowy's background was a classic preparation for the NYPD, and he'd risen quickly up the ranks and made it onto the bomb squad. He'd become one of the NYPD's two resident car-bomb experts since the April 1992 incident with the crazy lady in the van. Her name was Linne Gunther, and she was so angry that her tax dollars were paying for the Persian Gulf War that she loaded up a van, parked it across from the UN, and announced her intention to blow it to bits. THIS IS A PEACEFUL PROTEST, read one sign on her van; THIS VEHICLE IS LINED WITH EXPLOSIVES, read another. Volatile expressions of political dissent aren't completely uncommon in New York City, so the NYPD bomb squad handled it like any of the other 1,500 bomb calls a year. But this woman had a terrifying pedigree because she was the daughter of nuclear physicist Owen Chamberlin. Chamberlin had won a Nobel Prize in 1959 for discovering the antiproton, so who was to say his daughter wasn't capable of turning an inherited aptitude to destructive purposes? Instantly, the kook *du jour* had become a bomb technician's worst nightmare.

Gunther surrendered after a nerve-wracking twenty-four-hour standoff, and police found that her van didn't contain anything more explosive than a few cans of gasoline. But the encounter pointed out a weak spot in the NYPD's defenses: the car bomb. The NYPD's bomb squad had earned a reputation as one of the best explosives units in the world. Cops used robots to retrieve suspicious packages, and specially trained dogs to screen for anything volatile; they learned to dismantle the explosive booby traps that drug dealers rigged up to protect their stash houses. But a car bomb was pretty sophisticated stuff for most New York psychopaths. Why go to all that trouble, and worry about finding a parking spot, when you can just call your streetcorner gun runner for a bargain-basement automatic weapon? The NYPD's explosives experts tended to think of car bombs as the stuff of wild-eyed Arab terrorists, IRA members, or Steven Seagal movies.

After reviewing the tapes of the Gunther incident, Lieutenant Walter Boser, head of the bomb squad, was determined that the police department had to strengthen its guard. He assigned two of his most dependable investigators, including Don Sadowy, to become car-bomb experts. The job was a pyromaniac's dream come true. Every week they could take a few autos from the NYPD pound, drive or tow them to the shooting range at Rodman's Neck in the Bronx, and blast them back into scrap iron.

They met with Israeli, German, and British bomb experts, all of whom routinely handle exploding vehicles, and learned the tricks of the trade. After a year of study and practice, the NYPD had the capability to dismantle almost any car bomb, or neutralize it by rigging up a counter-explosion to blast an explosive device out of a vehicle.

Of course, all the training in the world couldn't have prepared the NYPD for the sneak attack used by the Trade Center bombers: a bomb with no prior warning. Just after noon on Friday, as the explosion ripped through concrete and bone, flesh, and steel, Boser had been seated at his desk in bomb squad headquarters. Sadowy was working on old case files and waiting for the opportunity to step out to the podiatrist. The office is an oasis of conformity amid the orgy of self-expression that is Greenwich Village. Painted in basic police-office gray, the shade of a late-fifties fallout shelter, it's lit by humming fluorescent tubes, floored in scuffed linoleum, and furnished with Depression-era furniture, perfectly coordinated to dull the senses and induce obedience. The walls are covered with bulletin boards. Just in case that drabness made anyone careless, mounted on the wall, just a few feet from Don Sadowy's desk, was The Plaque. The wood-and-bronze memorial commemorated the bomb squad employees who had been killed in the line of duty. Dudley and Storm, two black Labradors trained to sniff out explosives, padded around the office, adding a bit of cheer. That Friday had been just an average tour of duty when Sadowy picked up the receiver and muttered his usual greeting: "Bomb squad."

It was a federal agent calling from the Secret Service office located in the basement of the Trade Center, and from the panicked tone of his voice, it was clear that something was seriously wrong.

"You guys better get down here quick. Something exploded," he said. "I don't know what, but it's big. Fucking big!"

Now, forty-eight hours later, as Hanlin and Sadowy were passing by the Secret Service office, the detective realized why the agent had been so alarmed. The entire fleet of vehicles had been destroyed, and the office had collapsed.

"We've got to head the other way," Hanlin said.

Both men had studied the miracle of the Pan Am Flight 103 investigation. Terrorists had bombed the plane over Lockerbie, Scotland, in 1989, scattering evidence over 845 square miles of sparsely populated Scottish countryside. British authorities combed every inch of that boggy, hilly, rocky terrain—climbing trees, scaling rooftops, dragging lakes and marshes, and walking in spread-out ranks, twelve cops wide, across acres of woods and farmland.

They had a simple instruction: If it's not a rock and it's not growing, put it in a bag.

The minute scraps that had led them to the bomber were three tiny pieces of a radio cassette player which had been packed with explosives. Lockerbie proved that almost any bomb search could produce evidence. But standing on the brink of a giant crater strewn with concrete rubble, twisted metal, and human remains, who wouldn't be doubtful?

Just walking the crime scene was a dance across a minefield. The underbelly of the World Trade Center had just incurred the equivalent of an earthquake, a devastating shock that had reduced a giant parking garage to huge, teetering piles of concrete and gnarled metal. Now, two days after the blast, the scene was an avalanche waiting to happen. One wrong move could bury the investigators alive. To minimize the risk of a landslide, they frequently scuttled along on all fours to maintain their balance and distribute their body weight over a larger area. In the final hundred yards or so, the rubble was so dense that they frequently had to set their Porta-Lights down to get a firm handhold. Finally, after forty-five minutes of scrabbling through the darkness, they reached the B-2 level. It was a mess. About a dozen cars, all profoundly damaged, were littered near the edge of the hole. The blast had actually turned the B-2 level into a cliff, a concrete platform suspended sixty feet above the bottom of the cavern. Several of the cars were balanced on a thirty-foot slab of concrete that tilted in toward the crater at about a fifteen-degree angle, and was held in place only by steel reinforcement rods known as rebar. Then, Joe Hanlin thought, everything falls into darkness.

To a bomb investigator, it was an encouraging, exciting sight. The cars were so burnt and battered that they made both Sadowy's and Hanlin's hearts race. A car wouldn't be as badly charred as these wrecks unless it had been extremely close to the center of the blast. Suddenly it seemed almost possible. The vast expanse of the site had made the task seem unmanageable, incomprehensible. But up here, on this one small precipice, things were starting to look recognizable, almost familiar. There were some of the same mangled objects and burnt debris they'd seen in dozens of test ranges, battlefields, and crime scenes. It was doable, all right. A case this momentous had rewards as big as its risks, so the detective who found the breakthrough piece of evidence would earn the supreme satisfaction of solving the crime—while gaining the undying admiration of his peers, the mantle of The Guy Who Solved the Big One. Joe Borrelli had been just another Queens detective in 1977, until he managed to get credit for catching the serial killer known as the Son of Sam. By 1989 he was chief of detectives for the entire department. In today's media-glutted world, the payoff would come even quicker: a movie deal, an appearance on "Nightline" or "Geraldo," even a walk-on on the racy TV show "NYPD Blue." None of them would admit it, even under oath, but there's not a detective in the world who wouldn't grow misty-eyed at the thought of writing the book, *How I Cracked the World Trade Center Case.*

Hanlin and Sadowy both sensed something significant in the area, and homed in on the scraps of metal. Hanlin noticed a pattern to the debris, that the damage to the vehicles had gotten progressively worse as they moved across the concrete slab. On one end, the cars had only impact damage. As they moved closer to the lip of the crater, the autos were more seriously burnt and showed signs that they had been fragmented. He pulled down his respirator, pointed to the two cars closest to the ledge, and said, "It had to be one of these two," he said.

Sadowy, a car buff since his days at Brooklyn Automotive High School, was scoping out the spare parts. They were sifting through a junkyard that specialized in auto parts and construction debris. After a few minutes, Sadowy stood up straight and spoke.

"Look at this," he said, showing it to Hanlin.

Both men's eyes grew wider now, as they panned the wreckage for clues. Upstairs, outside, and beyond, millions of people around the world were waiting for something, anything, that would explain what happened, ease their fears. Yet on that battered chip of concrete, somewhere below Manhattan, Sadowy and Hanlin had entered a zone all their own—a world where chemistry, industry, and intuition allow men to divine a mystery. One of the chemists had sensed the excitement, and joined them. He picked up another large, hollow piece of metal, shaped like a giant thimble, and showed it to Hanlin.

"I think this is a transmission," he said.

"No, no," Sadowy said. "This is the housing to the differential." He lifted the bulky parts up and, with a bit of a struggle, showed that they fit together perfectly, like pieces from some macabre puzzle.

"This is forged steel," he told Hanlin. "Never in my life have I seen it ripped apart like this. To get blown apart this violently, they had to be sitting right underneath the bomb!"

There was no doubt now: they were within twenty feet of ground zero. Both men began desperately digging through the debris for any new, significant pieces of the puzzle. Sadowy moved a few chunks of concrete, and suddenly caught a glimpse of another piece of twisted metal. A few minutes of tugging freed it from the pile: a four-foot-long steel beam.

Sadowy carried the piece over to Hanlin. It was badly burned and twisted, but what the hell was it?

"What about this?" Sadowy asked.

"Hmmm," Hanlin said. "Maybe part of the frame?"

"Yeah, that could be."

Sadowy held up his light, so they could scour the piece for any identifiable markings. Hanlin rubbed his glove over the contorted metal, brushing off the soot and ash, and slowly a series of dots became visible. At first they thought the specks were abrasions caused by the explosion or a collision with other pieces of debris. Then Sadowy noticed a pattern. The dots formed a digit.

"I think that's a VIN number!" Sadowy said.

"What the hell's a VIN number?" Hanlin asked.

"I'm not sure what the letters stand for," said Sadowy, whose former partner and close friend worked in the NYPD's Queens auto-theft unit. "But I know that the auto-crime guys can use them to trace where a vehicle comes from."

Hanlin kept rubbing the frame, and now a series of digits emerged from beneath the dust: * . . . 1 . . . 3 . . . 9 . . .

"That's it!" Hanlin said. "That's the code!"

Sadowy just stood there and grinned.

Before they could fully savor the moment, a call came over the radio, warning all the searchers to leave the crater. The Port Authority was planning to move a subway train from one of the tunnels leading into the Trade Center, to test for damage. There was a danger that the vibrations might cause the mounds of debris to shift or collapse. The search team had fifteen minutes to leave the crater or risk being buried alive.

Hanlin and Sadowy were more concerned that their discovery might somehow get lost in the commotion. Williams had given them specific orders not to move any evidence. But if the rumbles of the train knocked the metal back into the crater, it might take weeks or months to find it. Who knew where the suspects might be by then.

"You think we should leave it here?" Hanlin asked.

"After all this trouble finding it?"

"You know we're going to catch hell if we move it," Hanlin said.

"If anyone tries to give us any heat for this, I'll take the heat," Sadowy offered.

They instructed the chemists to take their swab samples and told the photographer and sketch artists to document precisely where the pieces had been discovered, then headed out of the hole to find a way to lug the evidence to safety.

"How about one of those metal ambulance stretchers?" Hanlin suggested. "We could carry it part of the way, then fold the wheels down and roll it the rest of the way."

"That'll work," Sadowy said. The two of them decided to head aboveground to find a gurney. In the meantime they instructed the evidence techs to make their swabs and sketches, then move to safer ground.

Hanlin and Sadowy eventually returned with an orange fiberglass stretcher known as a Stokes basket, and loaded the vehicle pieces on top. Then they placed a plastic body bag over the metal to cover the evidence. Four searchers hoisted the entire package on their shoulders, like some archaeological expedition retrieving a holy relic, and began the long trek back toward the surface. They bobbed along the surface of their underground Acropolis for about twenty minutes—the Port Authority had agreed to delay its tests—and headed toward the nearest exit ramp.

About fifty feet up the ramp, the light from a television minicam flicked on, illuminating a pack of at least a dozen reporters and photographers desperate for any speck of information about the investigation. The journalists saw the body bag and figured that another victim had been recovered.

"Hold it," Sadowy shouted to the other searchers, who stopped dead in their tracks. "Let's go that way," he said, pointing to another, less populated ramp. They scurried to the second ramp, which hadn't yet been crowded by the press, and set the gurney on it. A station wagon from the NYPD's Crime Scene Unit backed down to pick it up, then sped off to the laboratory on East 21st Street.

Just as the van drove away, Dave Williams, the FBI supervisor, walked over, clearly furious.

"What the hell are you doing?" he screamed, his anger drawing the attention of more than a dozen investigators standing nearby. "I gave you a specific order not to move anything. What are you trying to prove?"

Sadowy tried to answer. "But—"

"You're going to face some serious consequences for this," Williams said. "One more move like that and I have you banned from this whole site!"

Williams stormed away without ever hearing Sadowy's explanation, and the crime scene station wagon sped the VIN numbers to the lab.

Inside the hole, the search would drag on for nearly a month. Each day the investigators would crawl to some barely accessible section of the hole and resume their work as archaeologists with police badges. It was incredibly painstaking work. Every speck of rubble had to be packed into a bucket, sifted through a metal sieve, and then through an even finer sieve. Oddly, the bomb squads didn't have their own sieves—the Port Authority laborers had constructed them. Anything other than concrete had to be marked, bagged, and sent to the laboratory. Damaged cars were all swabbed, then vacuumed for evidence and residue, so that the dust in the vacuum could be double-sifted for evidence. If the cars were too badly smashed to be opened, the investigators would saw them open to get to the particles inside. Evidence technicians would then record where each bucket, car, swab, and scrap of evidence had been unearthed, so it could be plotted on a master grid. For ten, twelve, even fourteen hours a day, Sadowy, Hanlin, and the others scoured that pit for clues, again and again and again. In time, six thousand tons of rubble were removed, at first hauled up three stories to the street level, until someone at the Port Authority realized that it could be lowered a few floors to the PATH trains and hauled away.

Slowly the evidence was pieced together: an embossed metal stamp with the initials AGL that came from one of the hydrogen tanks used to fuel the fireball; a piece of a Rockmaster blasting cap. They even reconstructed the dashboards of damaged automobiles, and recovered some of the parking garage's filing system. One particularly devastated area was the lunchroom where the Port Authority employees had died. The search team discovered decaying sandwiches from their half-eaten lunches.

The tediousness of the search was made even more frustrating by the fact that the searchers were never told what conclusions the scientists had drawn from all of this evidence. The FBI had brought a mobile laboratory from the FBI Academy in Quantico, Virginia, with all of the state-of-the-art toys, and they could test the molecular structure of each swab of residue with a high-resonance magnetic chromatometer. The scientists told the FBI what each item was made of. But the FBI never told any of its partners in the investigation. So each day, the investigators would read the newspapers when they stopped for a cup of coffee on the way to work, to find out exactly how they were doing.

The lack of communication reached comic proportions during the search for the phantom timer of the bomb.

The searchers sifted through the rubble for weeks, combed through every piece of dust, but came up empty. Then they did it again, and still came up with more questions than answers. They brought down clocks that matched the one in the lunchroom, so they could compare any gears or wires they found with it. They eventually found a scrap of wire, part of a C-cell battery, and a spring, which may have been part of an alarm clock. But these items weren't fused together. They had been found fairly far removed from each other. So there was no telling whether they had been part of some crude timing device or three unrelated bits of debris coincidentally found in the parking garage. The searchers had no choice but to keep digging.

The NYPD's Lieutenant Walter Boser, who was frustrated by the FBI's refusal to share information, finally broke with protocol and called an FBI lab technician himself. Boser had worked with the agent on dozens of prior cases through the years, and hoped that their rapport would be strong enough to persuade the agent to share some information. After a little cajoling, some prodding, and an appeal for law-enforcement solidarity, the agent told Boser what the FBI had learned days earlier: the World Trade Center bomb had been triggered by four twenty-foot fuses and lit with a ninety-nine-cent disposable lighter.

*   *   *

Evidence teams remained in the crater for twenty-six days, but nothing they found turned out to be as crucial as the VIN number. The day after Don Sadowy and Joe Hanlin lugged it out of the hole—just forty-eight hours after the explosion—a federal agent punched the digits on it into a computer. In an instant he discovered the model, make, and year of the vehicle, where it had been built, and to whom it was registered. For the FBI, those answers turned out to be a mixed blessing. The suspects were a group of New Jersey men who had been suspected of terrorism for more than two years, but had eluded repeated FBI investigations. Someday the bureau would have to explain how these clowns from across the river nearly toppled the World Trade Center right under the FBI's nose. But in the fearful, frenzied days after the explosion, the agents were just grateful they'd made progress.

The bombers had left a return address.

6

MARCH 4, 1993:
THURSDAY MORNING

FBI Agent William Atkinson was disguised in his khakis, loafers, and tan cotton golf jacket. A microphone was taped to his body, so he could secretly tape-record the upcoming conversation. In his left hand was a remote-control button to activate a hidden camera stashed in a bag hanging on the wall. Everything was in place for a successful undercover operation, except the cover.

Atkinson was posing as a midlevel manager for a rental-car agency, waiting to meet the man responsible for the van that exploded in the Trade Center a week earlier. Mohammad Salameh, who had reported the van stolen the day before the bombing, had no idea it had left enough recognizable pieces for the cops to trace. Salameh just wanted his four-hundred-dollar deposit back, and had been pestering the Ryder clerks for days. When FBI officials heard he was coming into the office on Thursday, they saw an opportunity to question, follow, and possibly arrest him. They chose Atkinson, a veteran agent from the Newark office, to play the role of a Ryder "loss prevention analyst." He was set up with a phony questionnaire devised to gather personal information about Salameh's background and associates. Salameh even called the office about 9:00 P.M., and said he was heading over. The operation was on. Now all they needed was a little secrecy.

But outside the DIB Leasing Agency, at 1558 Kennedy Boulevard in Jersey City, two television trucks were cruising by, and threatened to screw up the entire operation. *New York Newsday*, a city tabloid, had somehow found out that the van came from DIB. A reporter had interviewed one of the rental clerks on Wednesday afternoon—sixteen hours before Salameh was scheduled to come back. The paper's editors had called the FBI to confirm the information, but FBI officials had inexplicably decided not to ask the paper to hold the story. When *Newsday* came out on Thursday morning, every assignment editor in town sent someone to follow the story. Atkinson had heard radio reports about the *Newsday* story as he drove to the rental agency, and he feared that Salameh might also hear the news and flee.

Unfortunately for Atkinson, that posed a rather unsettling security risk. Here he was in his disguise—waiting to meet a guy suspected of trying to kill thousands of people—and outside, every Ted Koppel wannabe in New York was circling around, blowing his cover. Who knew if Salameh would come alone? Or armed? What if he saw the news trucks and realized this was a setup? There were sharpshooters positioned outside. Brian Dunbar, a detective from the New Jersey State Police, also was posing as a Ryder agent and was assigned to watch Atkinson's back. But if Salameh was crazy enough to blow up the Trade Center, who could say he wouldn't come rigged up with another bomb? As Atkinson adjusted his shirt, several of the plainclothes agents who had the place surrounded had to chase away the news vans, screaming, "Get the cameras out of here!"

This was not the way they taught it down at the FBI Academy in Quantico.

Then again, the suspects hadn't exactly been setting new standards for criminal brilliance. When the searchers found the VIN number, they figured it would be a sketchy road map to set the investigation vaguely in the right direction. Every detective was certain that whatever vehicle the terrorists had used to transport, carry, and conceal the bomb had almost certainly been stolen. Any crook sophisticated enough to cripple New York's tallest building would probably understand how easy it was to trace VIN numbers, wouldn't he? Detectives figured they'd have to use the van as a starting point—tracking down when and where the vehicle had been stolen, then contacting the owner and looking for witnesses to the theft. With a positive ID on the vehicle, detectives could also re-canvass the Trade Center parking-lot attendant, patrons, and passersby to see if they remembered the driver. By leaking a description of the vehicle to the press, a time-honored detective's trick, they might also stir up leads. Someone out there must have seen something, so a media blitz would turn up new leads by jump-starting the public's memory. Meanwhile, back in the hole, the evidence techs would search for more clues near the spot where the van had exploded, maybe a piece of paper or a fingerprint on an identifiable part of the car. A single fingerprint can be entered electronically into a federal computer library, to compare it against millions of other prints taken from criminals. If they found a print and the bombers had a record—Bingo! The hunt would be nearly over.

Instead, the bombers saved the detectives the trouble. The van, a 1993 Ford Econoline, had been rented by Salameh, using his real name, his own driver's license, and an address from the local Islamic Cultural Center. To make things even easier, he was well known by the Jersey City police and the FBI. Salameh was among the one hundred Arabs who had spent months protesting outside the courtroom at the trial of El Sayyid Nosair, the man accused of murdering Jewish militant Meir Kahane. The protests were boisterous without quite being violent, yet federal officials discovered evidence that the group supported armed opposition to the U.S., Egyptian, and Israeli governments. Salameh hadn't been considered smart or assertive enough to be a key player. At least until now. When FBI agents traced the van back to DIB Leasing, they discovered that Salameh had reported the van stolen the night before the bombing, and had been pestering the rental office because he wanted his deposit back.

Maybe the theft had actually occurred, but given the radical leanings of Nosair's supporters, the FBI wasn't about to underestimate these guys again. They stationed dozens of agents around the office building, on rooftops, in unmarked vans, even hiding behind trees. It was an elaborate trap set to catch Salameh, and Agent William Atkinson was the decoy.

Nine years in the Bureau had taught Atkinson the intricacies of undercover jobs. Stay calm, act natural, and try to enjoy yourself. Be cooperative but not too accommodating, or you might raise suspicions. Above all, make sure the detective inside you doesn't overwhelm the disguise. Atkinson took a few deep breaths, tried to think like a rental agent and make sure all the electronic devices worked. Atkinson was well known for his technical ineptitude, and was so bad with gadgets that he had to beg his son to program the VCR. There was no room for error here, Atkinson thought. He gave the remote button for the camera one last test, then checked to be sure the microphone wouldn't come untaped from his chest, when Dunbar saw a Middle Eastern man walking up through the parking lot.

"This has got to be him," Dunbar said, taking his place behind the counter just as the door swung open.

In walked Mohammad Salameh.

He was scrawny, maybe five feet six, and walked with a slight hunch. He was unshaven, with some scraggly growth on his face, but appeared incapable of mustering a full-fledged beard. He wore a checkered jacket, red and black. It was loose-fitting, but Atkinson didn't see any lumps or bulges to suggest that he was packing a weapon. Salameh looked as though he could use a good night's sleep. He also looked very determined.

"Hello," said Patrick Galasso, the Ryder manager. The plan was for Galasso to greet Salameh, then lead him over to Atkinson. Salameh seemed a little edgy, and gave Galasso a garbled explanation about having left the key to the van at home. Nervous but determined, Atkinson stammered through the first few lines of the most important performance of his life.

"I'm with the, ahm, loss prevention unit at, ahm, Ryder and I work out of New Brunswick and we try to settle claims without—"

Salameh, who appeared equally nervous, interrupted. "Yes," he said. But Atkinson continued with his script.

"—a lot of problems. But what we've done, we, there's a lot of stolen cars in New Jersey—"

"Yes," Salameh cut in.

"More than any other state in the union."

"Yes," Salameh interrupted again. "And New Jersey I called."

Salameh apparently had a script of his own, delivered in an almost unintelligibly thick Middle Eastern accent, so Atkinson just continued.

"What we're trying to do, we're trying to put an end to that, and we're doing it by help of our customer representative and our customers. Maybe you can help us, if I can just get some information."

"I will tell you now what's happened?" Salameh asked.

"All right, let me, let me just run through this and it will take you—"

Salameh cut him off again. There was a struggle going on to determine who would control the conversation. The detective in Atkinson wanted to plow right through Salameh's disjointed, garbled explanation. But Ryder clerks are trained to be polite and hear out the customer's side of the story.

Atkinson decided he'd better back off. Just let Salameh stare into his understanding blue eyes, and wait for this guy to calm down.

"Today's Thursday," Salameh said.

"Yeah," Atkinson said.

"Like this day, but in the night, ah, I go again to increase my language."

Whatever language course Salameh was taking hadn't yet done much good. Salameh's frustration with the paperwork was compounded by his tenuous grasp of English. Atkinson decided to hang back, let Salameh blow off some steam, and then resume his questioning. Don't want this guy to blow his fuse.

Through several more minutes of wrangling, Salameh explained that he had rented the van February 23, and it had been stolen from a shopping center two days later. He pulled out a receipt from the Pathmark plaza, where he had been shopping on February 28 at 9:28 P.M. Already the story had sprung a leak. Why would the victim of a car theft feel compelled to prove he was shopping? The detective within Atkinson decided to let Salameh box himself into a lie.

"How many packages did you have?"

"In, inside it?" Salameh asked, unsettled by the change in direction.

"Were you carrying," Atkinson said.

"Ah, three. Three bags. Three small, small, eh."

"Three bags," Atkinson said, letting the words hang there like an indictment.

"Yeah."

Atkinson decided to play rental agent again, lighten things up with a little joke.

"Three bags full, sorta like, ah—"

"What you—" Salameh interrupted.

" 'Baa, baa, black sheep, have you any wool . . .' "

"Yeah," Salameh said. Apparently that nursery rhyme had never been translated into Arabic.

"Yeah," Atkinson finished, "three bags full."

So much for jokes.

Salameh kept playing the role of pitiful car-theft victim, and the story kept taking on water. He said he'd rented the van on the twenty-third to help a friend move. Two days later, when it was loaded with a table and a few chairs, he stopped at the ShopRite grocery store on Kennedy Boulevard. When he returned to the parking lot, the van was gone. By now the story was sinking fast. Who's going to pay for three days' rental to move a single apartment's worth of furniture? And who would make a special trip just for a table and a few chairs? Salameh did add one nice detail when he said he originally suspected that the cops had towed the van for illegal parking. But he said he couldn't remember either of the addresses. Even at the scene, the Jersey City cops were skeptical, and Salameh was angry that they'd called his story "bullshit."

Once Salameh handed over the Jersey City police report, made on the day of the bombing, he seemed to relax a bit. He didn't appear to be armed or booby-trapped. It was time for William Atkinson, dutiful clerk for Ryder Truck Rental, to take control of the interview by doing what bureaucrats do best: bog his adversary down in a quagmire of mundane questions. Who else drove it? Did you put the special sideview mirror on the passenger's window? How did you get here today, taxi or bus? When did you file that police report? When it came time to spell Salameh's name on the form, Atkinson dragged it out so long it seemed like an Abbott and Costello routine. Salameh must have thought he was back in English class.

"Let me get, let me get, let me," Atkinson began, "I'll get back to this, but let me get your name. It's, um, Mohammad?"

"M-O-H, this is my name," Salameh answered.

"Okay, M-O-H . . ."

"M-O-H-A . . ."

"Uh-huh."

"This first name, this last name," Salameh said, handing Atkinson the incident report from the car theft with his name on it.

"All right."

"M-O-H-A-double-M-A-D," Salameh said.

"And middle initial?"

"A."

"What's that stand for?"

"Amin, A-M-I-N."

"S—"

"This is my—" Salameh began.

"How you, how you say your last name?" Atkinson asked.

"My last name Salameh."

"Okay."

"Yeah . . ."

Salameh soon grew tired of the bureaucratic merry-go-round of minutiae. When Atkinson asked, for the fifth time, why Salameh had rented the van, he began reacting like a man in the middle of a police interrogation instead of a business transaction.

"And to move your friend's furniture?" Atkinson asked.

"Yeah, not with us, move, ah, somebody to other, but I'm the driver. Now why I need the money, you know why?"

"Eh, why?"

"Because my friends need their money."

"Okay."

"How's the . . . what's happened to the money?" Salameh asked.

"Now anyone other, anybody else drive the van? Did you let anyone else drive the van?"

The detective inside Atkinson had outwrestled the Ryder clerk again. Atkinson reverted back to answering a question with a question. Salameh's façade was crumbling, too—the maligned crime victim giving way to the liar, scrambling to keep his stories straight. What Atkinson didn't know was that Salameh had a plan of his own, and that only desperation had forced him to return for his deposit money. In Salameh's pocket was a child's plane ticket to Amsterdam for a flight that left the next day. Salameh had bought it earlier in the week with his last sixty-nine dollars, then taken it to customs to get the proper visa. But Salameh desperately needed the four hundred dollars so he could upgrade to an adult's ticket and make his escape.

"Eh, what?"

"Did anyone else with you drive the van?"

"What do you, eh, eh . . ."

"Did you let any of your friends drive the van?"

Atkinson had Salameh in full retreat now, but the roar of trucks outside briefly buried the room in noise and bought Salameh a little time to think about his answer.

Finally he spoke up.

"No. Just me."

"No other drivers. Hmm."

"Because I have, just me, I have the, ah . . ."

Salameh was saved by the telephone. An FBI agent from the command center was monitoring the operation by talking to Dunbar on the telephone. Dunbar pretended the phone conversation was with another Ryder office.

"Hey, um, excuse me, Bill, but how much, how much longer?" Dunbar asked.

"Ah, if you could, I'd say a minute," Atkinson replied.

"Another minute," Dunbar said into the phone, " 'cause, um . . ."

"I only need, I need to give him the money, ah, to settle this claim and get him to sign the paper."

"All right," Dunbar told the agent on the other end of the line. "Because Bill and I will be done shortly. About ten minutes."

It was time to close the deal.

Atkinson had never been told by his bosses whether Salameh would be arrested or simply tailed. So Atkinson's mission was to keep Salameh from straying too far away, give him enough of his deposit that he wouldn't do something rash.

Now Atkinson's script called for him to give Salameh the money, end the operation, and get out of the office unscathed.

He reviewed the incident report with Salameh, the fastidious clerk making his last stand. But Salameh wasn't going to make it easy. First he claimed that he'd filled the gas tank, and insisted that Ryder should reimburse him an extra fifteen dollars. Next he mucked up the whole process again, by telling Atkinson he hadn't brought the key. To top things off, Salameh then decided that he could remember the addresses he was moving between: 26 Weldon and 34 Kensington. "I want justice. This is not justice."

The detective had to get a few more questions in after that, just to watch Salameh squirm, if nothing else.

"But what did you do after the van was, ah, stolen? How did you move?"

"Well, I didn't," Salameh shot back. It was Abbott-and-Costello time again.

"You didn't move?"

"Move for what?"

"You didn't move after the van got stolen?"

"No, I moved now."

"Oh, did you? How did you do it?"

"Yes."

"Did you get another van?"

"By my friends, yeah."

"Okay."

"Yes."

"All right. Moved aided by—"

"Yeah, by my friends."

"Okay."

"Yeah, I want tell you one—"

"Okay, just give me—"

"His name is Adel. A-D-E-L."

"Adel?"

"Yes. Mohammad."

"Uh-hum."

"His last name Mohammad. Yeah."

"Okay."

For a solid week the entire world had been searching for the evil genius who had carried off the Trade Center bombing, and when the guy finally made his entrance, he hadn't even bothered to put together a cohesive story. Atkinson wanted out of there, so it was time to start waving dollars around. The rental agency still wanted to charge Salameh $271.68 for the three days he'd used the van, meaning that only $138.32 of the deposit was unused. But the rental business is a people business, Atkinson explained, so he was willing to offer Salameh a few more dollars for his trouble.

"We're willing to go as high as two hundred dollars to settle the claim," Atkinson said, trying to make the offer sound generous.

Salameh might not have been skilled at English, but he knew his math. "Is not justice," he complained. "This is not justice!"

"Well," Atkinson said, trying to preempt an explosion, "but it's business."

"I know business, but eh, eh, I need justice, some justice. I paid four hundred dollars, he told me I need deposit."

"Right."

"I give him, ah, four hundred dollars."

"But you've lost our van," Atkinson said, careful not to mispronounce "lost" as "blown up."

Salameh ran through a series of excuses, blaming the police for delaying his reports and the Ryder officials for giving him an inaccurate rental agreement. He dragged things out by wallowing in the details, pointing to a clerical error on the contract, a problem with the keys, the fact that he'd called DIB to report the theft, but the office was closed. In desperation, he resorted to one of the same demands he'd shouted outside of Nosair's murder trial fourteen months before: "No justice! We need justice now!"

This encounter had dragged on for half an hour by now, despite Atkinson's efforts to speed things along. He decided to cut the guy a deal.

"All right, how about $250?" he offered, knowing that the extra fifty dollars wouldn't be much use where Salameh was headed. "Would that get you out of here, $250? Now we're taking, we're taking the burden."

"Now listen to me," Salameh said. "Now."

The phone rang, and Patrick Galasso, the authentic Ryder agent, picked it up. "Ryder," Galasso said. "Yes. Be right out. Okay. Over. Yeah."

From what he was saying, it sounded like the FBI agents probably were telling him to hurry things up.

Luckily, Salameh was beginning to calm down.

"I have a good idea," he said.

"Uh-hum," Atkinson replied.

"Eh, two days and a half, two days and a half," Salameh said, bargaining away the extra fifty dollars Atkinson had just given him.

"Two days and a half, and two days and a half?"

"Yes," Salameh said, obviously pleased with himself.

"Is two hundred dollars. Half of four hundred dollars is two hundred dollars."

"That's good," Salameh said.

"Okay," said the FBI agent.

"I see this is justice."

"Okay. That, that makes sense," Atkinson said.

"Yeah."

"Okay."

"And after I bring the key, you will give, give me gas."

"For the gasoline?" Atkinson said.

"The gas money, all right. Fifteen dollars I put in, in the gas."

Atkinson was anxious to leave, so he agreed. Naturally, that caused Salameh to go right on bargaining.

"You, ahm, ahm, eh, you, you give me the van without gas. Little."

"A quarter-tank," Galasso said.

"No, no, no, not the quarter-tank."

"Well, we'll—" Atkinson said.

"All right," Galasso said, eager to end the conversation.

"Fifteen dollars," Salameh said.

"Bring the key, bring the key," Atkinson pleaded.

"Fifteen dollars," Salameh said.

"Fifteen dollars, yeah," Galasso said.

"Bring the key," Atkinson added.

"I, ah, I think the van took twenty-five dollars, just fifteen dollars I take," Salameh said.

"No, no," said Galasso, unable to resist his bureaucrat's genetic need to quibble, "the van takes about twenty dollars."

Atkinson couldn't tell Galasso to shut up, but he wanted Salameh gone.

"Okay, bring the key and we'll give you twenty dollars . . . because really, how do we know the van isn't out there, you got the key and the van and two hundred dollars. We don't know if the van is really out there and you're driving it around. See, making a report, and you make two hundred dollars and we don't have the key, you know what I mean?"

Salameh seemed insulted by the very suggestion. "I'm, I'm a Muslim," he insisted. "I'm, ah, honest."

Finally, Salameh agreed to sign the form, take his copy of the rental agreement, and leave. But even in the glow of victory, he found a way to be a pain.

"All right, that's good," he said.

Atkinson, who was eager to shed the clerk's persona once and for all, was talking for the benefit of the tape recorder now.

"Okay, well, that's it, we're done. Our business is ended at ten-twenty-eight."

Dunbar, who was equally relieved, added, "You can say that."

"On March 4, 1993," Atkinson said. "I appreciate it."

Salameh was not about to leave easily.

"Oh," he said.

"Thank you," Atkinson said, fighting the temptation to boot Salameh out the door.

"Ah, thank you very much," Salameh said, stunned that he'd actually pulled it off. "I'm sorry about that."

"Yeah, Mohammad," Galasso said. "The key."

"Eh, ah, I will bring the key," he promised. "Maybe tomorrow."

"Okay," Galasso said.

"Okay," said Atkinson.

"Because I won't have time today, because we have Ramadan. We have, eh, break-fast afternoon."

"Okay," Atkinson said.

"Yeah," Salameh said.

"Okay," Atkinson repeated.

"I can't come, ahm," Salameh continued.

"Okay, that's no problem."

"Eh, ah," Salameh kept stammering. Was this guy lonely, stupid, or building up the courage to do something dramatic?

"No problem, whenever you can," Atkinson said. "Call, okay? Ahm, you know we're gonna be here."

"Thank you very much," Salameh said, still refusing to move from the office.

"Okay."

"This is, I see this is justice."

"Fine, it certainly is," Atkinson said.

"We're on Kennedy Boulevard," Galasso said, stating the obvious.

"Yeah." Salameh nodded.

"Okay," Atkinson said, using his voice to motion Salameh toward the door. "All right."

"Thank you for—" Salameh started.

"You're welcome." Atkinson abruptly cut him off.

"Thank you for, ah, see, what's your name?"

"Bill," Atkinson said.

"Bill, thank you very much," Salameh said earnestly.

"You're, you're welcome."

"Thank you," he said, finally moving toward the door.

"Okay?" Galasso asked.

"Thank you," Salameh said.

"Okay," Atkinson said. "Take care."

With that, Mohammad Salameh finally stepped outside the office, took a few steps into the parking lot, and was descended upon by dozens of agents in FBI windbreakers. After one week, a massive manhunt, and countless thank-yous, the first suspect was apprehended.

Atkinson's interview had also yielded other valuable information. In the course of all those annoying questions, Salameh had provided his address, 34 Kensington in Jersey City. Within an hour, a swarm of detectives were combing the place for evidence; they quickly realized they'd only scratched the surface of the conspiracy.

Inside was Salameh's former roommate, Aboud Yasin, who would yield a wealth of information. They also recovered Salameh's briefcase, which contained bank account information, and a chilling photo of Salameh standing next to a very familiar felon—El Sayyid Nosair, the "lone gunman" accused of assassinating Zionist Rabbi Meir Kahane in 1991. This was going to get messy.

*　　*　　*

Before the day was over, the FBI benefited from another stroke of luck, courtesy of an inquisitive storage-locker clerk. Doug Melvin, manager of the Space Station storage center in Jersey City, had grown suspicious a week earlier because two men had tried to have tanks of hydrogen delivered to his facility. They'd been turned away by a guard, who had recognized that the tanks were forbidden in the lockers.

Hydrogen is extremely combustible, so dangerous that it's not allowed in enclosed places such as tunnels or storage facilities, where it might easily be sparked and explode. So Melvin turned amateur sleuth.

Twelve years in the storage business had taught him to be wary. People rented storage lockers for two reasons: to stow things they didn't have room for at home, and to stow things they didn't want associated with their homes. Just a few miles south, a rented locker had become a tomb for Sidney Reso, an executive with Exxon. He had been kidnapped from the driveway of his home by his former janitor and the janitor's wife. In the process, they'd shot him, then left him to bleed to death inside a storage locker.

Melvin hadn't yet found a corpse, but he'd had plenty of contact with law-enforcement officers. He'd reported stashes of counterfeit money, phony designer merchandise, and drugs. Just last year he'd led cops to a locker crammed with illegal fireworks.

So when an assistant manager told Melvin about the hydrogen tanks, the amateur detective inside him awoke once again. Hydrogen? The only legitimate uses for hydrogen were in welding and medical research, and what laboratory or construction contractor would work inside a storage locker? Melvin smelled something peculiar, so he thought he'd better take a peek inside locker number 4344, just to be certain no other dangerous chemicals had been sneaked past the guards.

It was still Thursday, the day before the Trade Center bombing. If Melvin had been able to enter the locker that day, and alert FBI officials—who knows?—maybe the whole bombing could have been averted. But the Space Station sells privacy along with its storage lockers, so on-site managers are forbidden to enter any unit without permission from the company officials. Melvin called Space Station headquarters in Tennessee to ask for clearance, and after a brief discussion, his supervisors agreed to send him the master key. It would take four days to arrive in the mail.

The next day, when Melvin heard about the Trade Center bombing on the radio, he felt a strange stirring in his stomach. The news bulletin said nothing about the suspects in the bombing, or about the type of bomb that had been used. It made no mention of hydrogen; in fact, police didn't yet know what had been used to set the explosion. But you can actually see the Trade Center from most of Jersey City, and Melvin watched across the river as the smoke rose from the battered towers, and helicopters landed on the roof. There was no single, great epiphany. Instead, Doug Melvin was being overtaken by a slow, steady tide of suspicion. He had only a layman's understanding of chemicals and explosives, but he had a friend who was an engineer who had once worked for the government.

The weekend dragged by. Melvin kept tuning in to the television to watch reports of the bombing aftermath, to see if anything had linked the two Middle-Eastern-looking men from locker 4344. Finally, when the key arrived, Melvin and his friend went inside and found a storehouse packed with boxes, bottles, and bags of chemicals. Melvin's friend wrote down the names, looked them up in some chemical manuals, and told Doug that his suspicions had been well founded.

"This shit is dangerous," said the friend.

Melvin wasted no time in picking up the telephone and calling the FBI. "I think you guys better come over here right away," he said.

It took hours for FBI agents to empty the locker of the chemicals that were, in essence, spare parts for the bomb that had blown up in the Trade Center. In addition to urea nitrate, they found nitroglycerin and cyanide gas. Nitroglycerin freezes at fifty-two degrees Fahrenheit, but becomes extremely unstable and can be ignited by a sudden shift in temperature. If the nitro had exploded and released the cyanide, the explosion could have sent clouds of poisonous gas wafting through Jersey City and its neighboring town, Hoboken—two of the most densely populated cities in the state. One breath, an FBI agent said, would have been deadly.

Melvin was taken to a lineup where he identified Mohammad Salameh as the man who had rented the locker.

* * *

The investigation had been compartmentalized. The people grubbing around in the crater at the Trade Center knew next to nothing about what was happening in Jersey City as they went through the business of sifting, sorting, guessing, evaluating. As he came up for lunch on Thursday, his fifth day in the hole, Donald Sadowy leaned into the slope of the ramp. After spending the whole morning stooped over in the crater, he could feel the uphill climb cutting into the backs of his thighs. The focus had been intense, almost numbing, and his own aches kept his mind off the noise around him. He thought he heard applause; that was pretty silly, but as it grew louder, a puzzled grin crept over his filthy, sooty face. Then he looked up. The guys from the FBI and the ATF and the other agencies were leaning over the ramp, clapping their hands. The applause grew louder as more of them spotted Sadowy.

"What's going on?" he asked.

"They just made the arrest," he was told. "That VIN number you guys found broke the case."

Standing in the crowd was Dave Williams, the FBI explosives chief who had reamed out Sadowy and Hanlin for moving the crucial evidence from its original resting place.

"Congratulations," Williams said, as he simultaneously shook the policeman's hand and patted his back. "I guess I owe you an apology."

Williams put his arm around Sadowy's shoulder and stated the obvious: "Sometimes you have to do things based on your instinct, and not on procedures."

Then the FBI agent casually dropped a blockbuster:

"These people we had under surveillance six months ago, they were the guys who did it."

MANTA, ECUADOR
MARCH 4, 1993

Ed Smith sat in the back of the limousine and looked at the crowds lining the streets. The police were pushing back people so the car could get through. Many wept. A bank of television cameras filmed the coffin as it was slid from the back of the hearse. It is how we would greet a president, Ed thought. The headlines the next morning would read: *The Daughter of Our Country Comes Home to Be Laid to Rest.* Monica's father told him that he would build a little apartment in the Rodriguez home, so that Ed could come anytime to visit her grave and have his own place to stay.

THE CRATER
B-2 LEVEL
WORLD TRADE CENTER
MARCH 4, 1993

The bomb crater was quiet. The jackhammers pulverizing the concrete slabs had been shut down; the spider cranes lowering pipes had been halted; even the PATH trains that hauled out the rubble were held in the tunnels. For more than a week, twenty-four hours a day, all that noise had driven out the sinister feeling of the crime scene. Now it was deathly quiet again. The basement was full of drafts that cut through all clothes, air that was colder than the street, that felt like the breath of evil rising from the broken basement.

Then the voice of a woman cried out.

"Willie," she called.

Olga Mercado walked along the high rim and peered down into the dark morass—the concrete boulders, the twisted steel, the pulverized bits of building—and begged it to speak to her.

"Willie," she called.

All the other bodies had been pulled out less than two hours after the explosion. Other than Mercado, anyone else missing turned up in a few days. One guy had gone on a bender and not bothered to tell anyone. He had been presumed dead until he turned up, hungover. Another man was found upstate with a girlfriend and pleaded with the detectives to tell his wife that he had been injured in the explosion. The detectives declined.

Some of the news reporters had suggested that Mercado, too, had taken the opportunity to shack up with a honey. And the police briefly entertained the notion that Mercado was involved in the bombing: after all, they figured a truck had been involved in carrying the explosives, and Mercado worked at the truck depot checking in the food. But the people at the Port Authority knew this was the far side of unlikely: Mercado had been a great American success story, an engineer and college graduate from Peru who moved to New York and took night classes in English. He bought a home in a tough neighborhood in the East New York section of Brooklyn and worked two jobs to send his kids to Catholic schools.

His wife, Olga, had insisted that her husband might be alive, perhaps hit on the head, in a hospital where no one knew who he was. But she had gone to the hospitals and he was not there. She thought that the police might have arrested him and were not telling anyone.

Maybe he was just buried in the rubble, able to breathe, and was afraid to speak up, she had said.

Well, her Port Authority escort said, we can hope.

In Peru, people were famous for surviving earthquakes, she said.

Is that right? asked the escort.

She walked around the edge of the crater, and her escort, who had stood a half-step back, now worried that she might throw herself into the pit. He reached for her elbow and followed as she paced along the edge, her husband's name unreeling from her heart, into six stories of destruction: "Willie." She paused.

"Willie. *Es Olga, su esposa.*" Willie, it's Olga, your wife.

All work had ceased when she came down. She wanted to be able to hear him calling out her name, so the jackhammers and welders turned off their machines, and the workmen retreated to a polite distance.

She had been moved into a hotel across the street from the Trade Center, switched from room to room as reporters scrambled to keep the bombing story alive with the missing Mercado. She suspected that the search for evidence was delaying the removal of the rubble. The mayor, David Dinkins, and the police commissioner, Ray Kelly, both called on her to promise that everything was being done to find her husband. A specially trained dog was helicoptered down from Connecticut to help.

A tuition bill arrived from the school. Someone from the Port Authority hustled over to Inhilco, the company that employed Mercado in his work for Windows on the World, and within a few hours, they issued a thousand dollars in cash. Not all the Port Authority's engineering work involved steel and concrete.

Olga Mercado did not stay overnight in the hotel. She went home to East New York to be with her kids. At night, little Heidi, age three, wandered the house with a storybook she wanted her father

to read. When she heard her mother coming home, she would run
to the door. "Mami! Did you bring Daddy home?"

On March 15, a construction worker cleared away some rubble
and found a work boot. The police searchers were called in. They
delicately cleared away the ground-up concrete. Willie Mercado
was upside down, in his chair.

PART

ORIGINS

TWO

7

THE RABBI'S MURDER

*I came to Kahane's lecture because
there are many points I agree on it from him.*
—El Sayyid Nosair, accused assassin of Meir Kahane

The arrest of Mohammad Salameh was greeted in New York and around the country with relief. His home was the source of clues that quickly led to a roundup of his confederates. The bombers had presented themselves as the greatest clowns in the history of international terrorism—and American law enforcement as canny and powerful. Certainly, the Bureau of Alcohol, Tobacco and Firearms was glad to have a public success; four of its agents had been killed on February 28 in Waco, Texas, during the bungled raid on the home of the messianic gunman David Koresh. And the FBI's director, William Sessions, had been cut off from his own agency after his deputies claimed that he was abusing plane rides and had taken advantage of his status to install expensive security precautions at his home. He was filmed walking through the streets of downtown Manhattan with his loyal aide, Jim Fox, during the FBI's peak moments in the Trade Center inquiry.

Still, few could get over the groundbreaking stupidity of the bombers. Imagine a man returning to a rental-truck outfit to haggle over a couple of hundred dollars' deposit on a truck! But a darker, tragic question shadowed the farce: Could the Twin Towers bombing have been stopped, or was it the price of a free, open society? Sadly, the evidence now suggests the former. When presented with evidence of a wide-ranging, violently anti-American, anti-Western movement based in certain mosques, the FBI performed ineptly and the press indifferently.

The best evidence now suggests the banner of Jihad was

planted in the United States more than two years before Salameh and Abouhalima and their cohorts killed six people in the basement of the World Trade Center. At the time, few noticed. Now, however, we can mark the beginning of America's post–Cold War era at a moment, a November evening in 1990, and in a place, an ordinary, chain-run hotel in midtown Manhattan, that could have been in any American city.

On November 5, 1990, Rabbi Meir Kahane had come to the city to warn the faithful, once again, about their enemies. On this night, the alarm was sounded in the New York Marriott, an old hotel on the corner of 49th Street and Lexington Avenue. In years gone by, Kahane's venues had been the streets of Brooklyn, the marketplaces of west Jerusalem, and the dusty villages of the land that most of the world called the occupied territory, but that Kahane and his people called Judea, the land of Israel told of in the Holy Book.

The audience filed into the Manhattan hotel meeting room just a little past seven. They went up one flight from the lobby to Morgan Room Two, about one hundred true believers, old-line Brooklyn and Bronx Jews, politically alert and steeped in the bitter politics of the Mideast. Rabbi Kahane had been shaking money out of the trees for over thirty years, some of it funding a life of pickups in singles bars, some of it going for advertisements that created the impression that the Jewish Defense League was actually a huge organization, some of it supporting charity in Israel, some of it sponsoring murder and low-level war.

Just as the venues for Kahane's alarms had changed, so had the enemies. Once they had been Brooklyn blacks—whom he had called "savages" and "animals"—or the evil Soviet Communists, or Arabs living in the land Kahane believed was Israel by virtue of a title and deed granted by God Himself in the Scriptures. Kahane was an ordinary-looking man, of medium height and moderate weight, black hair gone to gray, possessed of a slight stutter and a history of murder, racism, adultery, and betrayal. Hardly anyone outside New York and Israel knew who he was. Because he was a scholarly man steeped in the Talmud, he could and did scorn most American Jews, who, in his view, gave bar mitzvahs where nobody understood the Hebrew words intoned during the services, but who still managed to spend ten thousand dollars on shrimp and salmon mousse. His voice, shrill and biting, had helped to polarize Middle Eastern politics for over two decades. He could raise hell.

Tonight his enemy was the entire United States. That fall, all signs were pointing to another downturn in the American economy. Nazis and skinheads were on the rise. And the Jews, Kahane warned, would be blamed for everything. He had explained it all in his column in the November 2, 1990, *Jewish Press*:

> Side by side with the economic monster is the even more im-
> mediate disintegration of the social and racial fabric of
> America. The U.S. is a nation made up of countless racial and
> ethnic groups, and the myth of the melting pot is on the
> verge of exploding in this era of nationalism and ethnocentrism.
> The hatred and fear between whites and blacks is palpable.
> Hatred between blacks and Hispanics and Hispanics and Anglos
> and Asians and blacks—and all against the Jews. . . .
>
> In the minds of the haters and the potential ones, it is the Jew
> who is the key to all the destruction of values and of America.
> Let us not bother to protest that it is not true: that is irrelevant
> to people who wish to believe and need to believe it.

In his talk, he restated the themes of the column, and then played a version of his most famous and resonant line: "They hate us with a passion out there—with a virulence that's frightening to see."

Outside the hotel, a yellow city cab circled the block. Its off-duty light was on. At the wheel was a tall man with olive skin and oddly contrasting bright red hair, a man named Mahmud Abouhalima, here on a mission. He had tried to park in front of the hotel, but the street was marked as a loading zone, and any cab out front was expected to carry away hotel guests going out for a night on the town; it was not meant as a permanent parking spot. Abouhalima wasn't interested in making any fares and he wasn't interested in explaining that he was waiting for someone in the hotel. He had returned from Afghanistan, having done his part for Islam by pushing back the infidel Soviet Union. He had spent American money, from the CIA and other covert sources, but had nothing but contempt for his sponsors. The Americans were as bad as the Soviet Union. Their day would come. The Cold War that had seemed to be lodged in an arctic-style permafrost was now melting. And the true Jihad would begin.

Inside the hotel, Meir Kahane could not have agreed more. He himself had been a minor player in the Cold War surrogacy—in the 1960s he'd been under contract with the CIA to rev up support among

Orthodox Jewish college students for the Vietnam War. Lyndon Johnson had publicly noted that many of the antiwar movement's leaders came from the establishment Jewish organizations. To Kahane, Jewish peaceniks were a direct threat to the U.S. government's vital support for the state of Israel. He wanted vocal Jewish support for the war, to counteract the visible opponents. He even cowrote a book about the need for Jews to back the war, and the CIA arranged its publication. Later, he was encouraged by Israeli intelligence in a campaign of violence against the Soviet Union and its offices abroad.

On this November night, Kahane announced that he was forming a new organization: the Zionist Emergency Evacuation Rescue Organization, or ZEERO. The advertisement for the meeting exhorted people to start showing up by 6:30 P.M.

"This time . . . Before the Flood . . . Before It's Too Late . . . Come Home! Come Home!"

The idea was to move Jews out of the United States, and into the security of Israel, before the American economy collapsed and a new Holocaust began. When he spoke to people who were not explicitly with him, his rallying cry had always been, "I say what you think. . . . No guilt, no apologies, and to hell with the rest of the world. Never again!"

No need for that tonight. He was among sympathizers, and he reminded them that he had been right, right, right.

"My whole life has been ideas which eventually were taken up by other people and succeeded," Kahane told the Marriott audience in conclusion. "Today, Jewish defense is an accepted thing. A patrol in a neighborhood is an accepted thing."

The audience applauded. In the back row, a slight, round-faced man wearing a black yarmulke appeared to join in the general agreement. He looked very Arabic, but those who took notice of him decided he must be a Sephardic Jew, the dark-skinned Jews of the Mideast, who were among the most loyal of Kahane's followers.

Kahane stepped away from the podium and a group of a dozen or so devotees crowded around. The round-faced man stepped up to the front. An instant later, a shot rang out. Kahane fell to the ground, and the people around him screamed as blood spurted from his neck.

"Call an ambulance, the rabbi has been shot!"

"What?"

"Call an ambulance, they have shot the rabbi."

The screaming reached someone with a cellular phone, and then hotel security. Then the round-faced man was seen rushing toward the door, with a silly grin on his face. An old Kahane supporter from Brooklyn, Irving Franklin, seventy-three, reached out to stop him. The man pushed Franklin aside and fired one shot into his back. People were scrambling up from the lobby to see what was happening. The round-faced man ran down the stairs and out the front doors of the hotel. He looked around for an instant, then saw a yellow cab, pulled open the door, and jumped in the back.

In the driver's seat of the cab was a Hispanic from the Bronx—not the tall, redheaded Egyptian, Mahmud Abouhalima, who was circling the block because he could not find a legal parking spot.

"Drive the cab!" screamed Nosair, pointing his gun through the Plexiglas divider.

The cabbie pulled away from the hotel, but got lodged in the midtown traffic. It was 9:07 and the streets were jammed. From the hotel, a few young men who had seen part of the shooting ran outside and screamed at the cab: "Stop him, stop him!"

The cab lurched down Lexington Avenue, but, two blocks later, got stuck behind slow-moving cars that were approaching Grand Central Terminal. The round-faced man jumped from the cab at 46th Street. The Jewish men who had been chasing on foot screamed, "Get him, get him! Somebody was just shot—get him!"

Carlos Acosta, a postal police officer, was locking up a temporary post office. He turned and saw a grinning, round-faced man running toward him with a gun in his hand. He raised the gun and fired at Acosta. The bullet hit Acosta in his armored vest, and was deflected into his arm. It was not his shooting arm. Acosta drew his own .357 Magnum and fired once, hitting the round-faced man in the chin.

* * *

The round-faced man was El Sayyid Nosair, a thirty-four-year-old immigrant from Egypt. He would tell police the next day that he hadn't shot Kahane, that, yes, he was an Arab, but that he and the rabbi were in agreement on many things. Nosair apparently had gone through the training camps of Abu Nidal, the Arab guerrilla warrior, a decade earlier, learning guerrilla warfare techniques, before settling in Pittsburgh. He met a heavy young Irish-American woman, unhappy with life. They married. Nosair was zealously devoted to his politics and religion—so much so that he was fired from a job in a jewelry store because he would not stop proselytizing the other workers. He had also experienced the raw side of being accused of sexual impropriety—a woman at his mosque had accused him of battery, and another person had accused him of assault. Both cases were heard in an Islamic court that cleared Nosair. But he and his new wife left Pittsburgh and came to New York.

Like Nosair, Meir Kahane knew how closely tied fundamentalist politics and religious orthodoxy could be. When he founded the Jewish Defense League, he recruited among Orthodox Jews. In a biography of Kahane, *The False Prophet*, author Robert I. Friedman recounts that Kahane once told an aide, Alex Sternberg,

> to use synagogues and large yeshivas for cover because they
> were an inexplicable universe to the FBI, let alone most
> Jews. "Put on a black coat and hat and walk into a yeshiva
> library and no one will question you," Kahane told
> Sternberg. Yeshiva libraries, Kahane said, were filled with
> musty shelves of seldom-used religious texts—a perfect
> place for a message drop. Most importantly, Kahane coun-
> seled, only Orthodox youths should be recruited into
> the underground. Not only could they inconspicuously navi-
> gate inside a yeshiva, but they also had characteristics
> that he thought were often lacking in secular Jews—self-
> discipline and adherence to a higher authority. "He be-
> lieved that if an Orthodox kid is committed to something,"
> said Sternberg, "he will do it with religious fervor."

They could have been talking about Nosair. Both Kahane and Nosair had emotional problems—Nosair was on Prozac, the antidepressant medication, and Kahane's duplicitous financial and personal life had long been a matter of private disgrace and wonderment among his inner circles. While living the public life of an Orthodox rabbi, and preaching fanatically against intermarriage, he had carried on multiple affairs, with both Gentile and Jewish women. One of these women, a young Catholic, threw herself off a bridge into the East River after Kahane sent her a letter admitting that he already was married and could not keep his vow to marry her.

Kahane's own family had cause to be troubled. Kahane spoke publicly against Sol Hurok, an old concert promoter known for bringing Soviet performers to the United States. One day in January 1972, Hurok's office was bombed. The JDL announced that it was responsible—before word came out that Hurok's secretary, a young Jewish woman named Iris Kones, had been killed. Her funeral was held at the Sutton Place Synagogue and presided over by Rabbi David Kahane, a cousin of Meir Kahane, who declared her death "the bitter fruit of a climate of violence."

Meir Kahane was troubled by the woman's death, but later wrote it off as a casualty in a larger struggle. Like Nosair, Kahane was passionately, intensely devoted to the politics of the Middle East, where the cycle of revenge and attack seemed unbreakable. A few weeks earlier, policemen in Jerusalem had shot nineteen Palestinians dead during a confrontation at the Temple Mount, the place Jews revere as the site of the Second Temple, and that Arabs worship as the Dome of the Rock, the place from which the prophet Mohammad ascended into heaven. In the early 1980s, Kahane had served forty-six months in an Israeli prison in connection with a plot to blow up the mosque that gives the Dome of the Rock its name.

After the police shootings, there were the usual vows of vengeance from the Arab world. A nineteen-year-old Arab showed up in a quiet Jerusalem neighborhood and cut the lung out of a young Israeli woman, then stabbed an old tree nurseryman in the heart. Finally, an antiterrorist policeman who lived on the street came out with his gun and put two shots in the slasher's thighs. When the officer grabbed the Arab to calm him, the young man reached around and jammed his knife into the policeman's belly, and the two clung to each other in a macabre *pas de deux* that ended when the policeman collapsed dead on top of the Arab, and into the knife. The Israeli army escorted the Arab man's parents, brothers, and sisters out of their home the next day, then blew it up. The man's relatives had nothing to do with his murderous deeds, but in the tribal war of the Middle East, a man's sins could be visited, by ricochet, through the generations. Great hatred, little room, as Yeats had written of Ireland.

Nosair and Kahane hated the United States for its secular relationship to the sad, screaming opera of Arab-Jewish relations. Meir Kahane's assassination was another run around that circle—but one played, for the first time, in the United States. Great hatred. Big room.

*   *   *

That night, separate ambulances carried Kahane and Nosair to the city's premier trauma center, the venerable Bellevue Hospital. Surgeons worked on the eerily similar wounds of their two patients, separated by a thin white curtain—both men were shot in the neck and chin area. Kahane's injury was mortal, Nosair's was not. The dead rabbi was put into a bag and brought a few blocks north to the city's main morgue. The chief medical examiner, Charles Hirsch, came from home to perform the postmortem. He walked past a crowd of chanting Jews who demanded that Kahane's body be released at once, without any incisions. Under Orthodox Jewish law, autopsies are generally forbidden. The body must be buried at once, with as little defilement as possible.

Hirsch, a thoroughly respected professional, did not need the situation spelled out. He looked at the entrance and exit wounds, and saw that it was a clean shot. There were no other external injuries. The case was straightforward and the man was an Orthodox rabbi. The medical examiner called the chief of the police crime-scene unit and asked if further examination of the body was warranted. The detective said no. Hirsch then made what he would later call the "worst decision of my professional life." He released Kahane's body without an autopsy.

An hour later, a letter arrived at the morgue on the letterhead of the Sutton Place Synagogue.

"I, Rabbi David B. Kahane, kin of the late Rabbi Meir Kahane, specifically prohibit an autopsy of Rabbi Meir Kahane on religious grounds."

David Kahane, who twenty years earlier had buried Iris Kones, the first victim to die at the hands of his cousin's JDL, now was again tasting the "bitter fruit of the climate of violence."

*　　*　　*

At 1:00 P.M. on November 7, 1990, it was eighty-four degrees in Tel Aviv and about to get much hotter. A long orange conveyor belt was stuck like a tongue into the belly of the El Al jet, and for five or ten minutes, suitcases and boxes and valises chugged down. Television cameras filmed a group of men in black hats and long coats peering into the cargo hold.

"Here he is!" someone shouted at last.

The big brown crate was eased onto the belt. The men in black hats lifted their arms to make sure the box did not topple off the side of the conveyor.

Meir Kahane, who had been expelled from the Knesset, the Israeli parliament, for his racist theories on Arabs, had returned. While he was loathed by left and moderate Israeli politicians, the engineers of his expulsion had been his old allies on the right, who saw in Kahane's grassroots support a threat to their ascendancy during the 1980s. Now that he was in a box, no one could begrudge him the full glory of a massive funeral. The remains were loaded into the back of a blue van and driven from the airport toward Jerusalem. As the van climbed the wooded hills outside the city, it passed an ordinary-looking highway guardrail. On the other side of the rail was a ravine. The previous summer, seventeen people had died there because an Arab man had grabbed the steering wheel and twisted the bus off the road. And not too many years before that, both sides of the highway were territories of a country called Jordan.

The funeral van pulled into the city and drove through the Mea Shearim neighborhood, where the most rigorous Orthodox Judaism has been observed for 120 years. Men wear long black coats and beards; married women shave their heads and cover them with wigs or kerchiefs. Some believe the state of Israel is an abomination of Scripture and instead await the coming of the Messiah.

This is where the power of Meir Kahane was at its greatest. He was a favorite of the Orthodox. Among his public obsessions was interracial intercourse, an evil in their world and, ostensibly, in his. Once he had written: "The Arab jackals defile the seed of the holy people, they strike at the God of Israel through the daughters of his people." Now, as his funeral van rolled through their streets, the men in long coats hurried behind. Posters had been pasted on the walls of their buildings in Kahane's memory. They cited the funeral oration given by young David when his friends were killed in battle: "How the mighty have fallen."

The van pulled onto the avenue known as Prophet Samuel. Here, in tiny apartments, live thousands of Sephardic Jews, descended from those forced out of Spain hundreds of years ago. They settled everywhere but in Eastern Europe, and finally came to Israel in the 1950s, with darker skins than those who had arrived earlier. Kahane deplored the idea that they were second-class Jews.

So here was his bedrock. Out with the Arabs; they are no good. Up with the Jews. Be proud. You can hear the same messages, with only the alteration of ethnic names, in Belfast, when Ian Paisley speaks to the Protestant working class about the lazy Catholics, or in Louisiana, when David Duke called on scratching-by whites to remember those good-for-nothing blacks. The near-poor can be bought cheap. Just a little respect does the trick.

Among those waiting on the street for the funeral procession was Chanah Shauder, a Persian Sephardic Jew. "He brings together something in my life and in his," she said. Her brother, an Israeli soldier, was captured by the Syrians during the Yom Kippur War. At the end of the war, the Syrians beheaded her brother.

On this street, Kahane founded a yeshiva in memory of the neighborhood rabbi's son, also killed by Arabs. And here, too, he dispensed cash favors to those in need. "Just before the high holy days, I needed three hundred dollars for a widow, and he wrote the check himself," a man was saying as the Kahane funeral van pulled into the yeshiva yard. Mordechai Eliahu, the chief Sephardic rabbi of Israel, announced that Kahane had given away $34,000 during the most recent Jewish holy days. Then he added, "He saved many Jewish women from Gentile hands."

The streets were clotted a quarter-mile in every direction with pensive male faces. The men paced about, listening to the loudspeakers carrying the eulogies for blocks. The women waited on the curbs. People in Jerusalem said it was the biggest funeral they could remember. All for a man who had been expelled from parliament for the poisoned views he held so publicly.

"Deep down," said Eli Peters, an eighteen-year-old student who had come to the funeral against the orders of his teachers, "Jews feel that what he's saying has to happen." A man whose dog Peters had walked had been stabbed a few weeks ago by an Arab who had a dream that he should go kill Jews. First he'd knifed a woman soldier, then a policeman, then the man with the dog.

"Even the most wicked Jew, if he is murdered by a non-Jew because of his Jewishness, is considered a holy person," preached Rabbi Meir Toledano. "To achieve security we must expel non-Jews who disturb our peace. Vengeance, with God's help!"

"Vengeance!" cried Yakutiel, a student of Kahane's at the yeshiva. The young man said his rabbi had been murdered by the press. The theme was repeated all day: somehow only Kahane's racist, insidious Arab-baiting had made headlines, not his generosity and love of the Torah.

Yakutiel, the student, concluded, "We'll let the machine guns talk, we'll let the knives talk. Shalom, Rabbi Kahane!"

Moments later, tens of thousands set off in procession to the cemetery. At the head of the line were two young men wearing T-shirts printed with a Star of David around a clenched fist, the symbol of Kach, the Kahane political party. They carried AK-47 assault rifles on their shoulders. The machine guns were mute. But the knives did talk. Two Arab workers discovered along the path of the funeral march were stabbed, dragged from shops owned by Jews.

"Leave them alone, they are good men," screamed one of the shopowners. Two other Arabs were beaten. The morning before, when word of Kahane's assassination had reached Israel, an old Arab leading his donkey into his olive grove was machine-gunned to death in a drive-by shooting. Another old man, out with the sunrise for farmwork, was shot by the occupants of the same car. Barbara Ginsburg, director of Kahane's Museum of the Potential Holocaust in Jerusalem, recalled that Kahane had advocated expulsion of Arabs from Israel, a policy known as "transfer." When Ginsburg heard of the killings of the two old men, she did not blink. "Rabbi Kahane wasn't right when he said transfer [the Arabs]," said Ginsburg. "First you kill them and then you throw them out dead."

By far the majority of the funeral marchers were subdued. But every few minutes a knot of teenagers came sailing along the route of the march, waving the yellow flag of Kach.

"Mavet Larevim," they chanted. Death to Arabs.

The chant had a lyrical, giddy tone, and a group of toddlers watching from a balcony in a day-care center took it up: "Mavet Larevim, Mavet Larevim," they squealed. At an Israeli television station, some of the young marchers stopped and threw rocks through the window. They tried to turn over a construction tool-shed, but it took too much effort, so they danced and chanted along the street.

At the cemetery, the crowds awaited the arrival of the coffin for nearly two hours. A Sephardic Jew argued loudly with a Hasidic man, who enjoyed a rare exemption from Israeli military service because of his religious studies. "You don't want to go into the army," he said. "You are deprived. You don't want to go into the army, so you end up not shooting any Arabs," he said triumphantly.

But this, many of the mourners said, was not what brought them to Kahane's burial. When Soviet Jews were being ignored and persecuted, he had stood up and made noise. "I remember a rabbi in the pulpit in Laurelton, Long Island, saying that this is not the Jewish way, what Kahane was doing," said one of the mourners, Hanna Kessler. "The Jewish way was to lie down and get slaughtered."

Kahane, she and other New York expatriates said, deserved

credit for the revolutions in the Soviet Union because of the wedge he drove with his demands that the Jews of the Soviet countries be set free. "A great Jew, a proud Jew, we don't have many of that caliber around now," said Miriam Lesser, a Brooklyn woman now living in Israel. Just then the procession arrived. Ahead of the casket was a new group of young men waving the flag of the Kach party.

When they saw news photographers and TV cameras on a high spot, they posed, chanting "Kill the Arabs." Then they heaved rocks at the journalists. "This is not what people really feel," said Irene Wechsler, another former Brooklynite. "We're grandmothers. Do we look like radical Kachians? I'm afraid of guns."

As she and the other old New Yorkers were walking from the cemetery, Nathan Morowitz, who had taught in a Howard Beach yeshiva with Kahane, spoke of his true charity. But the press never printed it, one of the women said.

"The news people were getting a whiff of fascism, so they stayed away," said Morowitz.

With that the chants rose again from behind them.

"Mavet Larevim! Mavet Larevim!" Death to Arabs, death to Arabs. The first desert stars cut into the night sky, and the old New Yorkers climbed the hill from the cemetery, shivering.

8

UNREASONABLE DOUBTS

A bullet-riddled rabbi. A roomful of witnesses. An Arab holding a smoking gun.

If any case in the history of jurisprudence ever possessed the essential components for a certain guilty verdict, it was the Kahane killing. There were more than one hundred people in the room when Kahane was gunned down. The suspect, El Sayyid Nosair, was arrested a few hundred yards from the scene—after running from the ballroom and leaving two wounded bystanders in his wake. When he was finally stopped, shot by a postal police officer who was locking up a post office three blocks from the hotel, Nosair's hand was near a .357 Ruger. In his pocket were bullets that fit the gun. You didn't have to be Sherlock Holmes to solve this one.

Joseph Borrelli, the city's chief of detectives, knew an open-and-shut case when he saw one, so he wasn't about to let anyone muddy the waters with conspiracy theories or tales of terrorist intrigue. There hadn't been any political assassinations in New York City in more than a decade, and Borrelli certainly didn't want one on his watch. So when reporters began raising the possibility that Kahane's killing might be part of some far-flung assault, or sponsored by an anti-Israeli group, Borrelli immediately tried to quash any speculation.

"At this point it looks like he was a lone gunman," he said the day after the shooting—even though he knew only the skimpiest details about Nosair's background, and the FBI hadn't told him about the boxes full of unusual evidence that federal agents had seized from the suspect's home in New Jersey. "Why he did it, we may never know."

Borrelli's counterparts in the Manhattan district attorney's office weren't eager to drag the Mideast conflict into the case either. Political trials get messy and complicated, and Kahane wasn't exactly the world's most sympathetic victim. If the DA made this a political trial, the defense attorney would start citing some of Kahane's more heinous pronouncements—his slogan "Every Jew a .22," and his plan to drive all "Arab dogs" from the occupied territories and the West Bank. Many jurors might hear those statements and figure that Kahane had gotten what he deserved. Better to play it safe— keep the jury focused on the hard evidence and try it just like any other simple homicide case. The detectives and the DA already had the corpse, the witnesses, the smoking gun—a veritable Holy Trinity of evidence. The authorities figured it was a case you just couldn't lose, so why get fancy?

Even William Kunstler, one of the nation's most flamboyant— and effective—defense attorneys, figured Nosair had little chance to win an acquittal. Kunstler nearly refused the case because his partner, Ronald Kuby, had an uncomfortable secret which he suspected would upset Nosair. Nosair's cousin Ibrahim El-Gabrowny came to Kunstler's office several days after the arrest. Though El-Gabrowny and his lawyer, Michael Warren, were both Muslims, they had no qualms about asking a Jewish attorney to join in the defense—at least not a Jewish attorney with Kunstler's astounding success at winning high-profile, antiestablishment cases. But Kuby had some particularly troubling secrets in his background, which he figured would prevent him from working on the trial.

"Ibrahim, I think there's something you should know about me before you decide whether we should represent you," Kuby said.

"Yes, what is that?" El-Gabrowny said.

"Well . . ." He hesitated, not knowing quite where to begin. "You see, in my younger days, in the uninformed passion of my youth, I was a member of a certain organization which you probably won't be happy about."

El-Gabrowny furrowed his brow, waiting for Kuby to continue.

"The organization was the JDL," Kuby said.

Kuby paused for a moment and waited for the weight of his words to land upon El-Gabrowny. It was bad enough that the Jewish Defense League was one of the most radical anti-Muslim, Zionist groups in the world. But Kuby, Warren, and El-Gabrowny all knew that the JDL had been founded by a militant Brooklyn rabbi named Meir Kahane.

El-Gabrowny said nothing. Kuby had developed a knack and a taste for high-profile cases during his years as Kunstler's chief assistant. The Kahane case would be a boon for Kuby professionally, and offer a prestigious opportunity for him personally. It would give the young lawyer a chance to repudiate a period of his own past that he regretted, even if he had to do it by defending an intolerant bigot like Nosair. Kuby made his plea to El-Gabrowny.

"And not only was I a member of this outlaw organization, but I even went to Israel to work toward its causes. I know now that these people are wrong, immoral, and racist. I saw firsthand some of the evil, intolerant things they did. I would be honored to work on the case and ensure that your cousin gets a fair trial. But I think you should know this. I don't want you to find out about it later on."

El-Gabrowny stared at Kuby's face, making certain this wasn't some sort of prank. He thought for a moment, and asked Kuby what had caused him to turn away from Kahane and his followers.

"Well, I saw what they did. I saw how their paranoia affected other people, how they had allowed hatred and fear to make them as abhorrent as the people they were supposed to be fighting. I learned that intolerance, from anyone, is inhumane."

El-Gabrowny waited another moment. "There's no possibility that you would change back?"

Kuby laughed, broke into a wide grin, and shook his head so briskly that his ponytail swayed from side to side. "Oh, no," he said, a look of shock coming over his face.

El-Gabrowny returned the smile. "Then I don't think it will be a problem."

Even after they had agreed to let the past remain buried, Nosair's supporters and attorneys figured his only viable option was to plead insanity. The press had already been provided with a wide array of convenient leaks from law-enforcement officials, designed to convict Nosair in the court of public opinion. Somehow, reporters learned that Nosair had been stalking the rabbi for a year, and was angry at work on the day of Kahane's murder because of job problems. Chief Detective Borrelli suggested that Nosair, who had a university education, had been despondent over finding only menial work in the United States—that he was a man with a bad case of shattered expectations. Defense attorney Michael Warren tried to counter this charge and prepare the public for an insanity defense. Warren told reporters about Nosair's long history of enduring anti-Muslim oppression, and that he had been suffering from depression and treated with Prozac, a prescription drug that allegedly drives some patients to suicidal and homicidal rages. The violent crime wave of the eighties and nineties had made psychiatric defenses harder to pull off, but Kunstler was one of the best, and he figured that he might be able to generate some sympathy for his client. A successful psychiatric defense would save Nosair the trauma of prison—even if it meant subjecting him to the surreal deprivation of a mental hospital—and probably shave a few years off his term of incarceration. With the corpse, the witnesses, and the smoking gun all lined up against his client, what other choice did Kunstler have?

But Nosair had other ideas. When Kunstler, Kuby, and Warren visited him at his cell in the city jail on Riker's Island, Nosair grew furious at the suggestion he should plead not guilty by reason of insanity. Nosair insisted that he wasn't insane. He also argued that he wasn't guilty. The day after the shooting, when he awoke in the hospital, Nosair had protested his innocence to detectives. The bullet wound in Nosair's throat had rendered him incapable of speaking, so he scrawled a desperate message across a detective's notepad.

"I am innocent," Nosair wrote in uneven, trembling script. "When I got shot, the man with the yarmulke stood beside me. When I was lying on the ground, he put the gun beside me."

Nosair repeated this plea to his lawyers in the Riker's Island interview room. If they wanted to represent him, they must plead not guilty and explain to the jurors that Nosair had been framed. If not, he'd find new lawyers.

Kunstler was a little unsettled by the sudden shift in the case's dynamics. It was clearly his kind of trial, a chance to infuriate nearly everyone by defending a man reviled by the public and already convicted by the media. Kunstler had built a career by acting as a crusading contrarian, defending cop killers, revolutionaries, and nearly anyone else whom the general public had deemed unworthy. He had beaten overwhelming odds before. He had defended the Chicago Seven during one of the most celebrated activist trials of the 1960s, and had negotiated on behalf of the inmates who rioted during the Attica uprising. In New York City, many police officers still sneered at the mere mention of Kunstler's name because of the infamous Larry Davis case. Davis was a Bronx drug dealer who was charged in 1987 with shooting an assortment of police officers and civilians. Kunstler and Warren defended him by putting the entire NYPD on trial, claiming that Davis had shot in self-defense because the cops had been buying drugs from him and this time had intended to kill him and steal his cocaine. A jury in the Bronx, New York's poorest, most crime-ridden borough, sided with Davis and acquitted him of the police shootings. He was convicted only of shooting a drug dealer.

But how could he overcome a case with a dead rabbi, a roomful of witnesses and an Arab holding a smoking gun? *Someone* had killed Kahane. If Kunstler wanted jurors to acquit Nosair, he had to convince them that someone else had pulled the trigger. But who? Where did you begin to look?

Kunstler's adversary in the case, Assistant District Attorney William Greenbaum, faced just the opposite dilemma. Greenbaum, whose skill as a legal technician had made him one of DA Robert Morgenthau's most dependable assistants, had to guard against overconfidence. From the minute police had arrived at the frenzied scene, the cops had treated it like the kind of case that terrifies prosecutors: a Sure Thing. With the cornucopia of evidence strewn about the hotel that evening, it looked like a connect-the-dots conviction. So people took things a little easier than usual, a little sloppier.

The crime-scene unit failed to seal off all of the chaotic murder scene. How could they have known that some of Kahane's followers, devout Hasidim, would actually cut out pieces of the curtains and carpet so they could bury his bloodstains with his body? The lead detective on the case, who'd figured it was open-and-shut, hadn't rushed out to interview witnesses and passersby. Instead, he went on vacation two days after the killing, and when he returned two weeks later, he then proceeded to canvass witnesses who had been inside the ballroom and outside the hotel. Midtown is one of the most transient parts of the city, with four major hotels within a few blocks. The chances of visitors still being around two weeks later were extremely slim. No one had thought to ask the Marriott security force to save the videotapes from the cameras mounted near the hotel's entrances and exits.

The city medical examiner, Dr. Charles Hirsch, might have pressed the Hasidim to allow an autopsy if this had been a shakier case. But the cops had the suspect and the gun, the roomful of witnesses. He settled for an "external examination" and agreed to testify that Kahane had, in fact, been shot and had, indeed, died.

The FBI handled the case in its usual fashion, with the greedy territoriality of a riled pit bull. Agents led a raid on Nosair's New Jersey apartment, and brought along more than twenty other law-enforcement officers to search for evidence. In all, the cops seized forty-nine boxes of evidence—providing strong links between Nosair and known terrorist groups, and even possible targets in the United States. But the agents failed to inventory some of the items properly. Every piece of evidence seized in a criminal case must be clearly tagged, logged, and tracked meticulously between the time it is discovered and the time it is used as an exhibit at trial. This precise "chain of custody" procedure is designed to minimize the chance that police officers might tamper with or doctor the evidence. But the officers who conducted the raid on Nosair's home simply threw some items into boxes without numbering or tagging them, making them inadmissible as evidence. It was the kind of oversight that would haunt the FBI after the World Trade Center was bombed.

The Feds did turn up some incriminating items. In Nosair's home there had been a file of newspaper clippings about assassinations, a pamphlet about bomb construction, a book about paramilitary training maneuvers, and a piece of sheetrock pocked with bullet holes, ostensibly used for target practice at some shooting range. There was also a newspaper story about Kahane's upcoming speaking schedule, with the November 5 speech at the Marriott circled, plus a suspected "hit list" that contained the names of a state senator, a federal judge, a former U.S. prosecutor, and Rabbi Meir Kahane.

Prosecutor Greenbaum still wanted to see what else was in the boxes, those troves of evidence the Feds chose not to turn over. But it appeared that he had enough to work with, and he didn't want to make this a political trial by dragging in the Mideast anyway, so the DA's office didn't fight the Feds on this one.

Greenbaum was the classic, reserved, by-the-book prosecutor, with a tightly controlled demeanor and a thinly veiled disdain for Nosair and Kunstler. His approach was to act as a simple vehicle for the evidence, not as an impassioned advocate, not as an angry champion for an innocent victim of slaughter. Greenbaum tried the case as if he were proving a scientific theorem. He laid out the facts like a physics professor explaining an equation that had long been accepted as the unshakable truth.

This smugness only made Kunstler angrier. Greenbaum was so

self-assured that Kunstler detected a bit of annoyance, as though Greenbaum were put out that he actually had to go through the trouble of trying the case. To Kunstler, the DA came to symbolize the single thing he had devoted his life to rattling: the Establishment.

While Greenbaum treated the evidence as a series of immutable truths, Kunstler viewed each fact as an organic, malleable creature, with a life and mysteries all its own. Bring it out into the light, put it under a magnifying glass, ask it the right questions, and oh, what a story it might tell! With his booming voice, wild gray hair à la Albert Einstein, lightning-quick mind, and provocative sense of humor, Kunstler had the stage presence to seize nearly anyone's imagination. He resembled some wizard out to dazzle the jury with mystical tales of tragic human emotions. The Kahane case would provide Kunstler with the opportunity to weave one of his most spellbinding stories yet.

It was a complicated plot with a brilliantly simple theme: the Jews did it, in a fight over money.

Kunstler, Warren, and Kuby changed Nosair's plea from insanity to not guilty. The lawyers began telling the public that they'd hired a private investigator, conducted their own inquiry into the rabbi's killing, and uncovered startling information. Kahane had been killed by his own disciples, Kunstler said, because of an internal feud over control of the organization's finances. In the months before the trial began, the defense lawyers worked furiously to prepare the case. Kunstler and Kuby asked State Supreme Court Justice Alvin Schlesinger to excuse himself from the case, saying that his Jewish upbringing would make it impossible for Schlesinger to give Nosair a fair trial. The judge angrily refused. Michael Warren and his assistant Shanara Gilbert even did a little detective work of their own. Kahane's biographer, Robert I. Friedman, received a call from Warren, who asked if the rabbi had any mortal enemies.

Gilbert pressed Friedman for the names of any possible suspects who might have wanted Kahane dead.

"Could it have been the CIA or the FBI?" Gilbert asked. "Could it have been the husband of one of Kahane's jilted lovers?"

The list of enemies was very long, Friedman told Warren. But then he took the question a step further and wrote an article for the *Village Voice,* suggesting that while Kahane was despised by many, no one hated him more than the people associated with Nosair. Although the killing had taken place in the heart of what is often referred to as the media capital of the world, Friedman alone raised questions about Nosair's radical views and his associates in Sheik Omar's mosque, and the connections with the guerrilla fighters in Afghanistan. Not a single one of the four New York newspapers pursued the leads exposed by Friedman—nor did CBS, NBC, ABC, CNN, or Fox Television. A solitary freelance writer had raised the alarm. The mainstream press dined on its regular diet of bread crumbs from the cops and circus performances by the defense lawyers.

In the month before the trial, Kunstler raised his showmanship to new heights, transforming the case into a miniature Mideast conflict in the center of America's largest city. On October 15 he held a press conference at the New York Hilton to announce his latest findings in the case, naming the Kahane supporters and other Jews who, he alleged, had conspired to murder the rabbi and frame the innocent Nosair. Kahane's supporters attending the press conference were outraged at Kunstler's audacity and rushed the stage. Before the Hasidim could reach the podium, an African-American bodyguard, hired by Kunstler and Warren, came up from behind the stage waving a 9-mm pistol. He held off the onslaught of protesters until a horde of police officers in bulletproof vests arrived to break up the disturbance.

The hype turned the courthouse into a cauldron of Middle East tension. Kahane's followers surrounded the courthouse entrances with picketers. Some were from the JDL, Kahane Chai, a radical group of Kahane disciples, the Kach party, and several other militant organizations. One Kahane supporter, Mordecai Levy, was out on bail, awaiting his own trial, when he attended Nosair's proceedings. Levy, head of Kahane's Jewish Defense Organization, had been convicted of shooting an elderly man with a high-powered rifle and was awaiting sentencing. Another Kahane disciple, Baruch Goldstein, would gain international infamy three years later, when he would massacre dozens of Arabs while they knelt in prayer at a mosque in Hebron, Israel.

The pickets demanded justice, screamed for Nosair's blood, and wrote graffiti in the elevators used by prospective jurors.

"Kill Nosair," read one message, scrawled in blue Magic Marker.

"Kill Kunstler," read another.

The Muslim protesters were equally determined, though somewhat less raucous. Among those protesting at the courthouse were Mohammad Salameh, Mahmud Abouhalima, and Bilal Alkaisi, three of the four men later charged with the World Trade Center attack and another bomb plot. Sultan El Gawli, an Egyptian who knew Nosair from a New Jersey mosque, also showed up. El Gawli had been convicted in 1985 for trying to buy plastic explosives so that Palestinian Liberation Organization members could kill tourists in Jerusalem on Christmas Day. Now that El Gawli had been released from prison, he was hoping to help his friend Nosair avoid the same fate.

The Muslim protesters also noticed an unfamiliar man who began attending their rallies, a burly Egyptian named Emad Salem. No one knew much about him, although he claimed that he had been a member of Anwar Sadat's special guard during his days in the Egyptian army, and he seemed to ask a lot of questions. In the months to come, Salem would become a fixture in the Egyptian community's radical fringe, watching and listening as Nosair's supporters plotted their revenge.

Behind the scenes, the Muslims worked furiously to raise money for Nosair's defense. Mustafa Shalabi, who ran guns for the rebels fighting the Soviets in Afghanistan, was helping to collect money for Nosair's legal fees. From the restaurants of Brooklyn to the mosques of Egypt, Muslims were asked to give what they could to help the hero El Sayyid Nosair. By the time the trial began, the fund contained $163,000, boosting the spirits of the Muslims at the courthouse.

"Allah Akhbar!" they shouted. God is Great!

The commotion outside Manhattan State Supreme Court, at 100 Centre Street, made the Kahane case the talk of Manhattan's legal community, and intensified the pressure on the prosecution. Greenbaum knew that juries were unpredictable, and there was no such thing as a sure-fire conviction. But he also had no doubt that Nosair would be convicted, because he had no doubt that Nosair had fired the bullet that killed Kahane. In addition to all the evidence, Nosair had made a confession to one of his cellmates at Riker's Island. The cellmate's history of violent crime made him too shaky a witness to present to the jury. No DA would be foolish enough to let Kunstler cross-examine a witness who had been arrested repeatedly for sexual assault on children. Nonetheless, as the mobs of protesters took their seats in the courtroom—the Jews in their yarmulkes on one side; Muslims, dressed in traditional white tunics and headdress, on the other—ADA William Greenbaum began the biggest case of his career with the unshakable faith that he was right.

"It was a perfectly planned crime," Greenbaum told the jury. "What better place to carry out an assassination than in a crowded room, so you can escape by slipping through the crowd?"

Greenbaum meticulously laid out his evidence—the rabbi, the witnesses, the gun. But to Kunstler, the most significant thing about Greenbaum's opening was what it lacked: a motive.

Greenbaum wasn't going to provide a motive? Fine. Kunstler would gladly offer the jury an assortment of theories about who might have had reason to kill the rabbi. Give them a little Shakespearean intrigue by suggesting that Kahane had been betrayed by his own lieutenants, men who lusted after Kahane's money and power. Point the finger at a mysterious doctor and a medic from a Jewish ambulance company. Kunstler's theories didn't have to be true or even especially convincing. All they had to do was sow the seeds of reasonable doubt, to be just as plausible as Greenbaum's explanation. And what scenario was the DA offering the jury? Nothing. Crazy Muslim shoots rabbi for no reason whatsoever.

As Greenbaum moved through his list of witnesses, Kunstler was irrepressible, always prodding, poking, insinuating, and raising new possibilities of a possible conspiracy or cover-up. He made the government pay for its every mistake, and even mistakes it hadn't made.

In addition to Kunstler's brilliant showmanship, Greenbaum was forced to battle with an openly hostile judge. Justice Alvin Schlesinger said he was just being tough but fair, keeping a firm grip on the proceedings. But many observers who viewed Schlesinger's treatment of the prosecutor thought Schlesinger was overcompensating for his religion—trying to prove that a Jewish judge could indeed give a Muslim defendant a fair trial. Others figured that Schlesinger was unaware that a police foul-up prevented Greenbaum from entering the boxes full of evidence from Nosair's home, and concluded that the judge was angry at Greenbaum for failing to enter such vital evidence.

Kunstler always figured that Schlesinger was mad at the prosecutor for the bail fiasco. In the days after Nosair's arrest, Schlesinger set his bail at $300,000. That infuriated many New York Jews, who wanted Nosair held without bail. Angry protesters picketed outside Schlesinger's home, until he finally revoked the bail.

"But I think the judge blamed the DA for failing to give him enough information," Kunstler said after the trial. "I don't think he ever forgave Greenbaum for that."

Ground zero. The February 26, 1993, blast blew a crater the size of a four-story building under the World Trade Center, paralyzing the Twin Towers' generators and nearly ripping open the wall that holds back New York Harbor. (The Port Authority of New York and New Jersey)

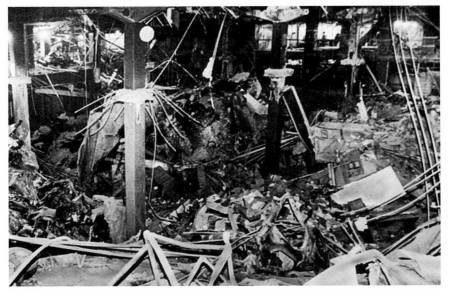

The search. With the crumbling floors shored up by supports, tons of rubble were sifted for clues to the bomb and for bodies.

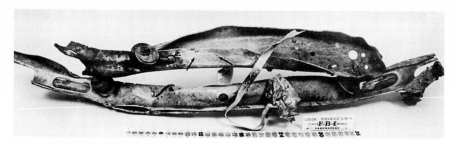

Needle in the apocalypse. A four-foot-long twisted, charred piece of metal broke the case. A series of dots punched in it helped identify the bomb-laden van.

The leader. El Sayyid Nosair, *above left,* allegedly the organizer of the terrorist cell, poses with bomber Mohammad Salameh.

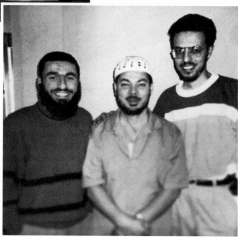

Brothers for Jihad. Bombers Mohammad Salameh, *left,* and Nidal Ayyad, *right,* pose with El Sayyid Nosair.

The face of terror. Nidal Ayyad was photographed with a Palestinian flag over his shoulder and gripping a hand grenade. FBI agents found this photo ripped to pieces in the trash.

Victors for Jihad. Mahmud Abouhalima lifts lawyer William Kunstler to his shoulders after a Manhattan jury acquitted El Sayyid Nosair of murder. (Stan Honda/*New York Newsday*)

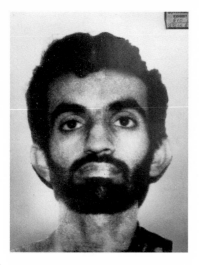

Ramzi Yousef. The mysterious bomber who was flown in from Afghanistan slipped out of the United States the day of the blast.

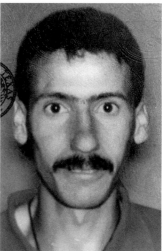

Ahmad Ajaj. He helped the terrorists build the bomb by phone from jail.

Abdul Yasin. The FBI questioned the American-born Yasin, and he left the country for Iraq the next day.

Four of the six killed in the blast are shown here in a group shot of the Port Authority Operations Department taken in front of the Twin Towers. The dead (circled, *left to right*): Bob Kirkpatrick, Steve Knapp, Bill Macko, and Monica Smith.

Remembering the dead. Edward Smith, husband of Monica Smith, lost his wife and unborn son in the explosion. (Alan Raia/*New York Newsday*)

Mourning the dead. A coworker weeps at a memorial service held for the dead directly above the blast site. (Richard Lee/*New York Newsday*)

The first blow. The terrorist campaign began with the 1990 assassination of the militant rabbi Meir Kahane in Manhattan. (Donna Dietrich/*New York Newsday*)

The sheik. Blind Egyptian cleric Omar Abdel-Rahman is the accused head of a nationwide terrorist network. (Daniel Sheehan/*New York Newsday*)

The informant. Emad Salem (*above*), the sheik's security adviser, was a double agent. (Taxi and Limousine Commission)

Inside the cell. Emad Salem (*right*), secretly working for the FBI, joins Mahmud Abouhalima's brother on a visit to the jailed bomber as he awaits trial. (Mitsu Yasukawa/*New York Newsday*)

Inside the courtroom. J. Gilmore Childers, a street-smart prosecutor with a no-nonsense style, led the case against the bombers. (Stan Honda/*New York Newsday*)

Jailed. Sheik Omar Abdel-Rahman surrenders to authorities after a stand-off at Brooklyn's Abu Bakr mosque. (Stan Honda/*New York Newsday*)

Whatever Schlesinger's motives, his rulings appeared inconsistent. When Kunstler asked for public assistance to pay for Nosair's psychiatrist, claiming that Nosair was too poor to pay for it, he failed to mention that Nosair had $163,000 in his defense fund. A tough judge could have fined Kunstler, found him in contempt, or accused him of fraud, but Schlesinger didn't even criticize Kunstler in the courtroom.

Michael Warren didn't receive the same celebrity treatment that Kunstler did, but Schlesinger also granted him indulgence on a major transgression. During the course of the investigation, Warren sent an official-looking subpoena to employees of the Marriott, informing them that they were compelled by law to speak to him about the case. It was a blatant lie. Defense lawyers aren't legally empowered to issue subpoenas; only judges and grand juries can. Yet when Schlesinger learned of the deception, he didn't fine Warren, find him in contempt, or threaten to file charges with the attorney grievance board. He gave the seasoned attorney a halfhearted lecture and warned him not to do it again.

Yet Schlesinger repeatedly chided Greenbaum in front of the jury, cutting him off in midsentence and lecturing him like a law school professor blasting a disobedient student.

In his chambers, Schlesinger yelled at Greenbaum for leaning against the wall and placing his foot against the wall. During jury deliberations, while Schlesinger entertained Kunstler at a Christmas party in his chambers, the judge chastised Greenbaum for spending too much time in the law library.

With his talent, experience, and a friendly judge, Kunstler was at his best.

The prosecution called Jay Goldberg, who had been five or six feet from Kahane when he was killed. Goldberg couldn't identify Nosair, but Kunstler seized on his statement that the gun used to shoot Kahane was black—as opposed to the silver revolver found by Nosair's side. Such inconsistencies of perception frequently occur in the chaos of crime scenes. But Kunstler treated this fact as though it were proof positive that conspirators had slain the rabbi and then tried to frame Nosair with a throwaway gun planted on the solitary Arab in the crowd.

The police officer who discovered the ammunition in Nosair's pockets had committed a minor oversight by forgetting to scratch his initials in the bullets. Crime-scene gaffes like this are usually written off as honest mistakes, but Kunstler again reacted with so much indignation that you might have thought he'd uncovered the secret to the Lindbergh kidnapping.

Greenbaum did a passable job of rehabilitating many of the witnesses Kunstler had picked apart. But he did little to restore jurors' confidence in the officer who found the bullets, leaving open the possibility of foul play by police. Suddenly the smoking gun found near Nosair was surrounded by a fog of uncertainty, and wasn't as damning as prosecutors had expected it to be. When the medical examiner, Charles Hirsch, took the stand, he explained that no autopsy was done because Kahane's family didn't want one. Under cross-examination by Kunstler, however, Hirsch acknowledged that he had performed autopsies on other Hasidim. Kunstler also got Hirsch to admit that he had decided against an autopsy before consulting with the Kahane family, and that without an autopsy there was no way to determine the exact trajectory of the bullet that killed the rabbi. The city medical examiner had actually let the body go without gathering all of the evidence, Kunstler pointed out, and the DA's office had allowed it to happen. The rabbi was still bullet-riddled, but Kunstler raised an interesting specter: Where exactly had the bullet that hit the rabbi come from? Who had fired the gun? And why was the government so eager to blame Nosair for murder, the most heinous of crimes, without conducting a thorough investigation?

As the trial went on, strange things happened to that roomful of witnesses, too. Although the ballroom had been crowded with more than one hundred people, the mob of two dozen spectators who gathered around Kahane after the speech had formed a kind of human shield obstructing the view of most people in the room. Only those spectators standing within ten feet of Kahane had actually been in a position to witness the shot being fired. When the lead detective on the case had returned from vacation and tried to interview people who had been in the room, he'd been surprised to find that a number of Kahane's followers were uncooperative. Most of those who did cooperate hadn't actually seen the shot being fired. Several had seen Nosair lurking near Kahane during the rabbi's last moments. Others had seen Nosair walking briskly from the room and firing several shots as he tried to make his escape.

The DA had promised jurors sixteen witnesses. But even though the ballroom had been crowded with potential witnesses, only one man was willing to point his finger at the defendant's table and say that El Sayyid Nosair had indeed pulled the trigger and killed Kahane.

Ari Gottesman, twenty-one, was a rabbinical student who had walked up to chat with Kahane after the speech. In response to Greenbaum's questioning, Gottesman acknowledged that he had stood next to Nosair.

"The man who shot the rabbi is over there," he said, pointing calmly at Nosair. "He shot Rabbi Kahane."

But on cross-examination, Kunstler forced Gottesman to open the tiniest window of uncertainty. Had he actually seen the bullets fired out of the gun in Nosair's hand? How could he simultaneously have seen Nosair's face, plus the gun, plus the bullet?

After playing rhetorical cat-and-mouse for what seemed like an eternity, Gottesbaum relented. He said he'd felt the gun move by him, heard the shots go off, and when he'd turned—a split second later—he'd seen Nosair with the gun in his hand, trying to hide it.

It wasn't much wiggle-room, but at least it was something. Kunstler had effectively neutralized the perceptions of a roomful of witnesses.

As he neared the end of his case, Greenbaum finally loosened up. Despite Kunstler's antics, he had shown that Nosair was in the room, carrying a gun and running to make a getaway; he had proved that Nosair tried to commandeer a taxi in his desperate effort to escape. To stoke the jurors' sympathy for the shootings' victims, he also called Irving Franklin, seventy-three, a man who had been wounded in the buttocks during the melee.

"Would you please drop your pants so we can see the wounds," Greenbaum asked, as the judge, the jury—and even Kunstler—burst into laughter.

Franklin never did drop his drawers, but after fifty-one witnesses and fifty-six exhibits, Greenbaum rested his case.

The defense began its case immediately, calling paramedic Gideon Zahler to the stand to bolster Kunstler's homicidal-physician theory. An unusual thing had happened to Zahler as he attended to the fallen Kahane on the ballroom floor. As Zahler had placed the rabbi's head back and tried to insert a breathing tube, he was stopped by Stephen Stowe, a doctor and Orthodox Jew who volunteered with a Jewish ambulance company that raced to the hotel after hearing of the shooting. Stowe, as the ranking medical man on the scene, had taken control of Kahane's care. Throughout the prosecution's case, Kunstler kept hammering away at this unusual tug-of-war between medical personnel at the scene, piquing the jury's interest. Lieutenant Kevin Haugh of the Emergency Medical Service recalled that someone had placed a 9-mm handgun into his ribs as he knelt down to treat Kahane. Haugh said that the person with the gun had told him not to interfere with Dr. Stowe, who had pushed Haugh aside several moments earlier.

To make a bizarre scene even stranger, EMS technician Eva Marie Cusick testified that Stowe had refused to allow a tube to be placed in Kahane's mouth. Cusick also said that Stowe had "hyper-extended" Kahane's neck as he lay bleeding, and manipulated his spine "horribly." Stowe had denied any wrongdoing when Greenbaum put him on the stand, but Kunstler pointed out damaging facts from the doctor's background: that he had been the subject of four prior complaints by EMS workers, and had once been forcibly removed from an EMS scene by police.

When Kunstler questioned Zahler, he testified that he, too, had seen Stowe prevent medics from intubating Kahane. On cross-examination, Greenbaum led Zahler to acknowledge that Kahane was already clinically dead by the time the EMS arrived.

Could anything have saved a man who had been shot in the neck at close range? Did the EMS crew's handling of the patient contribute to Kahane's death or detract from the guilt of the shooter? The answers to those questions didn't really matter; the mere act of raising them helped Kunstler sow more doubt in the jurors' minds. If he couldn't bring Kahane back from the grave, he could at least raise questions about who had put him there, and whether bullets had been the sole cause of death.

Kunstler was out to try his own murder case now, to prove that he was not only a better defense lawyer than Greenbaum, but a better prosecutor, too. Judge Schlesinger had forbidden Kunstler from asking detailed questions about disputes within Kahane's organization, saying that most of his inquiry would be irrelevant, sheer speculation. With his skillful cross-examinations, though, Kunstler still managed to sneak in a few thinly veiled references to internal strife within Kahane's inner circle. Irving "Izzy" Katz described himself as a close friend of Kahane, but Kunstler pointed out that he also owned a 9-mm handgun, much like the one that had been pointed at Lieutenant Haugh. Katz acknowledged that he had collected money for Kahane's religious schools in Israel. But in 1991, Katz had been stripped of the authority to make withdrawals from the Kahane organization's bank accounts. There was no evidence whatsoever to link Katz to the shooting, but Kunstler's implication was clear: might Katz's resentment have led him to kill Kahane?

The final two defense witnesses were both employees of the hotel. One was a security guard who did not remember seeing Nosair at the scene, but had seen a small, bearded man run from the ballroom carrying a backpack. The other was a clerk who said she'd received an unusual telephone call on the day of Kahane's death. The caller had wanted to know about security arrangements for the rabbi's speech, she testified. He had never identified himself, but had spoken with "a Brooklyn Jewish accent," she said.

The defense team considered putting Nosair on the stand, but decided against it. Greenbaum entered into evidence a videotape that showed the scene at the ballroom until several seconds before Kahane's killing. Kunstler repeatedly pointed out that the video depicted Nosair leaving the ballroom, and that the tape failed to show any of the witnesses who had put Nosair at the scene.

"Why put [Nosair] on the stand, and subject him to cross-examination, when the videotape tells the same story, irrefutably," Kunstler argued. "[Nosair] is so excitable that he might turn off some jurors. It's just not worth the risk."

The defense rested.

Despite Kunstler's performance, most observers still expected an easy conviction. Greenbaum took no chances, however. In his closing argument, he even tried to break out of the fortress of forensic evidence he had offered jurors, and showed them a touch of humanity. He talked about the calculated nature of the killing, and warned jurors that a man such as Nosair shouldn't be allowed to endanger the streets of America.

"With your verdict, tell him, 'Not here, Nosair, not here!' " Greenbaum pleaded.

Warren delivered the defense team's closing argument, and offered a flourish of his own. He portrayed Nosair as a hardworking, levelheaded man who had gone to Kahane's speech because he was trying to understand his adversaries' point of view. When Kahane was killed by his own people, they did what came naturally: they blamed the only Arab in the room.

In a moving closing argument, Warren presented a different El Sayyid Nosair—Nosair the family man. He pointed out that Nosair had carried his driver's license in his wallet, along with "pictures of his beloved children."

"That's not an assassin, that's a victim," Warren said.

Then, on Wednesday, December 17, 1991, after six weeks of trial, it was up to the jury.

During jury selection, Kunstler had looked for people who might share his skepticism about the government's claims. He wanted brown people, young people, people whose lives were difficult and uncertain enough that they'd be willing to suspend their disbelief. And once again, Schlesinger gave Kunstler virtual free rein. During the first two days of jury selection Schlesinger allowed Kunstler to have every caucasian removed from the panel—even though attorneys are forbidden from using race to disqualify potential jurors. In most high-publicity cases, judges ask for a large pool of jurors and perform an elaborate process, called voir dire, to weed out any potential jurors who might have prejudices toward one side or the other. But Schlesinger was inexplicably eager to speed through jury selection, and denied Greenbaum's request for a large pool of potential jurors. Before the trial, when Greenbaum asked how long voir dire would take, Schlesinger snapped back, "It will be a lot less time than you think."

At one point during voir dire, Schlesinger's haste led to an amateurish error: he forgot to make the potential jurors take an oath before he began questioning them. Later, he also denied the prosecution's request that potential jurors fill out a questionnaire to screen them for any religious or political predispositions that might taint their view of the case. It is a common procedure in cases involving emotional issues such as religion, abortion, or politics, but Schlesinger ruled that it was unnecessary. Even when the defense attorney, Michael Warren, joined in the request for a questionnaire, Schlesinger refused, saying "to show the impartiality of the court, both your requests are denied."

When the jury finally was chosen, it was comprised of five whites, one Latino, and six blacks—and at least one of them had the skepticism Kunstler had sought. During the testimony of eighteen-year-old Sholem Gubin, the juror told Judge Schlesinger that the witness was being coached by a man in the back of the room, and that the two men were trading hand signals. The man, it turned out, was Gubin's teenage brother, who was motioning for him to speak louder so he could be heard in the packed, cavernous courtroom. After two days of deliberations, it was clear that Kunstler had succeeded. The jury was struggling. They twice asked to view the videotape, and looked visibly drained when they emerged from the deliberation room for their meal breaks. They asked for testimony about the black gun and the bullet fragments found in the wall behind Kahane. Never did they deliberate for more than two hours without asking to view more evidence.

On Friday a female juror sent a note to Judge Schlesinger, complaining that a male juror had called her "a jackass." She asked to be excused from the panel because "we're starting to hurt each other in here."

Judge Schlesinger refused to let her leave, and the testy deliberations dragged on. Kunstler figured the jury would be out for several more days, so he left the courthouse on Saturday and spent the evening at a poetry reading with his daughter. When he arrived home, his wife conveyed the startling message that Nosair had been acquitted of murder.

Kunstler rushed down to the State Supreme Court in lower Manhattan, where dozens of angry Hasidim were already demonstrating, carrying a mock electric chair and angrily crying out, "Jewish blood isn't cheap!"

Most of the jurors quickly left the courthouse, anxious to put distance between themselves and the fitful, stunning decision. After wrangling over the evidence, and playing the videotape over and over again, they could only find Nosair guilty of gun charges for shooting Franklin and commandeering the taxi. The legal community was stunned that jurors had been swayed by a defense so theatrical that attorney Alan Dershowitz called it "amateurish." The Hasidim were livid at the police and the DA's office. Those jurors willing to speak about the case defended their verdict. Alexia Barre, a juror from Chelsea, complained that there was something fishy about the case, that she sensed there was more going on than the prosecutors had told the jury. She was half right.

"If they want somebody to blame, I think they should look at the police," she said. "They destroyed evidence, obliterated fingerprints, they never did a trajectory test. They simply didn't give us enough evidence to convict."

Another juror, Bernice McClease, later seemed to be under the mistaken impression that the jury had actually convicted Nosair of murder. McClease considered the trial a profitable experience because she had spent her lunch breaks outside the courthouse, selling home-baked peach cobbler for one dollar a serving.

"The court officers bought some, too, a nice big bowl of it," she said. "We did convict him of killing the rabbi," McClease insisted two years later.

The maximum sentence Nosair faced was seventeen to twenty-five years, instead of the thirty-five years to life that a murder charge would have brought. As the Hasidic protesters screamed angrily, Kunstler, Kuby, and Warren hugged to celebrate. They had won the case everyone thought was unwinnable. After a cheerful press conference, a tall, redheaded protester bent down and hoisted Kunstler onto his shoulders. The redhead, Mahmud Abouhalima, then walked down the stairs, carrying Kunstler to Warren's waiting car.

"Nosair's a filthy murderer," screamed one of the protesters.

"Kahane's blood is on your hands, Kunstler," yelled another.

On sentencing day, Schlesinger was crankier than ever. He blasted the jury for its decision, saying the verdict "defied reason." Schlesinger seemed angry, and Kunstler wondered whether the judge also felt guilty that his harsh treatment of the DA might have swayed the jurors.

He sentenced Nosair to the maximum.

Ironically, Nosair was sent to the Attica State Correctional Facility, the prison where Kunstler had represented inmates during the riot of 1971.

Nosair's cousin, Ibrahim El-Gabrowny, went to visit him in prison on May 6, 1992, along with Mahmud Abouhalima and the inquisitive newcomer, Emad Salem. Nosair was still stunned and angry that he'd been convicted of anything. He admitted that he had indeed killed Kahane. An angel had come to him in a dream and ordered him to murder Kahane, he said. But he was furious at the judge, the Jews, and the system itself. He told El-Gabrowny he couldn't bear to remain in prison. He ordered El-Gabrowny to devise a plan, to build bombs, to start securing safe houses, to kill the judge and the prosecutor who had done this to him.

If FBI agents had looked carefully, they would have realized that Nosair had already begun preparing for those actions before Meir Kahane was killed. Inside those boxes seized from Nosair's home the day after Kahane's murder was a virtual terrorist starter kit. Inside Nosair's home, written in Arabic, was a formula to a bomb made of urea nitrate, the same diabolical cocktail that caused the devastating explosion at the World Trade Center two years later. There were Arabic speeches, too, sermons by the radical Sheik Omar Abdel-Rahman, who urged his followers to "destroy the edifices of capitalism." But FBI interpreters were busy translating documents pertaining to Saddam Hussein and the Gulf War. The Nosair evidence, seized in November 1990, wasn't translated until 1993, after the Trade Center had been attacked.

Once Nosair went to prison, the FBI also knew that he was actively directing his supporters to begin the holy war to free him. FBI agents learned about Nosair's plans because one of El-Gabrowny's closest confidants, Emad Salem, was a government informant. Salem, the weight-lifting Egyptian, actually had been introduced into the New York Muslim fundamentalist community during the trial to give FBI agents an inside look at the militants' activities and plans. He won the confidence of El-Gabrowny, Abouhalima, and other militants, and began to tell his handlers that the group was preparing to launch a brutal war of terror on the United States, starting with targets in New York City.

Salem urged the agents to take this plan seriously, and open a full investigation into Nosair's supporters and connections. If they had heeded his warning, they might have taken a closer look at the speeches they seized in Nosair's home in 1990, and at some of the photos found there as well. Strewn among the *Soldier of Fortune* magazines and fundamentalist Islamic literature at Nosair's home were unusually detailed pictures of famous structures: the Washington Monument, Saks Fifth Avenue department store, the Empire State Building, and the World Trade Center. But the speeches, the photos, and the bomb formula remained in the boxes, unexamined, gathering dust in an FBI storage room.

FBI agents simply transcribed Salem's account of the May 6 prison conversation, told him to keep an eye on El-Gabrowny, and failed to recognize the full weight of Nosair's words when he ordered El-Gabrowny to help him.

"Get me out of here!" Nosair demanded.

9

A HOSTILE
TAKEOVER

Tears streaked down Abd-el Walli Zindahni's face as the brawl in Brooklyn's Abu Bakr mosque grew louder. Zindahni had been invited to a summit at Abu Bakr on March 6, 1993, to mediate a fierce philosophical disagreement between different factions of the congregation. But after several hours of shouting, curses, and threats, the entire meeting had disintegrated into an Islamic gang fight. Nearly two hundred people had packed the mosque to debate about which imam would lead the Abu Bakr congregation—the moderate Sheik Ab el Maged Sobh Masjib or the radical Sheik Omar Abdel-Rahman. The board was controlled by the militants, and they had recently announced that they were ousting Maged Sobh and replacing him with the blind, militant Shiek Omar, who was famous for preaching that Muslims should rob Western shopkeepers and murder Middle Eastern rulers who didn't impose Islamic law.

The vast majority of Abu Bakr worshipers were stunned by the coup. Imagine how a peaceful Christian congregation would react if it was one day taken over by a right-wing revolutionary. Abu Bakr members were offended or frightened by Sheik Omar's radical, highly politicized brand of Islam. They drew up a petition demanding that Sheik Maged Sobh be retained, and gathered signatures from 150 members of the Abu Bakr community. By March, as the growing tension threatened to destroy the mosque, a special meeting was scheduled to decide the issue, and Zindahni agreed to step in as an arbitrator. It was a daunting job.

"In the name of Allah, let us all please try to work together," Zindahni exhorted the worshipers, who sat shoeless on the carpeted floor. "We are all here for the same purpose. I ask you to open your hearts so that we may resolve this misunderstanding."

But the radicals scattered throughout the mosque frequently interrupted Zindahni's words. The moderates grew immoderate, and joined in the din. The conflict splitting Muslim communities across the globe was now being played out in the basement of a small brick row house on Foster Avenue, a quiet residential street in Flatbush, Brooklyn, and before long both sides became enraged. Within an hour the shouts and taunts grew so loud that the police were called to try to restore order. In the back corner of the room, two moderates had a militant in a headlock and were pummeling him with their fists. In the front, three militants had pinned a moderate to the wall and were throwing intermittent blows.

"Brothers, brothers, please!" Zindahni pleaded, his cries barely audible above the brawling. "We are all Muslims, please! Stop this, please!"

But the fight had actually been simmering for nearly a year. It escalated in October 1992, in the very same room, during Abu Bakr's annual elections for its board of directors. Normally, election day was calm, an exercise in democracy that most of the mosque members had never experienced in their homelands of Palestine, Syria, Egypt, and Jordan. Here, in the working-class communities in Brooklyn, they looked forward to the ritual with pride—even though most of the races for the mosque's board of directors contained little opposition and even less suspense. The elders who were usually elected to positions on the board continued the mosque's low-key array of programs and religious services. And members of the insular Muslim community went on with their daily lives, paying little mind to the Jews, Catholics, and Protestants who were their neighbors. Election day 1992 had all the makings of yet another uneventful race until just days before the balloting.

Then, in October 1992, Mahmud Abouhalima, called "the Red," and his army of fellow extremists showed up unexpectedly and in overwhelming numbers. Without warning, Abu Bakr found itself the victim of a hostile takeover, the latest battlefront in a global struggle over the future of Islam. The traditionally calm campaign speeches were suddenly spiked with invective and sparked shouting matches. Abouhalima had organized an election machine worthy of a Chicago ward heeler. He entered fifteen of his own candidates, and brought nearly one hundred supporters to capitalize on a loophole in the election bylaws and seize control of the mosque.

The Red's hard-bitten allies blended in easily at first. He himself drove a cab, so he and his colleagues shared the overburdened look of people whose lives were a daily struggle. But they had a wholly separate agenda, and their presence transformed the election into a fight for the soul of Abu Bakr. Abouhalima's combative past gave him a distinct advantage in terms of battle experience. Passengers whom the Red chauffeured through the streets of New York might have mistaken him for just another angry but ultimately harmless crackpot coursing about the byways of the city. At times he would rant about political injustices, quote the Koran, rail about the materialistic decay of Western society. On the streets of New York, there is a name for people who always complain, vow bloody retribution, and seem liable to explode at any moment: they are called New Yorkers.

The Red was also smart enough to prevent himself from actually scaring most of the non-Muslims he'd encounter. He was an astute judge of character, perceptive enough to notice when his fares grew wary, and charming enough to retreat to the persona of Mahmud the family man: father, teetotaler, devout Muslim. In Abu Bakr, however, the faithful knew that the two faces of Abouhalima's psyche were fused in volatile and contradictory ways. And they realized that his plans were to turn Abu Bakr into an outpost of violent Muslim extremism. "Islam is the solution," Abouhalima told a worshiper on the day of the election. "But we must have the courage to fight for what is just, to fight in Allah's name."

Abouhalima's unusual appearance—red hair and freckles, beefy six-foot-two-inch build—made him the center of attention almost everywhere he went. In Middle Eastern folklore, red hair and freckles are called "crusader blood," and Abouhalima tried to live up to this legacy by acting as a missionary bent on toppling Western culture. He was born in Alexandria in 1959, and raised in the Nile Delta town of Kafr-el-Diwar, the son of a brawny textile factory worker. The town was destitute and crowded; like most of his neighbors, Mahmud lived in a stark concrete bungalow. Kafr-el-Diwar had a tradition of political dissent; in the year the Red was born, a rebellion by textile workers turned bitter, violent, and bloody, so Abouhalima was raised to be acutely aware of his impoverishment. The children of Kafr-el-Diwar were also left no doubt about who was to blame for their despair—the corrupt political leaders who allowed the Egyptian people to be exploited by materialistic Westerners.

Abouhalima was an above-average student, and by 1980 he began classes at Cairo University, studying education. The oppressive poverty in Cairo and the pro-Western policies of the Sadat regime infuriated Abouhalima, however, and he was quickly drawn to the revolutionary ideas of the Gama al-Islamiya student movement, a fundamentalist group widely feared in Egypt for its violent attacks on tourist buses, civilians, and public officials. The group had been banned from Egyptian campuses in 1979, because they opposed Anwar Sadat's historic 1978 peace treaty with Israel. But the outlaw status only made Gama al-Islamiya seem more heroic to students such as Abouhalima, who flocked to hear speeches of Islamic revolutionaries including Sheik Omar Abdel-Rahman. Abouhalima was particularly inspired by Abdel-Rahman's call to overthrow the country's secular leaders and restore Egypt to its place as the spiritual center of Arab culture, promising "We must make the blood of the infidels flow."

All that lofty talk about one worldwide Islamic nation made Egypt's oppressiveness seem that much more constricting to the Red. In September 1981, Sadat stunned Egypt and his Western allies by arresting three thousand intellectuals, priests, writers, politicians, and Islamic fundamentalists. Abouhalima decided to go abroad. His goal was to meet with other Muslims already living in the West, to see how they kept their faith in a hostile culture, and how they might help Islam gain greater influence in Egypt, Europe, and beyond. The network of Egyptian émigrés could also raise money for political activities back in their homeland. In 1981 he toured the Netherlands, Finland, and West Germany.

Just nine days after Abouhalima left the country, the fundamentalists struck back, and Egyptian society was forever changed. On October 6, 1981, as President Anwar Sadat sat watching a parade in Cairo, a half-dozen commandos in military uniforms attacked him with machine guns and grenades. The revolutionary group Islamic Jihad was held responsible for the assassination, and Sheik Omar Abdel-Rahman was forced to stand trial. The day after the killing, an attorney in the German city of Stade filed an application for political asylum on behalf of Abouhalima. Three weeks later, in Munich, Abouhalima filed another application for asylum, this time in person. His landlord verified that the Red had been living in Munich since October 1. But that alibi didn't absolve Abouhalima in the eyes of Egyptian authorities. Nor did his claim that he was aboard a boat in the Baltic at the time of the assassination. *Al*

Achram, an Egyptian newspaper closely allied with the government, published the names of dozens of suspects and Jihad members wanted for questioning in connection with the assassination. One of the names was Mahmud Abouhalima.

During his immigration hearing, Abouhalima acknowledged that he belonged to the outlawed activist group Muslim Brotherhood, but he denied taking part in acts of violence. Abouhalima pleaded with the immigration officials, saying he would be persecuted for his political opposition. The Germans ruled that membership in a political organization did not prove persecution, and his request was denied.

Abouhalima's visa would not be renewed, but he had no intention of returning to Egypt. From his bleak apartment at Ehrenbreitsteiner Strasse 11—a building near the Olympic Village where Arab guerrillas had attacked the Israeli team in 1972—he began a frenzied offensive to remain in Germany. Abouhalima tried to get a student visa, but his two semesters in Cairo were not accepted in Bavaria. Just as Abouhalima was starting to lose hope, he discovered an opportunity to prolong his stay in Germany. Her name was Renate Soika. She was a lonely, sickly woman of thirty-three who had never fully recovered from tuberculosis. She lived on welfare, and was considered mentally unbalanced by her relatives and neighbors. Soika was still heartbroken from a failed romance with a man who was an alcoholic, and friends described her as "desperate for a husband." Soika was taken by Abouhalima's political passion. To her, he was a dashing figure—a tall, Third World hero who was fighting for justice and who must be saved from persecution in his homeland. To Abouhalima, Soika's problems and flaws were completely overshadowed by the chance she offered him to secure a four-year visa and thus avoid deportation. On December 27, 1982, they wed, and Abouhalima was granted a permit to remain in Germany until 1986.

They moved into Munich's West End, a flat at Landsberger Strasse 79, a neighborhood where 35 percent of the residents are immigrants. He forced her to quit her job, so she could fully concentrate on keeping the house. He bought her flowers on her birthday. Abouhalima searched for work and, after some difficulty, had to settle for a job as a dishwasher and barbecue cook at Kaufhof, a department store. When that fell through, he grew so desperate for work that he took a job at Hanhof, a restaurant in the artists' quarter that specialized in a dish no Muslim could ever sample—

pork. Meanwhile, he resumed his studies at night school, learning fluent German and working toward his teaching degree.

But Abouhalima's real mission in Germany was to network with fellow Muslims. Munich's Muslim community is dominated by members of Gama al-Islamiya. Nearly every day Abouhalima would spend hours in the mosque, praying and socializing with men whose aim was somehow to restore Islam to its preeminent place in world culture. The Red even befriended several members of the Black Panther movement. The black separatist movement begun in the United States during the 1960s had eventually established a small contingent in Germany, consisting mostly of U.S. servicemen who had brought their philosophy over with them. Abouhalima was fascinated to hear them talk about America: their horror stories about racism in the United States bolstered his conviction that America was a citadel of injustice. Soika could always tell when the Red had just met with a Panther, because his conversation would take a particularly anti-American hue.

"This mighty, decadent infidel must learn," he said on numerous occasions. "Islam will not be held down forever."

Soika went to the mosque on several occasions, but resisted Abouhalima's forceful suggestions that she become a full-fledged Muslim and bear him children. He was infuriated when Soika refused to start a family, but nonetheless he continued his effort to convert her.

"You should come to the mosque," he would tell her. "Islam is a beautiful religion."

"Pray six times a day!" she said, incredulous at the very suggestion. "That's not for me."

So Soika wasn't completely surprised when she returned home from a lengthy hospital stay in 1985 and found a Muslim woman living in her house. The interloper's name was Marianna Weber, she was twenty-two, pregnant with the Red's child, and said she was his new wife. Abouhalima later explained that Islamic law permitted polygamy in certain situations, and suggested that they live together as a family. But Soika was devastated by the betrayal. She filed for a divorce in 1985, and Mahmud, his immigration status in peril, packed up his new wife and child and headed off to begin a new life. He secured a three-month tourist visa, then moved to the New York City borough of Brooklyn.

He detested the materialism of Western culture, its atheism, promiscuity, and vacuous obsession with status and wealth. But many Middle Eastern activist groups believed it was helpful to station members abroad, where they could help raise money and support for the causes back home. Abouhalima soon learned that Americans were lax about much more than moral codes. He worked at several jobs in New York's thriving underground economy, as a laborer, an electrician, and a chauffeur. In July 1986 he was granted a livery license by the New York City Taxi and Limousine Commission, even though his visa had already expired and Abouhalima was in the country illegally.

Driving a taxi suited him perfectly. Locked in the solitude of his cab, the Red roamed the city freely, reading the Koran, listening to the sermons of Omar Abdel-Rahman and other fundamentalist preachers, and proselytizing his passengers.

By 1988 the Red was earning more than five hundred dollars a week, sending some of the money back to relatives in Egypt, donating funds to political groups in the United States and back home, and living barely above the poverty level in Brooklyn.

Abouhalima was becoming better known in the Muslim community centered on Atlantic Avenue in downtown Brooklyn. He worshiped at two mosques, and became active in an organization that helped refugees from the Afghani war resettle in the United States. The organization, known as the Alkifah Refugee Center, was run by several men closely linked with the Egyptian Jihad, the group accused of assassinating Sadat. At the center, the Red worked with Afghani refugees and learned firsthand of the Muslims' heroic, historic struggle. He also befriended El Sayyid Nosair, a fellow Egyptian at the center, who worked for the city and shared Abouhalima's political beliefs. They spent hours talking about the atrocities Soviet soldiers were committing on innocent Muslims—using mustard gas, tanks, and machine guns, wiping out villages, slaughtering women and children. Abouhalima longed to join in the fight. But he was already in the United States illegally, and knew that if he left he might never be allowed to return.

Then the Red got another break, again thanks to the laxity of the American bureaucracy. Abouhalima had learned of a loophole in U.S. immigration law that allowed aliens to enter the country under the guise of agricultural workers. He contracted some associates in New Jersey, filled out a few forms, and paid several hundred dollars for supposed "administrative fees." The Red, who had never grown anything more than a beard, was legally declared a farm worker, and was granted his coveted green card.

For the first time in six years he could stop worrying about deportation. Now he was free to pursue actively his dream of a true Islamic state. For a young Muslim in 1988, the place where he could make a difference was clear: Afghanistan.

Ever since Soviet tanks rumbled into Afghanistan on Christmas Day 1979, in an effort to prop up a teetering Communist government, Afghanistan's predominantly Muslim population had become Islam's latest martyr. A small resistance movement was given arms, aid, and encouragement from the United States, and became a rallying point for Muslims around the world. Respected Muslim scholars such as Abdullah Azzam declared it a Jihad, inspiring fundamentalist dreams that the soldiers of Islam would force the Soviets out and keep marching through Central Asia and the Middle East—to Iraq, Egypt, Tadzhikistan, Pakistan, and beyond.

One of the most popular preachers about Afghanistan was Sheik Omar Abdel-Rahman. To Americans, Sheik Omar appeared an almost comic figure. His trademark red cap looked as if it had been swiped from Kris Kringle, and his dark black glasses were vintage Ray Charles. Beneath that garb, however, militant Muslims recognized a man of great charisma and wisdom. The red velvet cap was a sign of distinction, worn only by graduates of Al-Azhar, the Islamic world's most prestigious university. Sheik Omar's blindness kept him from active combat, but also freed him from distractions and had allowed him to become one of the most accomplished religious scholars in all of Islam. In addition, he had sent two of his own sons to battle, and he made frequent visits to Afghan rebels on the front.

To the CIA, which pumped more than $2 billion into the fourteen-year Afghani resistance effort, Sheik Omar was what intelligence officials call "a valuable asset." Never mind that he was widely suspected of inspiring the Sadat assassination (although he was acquitted of the charge). His speeches helped recruit many of the twenty thousand Muslims who came to Afghanistan from around the world, including Mahmud Abouhalima. The Red considered it an honor to fight at the behest of his spiritual leader, and spent several weeks in Peshawar, Pakistan, gaining military training funded by U.S. taxpayers.

On the battlefield, the Red was part of a clique of foreigners whose fearlessness stunned even the Afghanis. The Arabs were viewed with some suspicion by Afghanis, as zealots whose motives went beyond merely ousting the Soviet invaders. But their single-mindedness and effectiveness on the battlefield was impressive. Abouhalima volunteered to perform the suicide mission of mine-sweeping. Equipped with only a stick or a reed, he would advance in front of the troops and probe the earth, ever so gently, to see if the Soviets had placed any mines.

Abouhalima somehow survived several tours in Afghanistan between 1988 and 1989. Once he returned to Brooklyn for good, the Red began wearing his combat boots and fatigues on the city streets. He became more deeply involved in the Brooklyn-based Alkifah Afghan Refugee Center, which provided financial support through the Alkifah Fund to the refugees brought to the center, and helped persuade Sheik Omar to move to Brooklyn—despite the sheik's U.S. status as an undesirable alien. The sheik was impressed by the number and enthusiasm of fundamentalists in the New York and New Jersey mosques, and when he came to Brooklyn, Abouhalima quickly positioned himself as the sheik's chauffeur and bodyguard.

By late 1989, though, the Soviets were steadily withdrawing from Afghanistan, and the United States had little use for the rebels. The CIA was lauded for shrewdly recruiting and deploying them, saving the U.S. military from the politically volatile task of committing America's sons and daughters to the fight. The American public, conditioned to viewing the world in the stark Us-versus-Them mentality of the Cold War, was relieved to see the Soviets vanquished and the fight ended. And unlike the CIA's other ill-fated policies—in El Salvador, Cuba, and Nicaragua—they'd even managed to back the winners this time.

For the Red and the Muslim freedom fighters, known as *mujahedeen,* driving the Soviet tanks back across the Hindu Kush mountains was just the beginning. Weren't the streets of Cairo and Kafr-el-Diwar still littered with the wasted lives of the permanent Muslim underclass? Hadn't the leaders of the Arab world built gigantic personal fortunes at the expense of their people's well-being? Didn't the Israeli government still brutalize Palestinians on the West Bank? In Bosnia-Herzegovina, didn't the West stand idly by as the Serbian army slaughtered and raped Muslims under a genocidal policy that was later given the perverse, macabre name of "ethnic cleansing"? And didn't America, the nucleus of world capitalism, deserve much of the blame for the Muslims' status as one of the world's downtrodden peoples?

Before Afghanistan, the Red could coexist grudgingly with those fellow Muslims who argued that Islamic leaders must go slowly, work within the system, and hope to improve marginally their lot in the world. The moderates, such as Sheik Maged Sobh at the Abu Bakr mosque, said that armed conflict was only the last resort of Jihad. They believed that one of the definitions of *jihad* was "to lead a good life." To them, *jihad* meant practicing charity and self-discipline in their daily lives, being generous and kind to the disadvantaged, and spreading the word of Allah. If Islam was attacked, the moderates believed it was morally permissible to take up arms in self-defense. Otherwise their approach was to work within the system, and to try to improve the community by leading more virtuous lives.

But Muslims had been trying conciliation for centuries, and in the words of the militant leader Zaid Shakir, it amounted to "swashbuckling with a flimsy sword." By working within the system, they had been doubled-crossed by Sadat, humiliated by Israel, plundered by America and the Soviets. Shakir—whose pamphlet "Muslims and the American Political Process" was widely read by militants in Abu Bakr and in the Al Salaam mosque in New Jersey— said it was pointless for Muslims to try and work through the system. American politics were so factionalized that they virtually demand compromise. But the fundamentalist Islamic state that Shakir and Abouhalima longed for was based on moral absolutes in which public policy and private lives must be conducted by strict adherence to the Koran. The fundamentalists believed that Muhammad had strictly forbidden compromise with nonbelievers, saying that "We disassociate ourselves from you, and from that you worship other than Allah: we have rejected you, and there has appeared between us and you enmity and hatred forever until you believe in Allah alone!" (Koran 60:4). That left only one viable alternative for politically conscious Muslims, according to fundamentalists like Shakir: "extra-systemic activity, ranging from noncooperation to guerrilla warfare."

In Afghanistan, armed Muslim resistance succeeded in less than a generation. So why change strategies once the Afghani veterans dispersed to the Sudan, Egypt, Jordan, the Balkans, and the United States? Abouhalima, Nosair, and other Muslims began training at a Connecticut firing range. There, the Red and several dozen other trainees would dress in white Afghani garb, bow their heads in prayer, then practice firing the Kalashnikov and AK-47 automatic weapons smuggled in from the front. The Red also took a more aggressive interest in the workings of Alkifah Afghan Refugee Center. He brought a fellow Egyptian to the United States to head the Alkifah Fund, a man named Mustafa Shalabi. The two men became inseparable, finding jobs and apartments for young refugees, and traveling to mosques and Islamic cultural centers to raise money for their cause. The Red viewed it as a way to sustain the contacts he had made in Afghanistan, and import the enthusiasm and zeal they had shared.

But coalitions forged in battle are often strained by the burdens of victory. Before long, even the Afghani veterans began feuding about the future direction of their movement. The Red and Shalabi believed the best way to capitalize on their momentum was to recruit veterans, regroup, then mobilize in the United States. Sheik Omar had other ideas. He believed the time had come when he might finally realize his deepest ambition: to transform Egypt into an Islamic state. For nearly a quarter of a century, Abdel-Rahman had been at odds with a succession of Egyptian rulers. As early as 1967, he began preaching about the shortcomings of the government, and was first arrested in 1968 for calling President Gamal Abdel Nasser a "pharaoh." His 1981 arrest for allegedly inspiring Sadat's assassination brought the sheik widespread support among the nation's Muslims, and his acquittal in 1984 left the blind cleric more celebrated—and more resolute—than ever.

Once the Soviets had been ousted from Afghanistan, and the United States had provided Muslims with arms, money, and training, Abdel-Rahman was convinced that his moment of destiny had at long last arrived. His singlemindedness seemed at first just an irritating diversion, an obsession that Abouhalima and Shalabi dismissed as a philosophical difference of opinion. Shalabi and Abouhalima were both Egyptian, too, and shared Abdel-Rahman's bitter hatred for Egyptian president Hosni Mubarak, but were willing to set aside their patriotism for the larger aims of a worldwide Jihad. Surely the sage Sheik Omar, who had led the mujahedeen so valiantly, would not be so small-minded as to overrule them. As the months went by, though, the dispute festered, spawning bitter arguments about how to allot money, weapons, and manpower.

The success of the Afghani movement had generated widespread support for the Alkifah Fund, and by 1990 it was receiving more than $100,000 per month from Muslims across the country and around the world. Sheik Omar suggested that Shalabi set aside half

the cash for efforts to overthrow President Mubarak. Shalabi resisted. The sheik insisted, but Shalabi, who was a close associate of
the Jordanian sheik Abdullah Azzam, stood fast. Abouhalima was
heartsick over the dispute, which placed him in the middle of a
battle between his spiritual adviser and his closest friend. Enraged
by Shalabi's display of insolence, Abdel-Rahman then began accusing him of wrongdoing, questioning whether the money in the fund
had been misused.

In the spring of 1991, Sheik Omar directed his handlers to circu-
late a pamphlet to all of the metropolitan area mosques, urging
Muslims not to contribute to Shalabi.

"He is no longer a Muslim," read the handout. "We should not
allow ourselves to be manipulated by his deviousness."

Shalabi's supporters were angered by Sheik Omar's unsubstantiated
claims, and rallied to his defense. They circulated their own flyers,
rebutting the sheik's charges. Abdukalder Kallash, president of Abu
Bakr's board of directors, made a personal appeal on Shalabi's behalf.
Kallash, a devout moderate Muslim, approached Sheik Omar in the
spring of 1991. The sheik had just finished preaching at a Jersey
City mosque, urging all Muslims to unite in the struggle to topple
Mubarak. Kallash agreed with the goal and respected the sheik as
a scholar, but he thought it was unfair for the sheik to siphon
money from the Afghan fund and send it to Cairo.

"The Koran tells us you must be kind to your neighbor," Kallash
said. "Yet you have been invited into your neighbor's home and
now you are trying to take over that home. How can you say that
is just?"

Sheik Omar was startled by the show of defiance, especially from
a man as low-key as Kallash.

"Shalabi is wrong," he said, then walked from the room.

Six weeks later, Shalabi was dead. His body was discovered in
his home in the quiet Brooklyn neighborhood of Seagate, beaten,
shot, and stabbed repeatedly. More than $100,000 in Alkifah funds
were missing from the apartment. The body was identified and
claimed by Mahmud Abouhalima, who told authorities that he was
Shalabi's brother. There were no signs of forced entry, so police
suspected that Shalabi was killed by someone he knew well enough
to welcome into his home. Detectives also found a single red hair
in the dead man's hand.

Shalabi himself was towheaded, so they were careful not to jump
to conclusions too quickly. But within a week, FBI agents, disguised

as repairmen from a utility company, entered Abouhalima's home in Brooklyn. They were searching for blasting caps, which an informant said the Red was planning to use in a terrorist bombing. The agents searched in vain but found no caps, so they planted several listening devices and then left. A neighborhood street kid had seen the suspicious-looking agents and told Abouhalima, who quickly deduced that he had been raided by the FBI.

Abouhalima's increasingly militant behavior made him a prime target for FBI officials in New York and New Jersey. But the Red was so elusive that agents began calling him the Teflon Terrorist. FBI agents were certain by now that Abouhalima had driven his cab to the Marriott East Side Hotel in midtown Manhattan on the night of Meir Kahane's murder, presumably to act as Nosair's getaway driver. But the Feds couldn't prove their theory. They dragged the Red in for questioning, reminding him of his dubious immigration status. Abouhalima refused to implicate himself or turn against his brother Muslim. Instead he attended the trial each day to support Nosair.

In September 1992, the FBI launched a full-scale investigation into a report that a group of Egyptians was planning to assassinate the secretary-general of the UN, Boutros Boutros-Ghali, and Egyptian president Hosni Mubarak. Twenty-six Egyptians were given subpoenas, ordered to appear before a grand jury, then questioned by FBI agents when they arrived at federal court. On the wall of the interrogation room was Abouhalima's photo.

None of this attention from law-enforcement officials deterred the Red from his mission. He continued to chauffeur Sheik Omar and escort him to mosques, fund-raisers, and social gatherings. He kept up his mobile ministry, preaching Jihad to whoever happened to be in the backseat. In October 1992, he embarked on his next battle—the small but important effort to take over Abu Bakr.

The Red and his three dozen closest operatives had already honed their electoral techniques on two other New Jersey mosques, so, when they turned to Abu Bakr, their opposition never really had a chance. Abu Bakr's moderates had heard rumors about a takeover at the election, but they simply weren't as well organized, or highly motivated, as the Red. The president of the board, Abdukalder Kallash, had used years of artful diplomacy to ensure Abu Bakr's status as an outpost of Islam's peaceful mainstream. Now, as he realized that status had been doomed by an electoral ambush, he could only watch in dismay when the first of the Red's zealots straggled into the basement of the mosque, removed their shoes, and seated themselves on the Kelly green carpet. Abu Bakr functioned as a de facto Muslim community center as well as a place of worship, so newcomers were welcome and frequent. The mosque's "regulars" were a resolute collection of Middle Eastern émigrés, many of whom had fled the oppression of their homelands only to end up toiling on the unforgiving fringe of the American service economy. They were convenience-store merchants, cabdrivers, restaurant owners, homemakers, city employees, garment manufacturers, delivery-truck drivers, service-station attendants. Abu Bakr had a few glowing success stories—Kallash ran a travel service, Hamed Nebawi owned several restaurants, and other worshipers had landed well-paying civil-service jobs. But for the most part, the faithful barely scraped by, working extended workweeks at tasks, and wages, that most native-born Americans considered beneath them.

On election day, however, many unfamiliar faces straggled into Abu Bakr. The strangers, who had been mobilized by the Red and the militants, sat quietly, filled out their ballots, and left quickly. Abouhalima himself arrived in the midafternoon, wearing a satisfied smile. In the front of the room, Kallash and several board members sat at a dais reading each voter's ballot. Behind them was a chalkboard to tally the vote totals, and the Red was pleased to see that fifteen of the twenty-three candidates were people he'd installed on the ballet only several days earlier. And when the results were announced, he was happier still.

The top vote-getter was Ibrahim El-Gabrowny, Nosair's cousin, who had persuaded William Kunstler to defend Nosair in the Kahane assassination. El-Gabrowny, a building contractor, was well known in the community and had ingratiated himself with Abu Bakr members by renovating the mosque's second-floor imam's residence. Four of the Red's other candidates also won, effectively seizing control of Abu Bakr's seven-member board.

Kallash's voice was heavy with regret as he read off the totals. He had resigned from the board after ten years because his family and business concerns were becoming too time-consuming for him to concentrate on Abu Bakr's community. Kallash had tired of arguing with the small clique of extremists, but he never figured that they'd succeed with their bloodless coup. Kallash worried that the mosque he had nurtured so carefully would soon be transformed from a house of worship into a paramilitary safe house.

"Please," he told El-Gabrowny, after announcing the electoral victory. "Respect what we have done here. Respect the wishes of the people who have supported this mosque."

"We will respect Allah's wishes," El-Gabrowny said, then walked out of the mosque gleefully with his friend Mahmud Abouhalima.

But there are starkly different ways to interpret the Koran, and Abouhalima's vision brought drastic changes to Abu Bakr. Over the next several months, several of Abu Bakr's community-service programs were phased out to save money. The youth program dumped its courses in Arabic language, history, and culture. In its place, the new regime began offering teenagers karate lessons. Meanwhile, El-Gabrowny and Abouhalima would encourage young Abu Bakr members to join them at their Connecticut firing range for classes in the use of hand grenades, pistols, M-16 assault rifles, and Kalashnikovs.

The daily prayer meetings also took on a strident new tone. Abouhalima and El-Gabrowny soon introduced a new preacher into the community: Sheik Omar Abdel-Rahman. Instead of offering practical ethical advice about the daily struggles of Brooklyn's immigrant community, the blind sheik preached about global conflict and his dream of a worldwide Islamic state. Instead of advising them how to live moral lives in a society dominated by materialism, self-interest, and corporeal pleasures, Sheik Omar urged them to overthrow the infidel in Egypt—a crusade that seemed far removed from the lives of the Muslims who lived and worked in Brooklyn, some of whom weren't even Egyptian.

Sheik Omar had once been booed off the pulpit at the Al-Farouk mosque on Atlantic Avenue because he was harshly critical of Iraqi leader Saddam Hussein during the Gulf War. Abu Bakr's worshipers were more polite, but were clearly distressed by his ranting style and combative, violent message. Some left the mosque. Others decided to draw up a petition asking that the moderate Sheik Maged Sobh be restored and Sheik Omar eased out of Abu Bakr.

When mosque members met on March 6, 1993, to decide the matter, it was clear that the feud would get ugly. As the mosque filled with people, the militants gathered in several small clusters, while the moderates formed their own small cliques. Conspicuous by his absence was the Red, who was already back in Egypt. Four days after a bomb blew a four-story crater in the World Trade Center, Abouhalima flew from Kennedy airport to Saudi Arabia, then traveled to his parents' home in Egypt. Throughout the entire stormy meeting, no one dared mention the rumors that the Red was involved in the World Trade Center bombing, or the fact that FBI agents had questioned virtually every Egyptian in Brooklyn, searching for Abouhalima. In the Red's absence, however, more than one hundred of his friends packed the mosque to lobby in favor of Abdel-Rahman.

The debate at the meeting focused on a question of protocol: Did the board of directors have the power to overrule the wishes of the mosque members? But all the maneuvering about technicalities simply boiled down to who would preach, Sheik Omar or Sheik Maged Sobh?

In the days leading up to the meeting, Usama Toobi, an extremist, argued that Sheik Omar deserved to lead the community because he was a more accomplished scholar.

"[Sheik Omar] is a man who can take us to the future," Toobi said. "He can help us free our people from Mubarak and the other infidels." Many of the militants had been tortured in Egyptian prisons, so they were infuriated by Sheik Maged Sobh's laissez-faire attitude toward Egypt's rulers. The sheik, who waited in the upstairs quarters of the mosque during the stormy meeting, had made it clear that he was not inclined to criticize the Egyptian government.

"Dr. Omar says Mubarak should be overthrown. Well, he's entitled to his opinion," Sheik Maged Sobh said. "I'm not entitled to judge Mubarak's administration, but I hope he will do justice."

Several hours into the debate, the mediator Zindahni thought he had managed a compromise. He proposed that the fiery Sheik Omar would continue as a visiting preacher, while Sheik Maged Sobh would remain the sheik-in-residence. But the militants, who controlled the board of directors, would agree only if several conditions were met. They demanded the power to edit and rewrite Sheik Maged Sobh's sermons, or to completely replace them with sermons of their own. The board members also wanted the power to fire Sheik Maged Sobh at any time, for any reason, no matter the length of his contract. Sheik Maged Sobh's supporters were outraged by the very suggestion. No one had tried to write his sermons for him since he was an imam in training, more than twenty-five years earlier. Even then, his editors had been respected Islamic scholars— not a group of young extremists. Sheik Maged Sobh had his pride. He also had any number of mosques he could return to in his native

Egypt. As his supporters grew angrier, Zindahni realized there was no hope. Tears began welling in Zindahni's eyes, then rolling down into his thick, gray and black beard.

"Maged Sobh is not their puppet!" came a shout from the crowd.

The meeting ended in a skirmish of shouts and punches. Sheik Omar was installed as the resident imam. During the next three months, Abu Bakr lost seventy-five percent of its membership, as moderates fled a mosque tainted by its association with several bombing plots. Many of those worshipers who remained loyal to Abu Bakr refused to support the radical new leadership financially, and stopped making donations. The mosque fell into disrepair, and quickly became dirtier, emptier, and roach-infested.

A few loyal moderates remained, even though they opposed Sheik Omar's violent message. One, Ezzat el-Sheemy, continued to make fleeting attempts at moderating the new regime's policies. El-Sheemy, a native of Egypt who now worked as an accountant for the City of New York, was no friend of Mubarak or the leaders of the West. But he was a practical man by nature and by trade, and couldn't understand why the new board members were willing to alienate their own financial supporters. One day he asked a board member why Abu Bakr didn't spend a little more money on building upkeep and a little less on teaching its young people karate and battle techniques.

"They are only children. Why are you training them for violence?" el-Sheemy said.

"Be quiet," he was warned by the board member, an ally of the Red, "or you'll end up like Shalabi."

10

THE BOMB FACTORY

More than half of Jersey City is a conglomeration of factories, streets, and railroads, with about 200,000 people wedged between two rivers. It's the state's most densely populated melting pot. Life here is lived in mostly modest houses chopped into cheap apartments. Spanish is spoken nearly as widely as English, and people from all over the world jam into these neighborhoods. Their lives are connected by tunnel and train to Manhattan, with the World Trade Center towering on the Hudson River's opposite shore.

The Space Station, which comprises four nondescript prefab buildings built for storage, fits inconspicuously within this bleak landscape. Garbage trucks roll from the disposal company yard across the street; two guard dogs yap at patrons swinging in and out of taverns on either side. Traffic clogs Mallory Avenue. Pool tables occupy the cement-block building on the corner. This industrial pocket could have been effective camouflage for espionage for an entire coven of saboteurs. The conspirators could have moved invisibly among the thousand self-storage cubicles at the Space Station. Their names and accents would have blended, their faces probably forgotten. But Mohammad Salameh simply showed up there too much.

Nearly every day for months, he visited locker number 4344. He waited at the security gate for deliveries, and stopped in the office for the elevator keys or to use the telephone. Usually he was alone while others stayed out of sight. In the self-storage business, where customers generally show up less than once a month, the man known as Abrahim Kamal made himself conspicuous.

On February 25, 1993, a sunny, brisk Thursday, Salameh was there again, this time with Ramzi Yousef, shivering in the driveway outside the Space Station office. Clouds of breath spurted into the air as they argued with assistant manager Dave Robinson. Three big red cylinders of compressed hydrogen gas waited on the bed of a delivery truck, but Robinson didn't want them unloaded. He was afraid they might explode.

The bomb makers had a fit. This was the final ingredient, the crowning touch. Months of work depended on those four-foot-tall containers. But Robinson just kept telling them, "You can't have flammable gases here."

Robinson, of course, had no idea that stashed in the cold cement locker a few hundred yards away were enough explosives to blow the Space Station into orbit.

The two men had come in around noon that day and sat down on chairs in the little office, watching out the window for the delivery. Robinson, who was a new assistant, didn't know many customers, but he'd seen Kamal around. He tried to make small talk, the way he usually did with people waiting in the office. Otherwise they just sat there and stared, and that felt weird.

"What do you guys do for a living?" Robinson asked.

"Manufacturing," Salameh replied. Yousef added that they had a factory.

Robinson was curious about their accents. He asked Yousef where he was from. Salameh interjected, "Israel."

"You were born in Israel?" Robinson asked Yousef directly.

"Yes," Yousef replied, nodding. They passed the time talking about languages. Yousef said he spoke Hebrew and Arabic. Salameh said he was from Turkey.

"What do you guys manufacture?" Robinson asked.

Yousef said something to Salameh in a language Robinson guessed was Arabic. Salameh answered, "I don't know how you would say it in English."

The word they would have had to translate was *bomb*. It was their only product line. Their factory was set up about two miles away, in a converted garage, where Salameh and Yousef and their cohorts were cooking up home-brewed nitroglycerin from chemicals hidden away in locker number 4344.

About a half hour later, a truck pulled up at the security gate and both men abandoned their plastic chairs. From inside, Robinson and Blessing Irgiri, the other assistant, could see the gas tanks on the back of the truck and a red triangular hazard sign on its side.

"Go out there to find out where they're taking that cylinder gas, okay?" Irgiri asked Robinson, since he was the new assistant.

Salameh was on the truck step, motioning to Irgiri to raise the security gate as Robinson came down the asphalt drive. "You can't have that truck in our facility," Robinson told him, and the debate began.

Salameh tried to persuade Robinson to let him leave the tanks until a van picked them up. It was almost 1:00 P.M. by then, and the truckdriver, Dennis Walsh, was getting impatient. He climbed out of the cab. "What's the matter? I got deliveries to make."

"Well, you can't deliver in here," Robinson snapped back.

Walsh joined the argument. "As long as the protective caps are on the gas cylinders and there's no open flame around, nothing can happen," he told Robinson. Robinson shook his head.

Salameh trudged back into the office to use the pay phone. He talked briefly, hung up, and stomped back outside. "Don't worry, we'll have it moved shortly," Salameh announced.

"How shortly?"

"Within twenty minutes."

Now it was Robinson's turn to go back inside. The manager had left early that day, and Irgiri was the senior man. It was his decision. "They cannot take it inside," Irgiri declared. "Make sure they come and pick it up."

Back down the drive came Robinson. "It has to be out of here in twenty minutes. If it's not out of here, we're going to put it out," he told Salameh. Something about this scene bothered Robinson. He made a mental note to tell the manager about this delivery.

The ten-by-ten-foot storage room Salameh had rented was on the second floor of the fourth building, behind the office. Salameh directed Walsh's truck down the drive to garage number 24, and Walsh pushed three four-foot cylinders off the flatbed and into the garage entrance.

"How dangerous are these?" Salameh asked him. Despite what he'd promised Robinson, Salameh told Walsh he might want to roll the tanks into the elevator and move them upstairs.

"Well, you know, I don't do that," Walsh replied, leaning on his truck to fill out the delivery form. "As long as you have the protective caps on them and you watch that they don't fall over—because they're heavy, they could hurt you if they fall on you—there's no danger."

He handed Salameh the shipping papers and invoice. Salameh neatly printed "A. Kamal" on the invoice and handed it back with money orders totaling $772. Back in the office, Robinson watched as the truck disappeared through the gate. He peeked outside, around the building. The cylinders were propped up against the garage entrance, and he was relieved. He wouldn't have been if he could have seen inside locker 4344.

Just up the stairs was a horror chamber of chemicals. Empty bottles and canisters were scattered around nearly empty drums. Over the past two months their contents had been shoveled into metal buckets and gingerly carried by car to their makeshift laboratory. Two bottles of nitroglycerin and four containing RDX, the main ingredient in plastic explosives, sat next to canisters of sulfuric acid and bottles of sodium cyanide. The acid and cyanide could be combined to form hydrogen cyanide, a lethal nerve gas.

The locker was unheated, the weather below freezing, and the explosives extremely unstable below fifty degrees. The simple molecular friction of freezing or thawing was enough to detonate the nitro and the RDX. If the storage locker exploded, Robinson's worries would be over. If he survived the blast, one breath of nerve gas would kill him and much of Jersey City.

Compelled by courage or emboldened by ignorance, Salameh and his cohorts had worked inside this concrete bomb chamber for three months. That Thursday morning they were making the final arrangements. They carted explosives, fuses, lab equipment, and chemicals from the lab back to the locker. With the gas tanks finally waiting downstairs, they teetered toward the grand finale. As the holy month of Ramadan began, Jihad would come to America. Now Mr. Kamal and the Israeli just had to wait for the yellow van and Mahmud Abouhalima's blue Lincoln to drive through the Space Station gate one more time.

*   *   *

Salameh had always operated in Mahmud's shadow, despite his own devotion to the cause and Mahmud's own failures. The months of work and planning for Jihad took a toll. Tension between them would tighten. Abouhalima, the great Afghani war hero, barked orders over the telephone, claiming he was eluding the FBI, while

Salameh took the risks. It wasn't Abouhalima who stood just yards away from oblivion every day, working in that cold locker. It wasn't Abouhalima who went into the hotel ballroom the night the rabbi was killed. Still, in their *gamaii,* or group, Abouhalima outranked him. Salameh, as cousin to the much-respected El-Gabrowny, had family status. But Abouhalima had respect. Over the years, Salameh had so badly wanted that same respect that to some of his fellow Muslims he had become increasingly arrogant. They didn't know why; to them, Salameh had little to be arrogant about.

Back home in Jordan, Salameh had left behind an unremarkable life. His family of thirteen was crammed into a four-room apartment in Massoum, a bleak suburb of Amman. He was the oldest, and least accomplished, of eleven children. He was never ambitious or political, and his own family didn't think he was particularly bright. He had few interests and low test scores. His ten younger siblings all attended professional or vocational schools, but not Salameh. The only way he could attend a university was to study *sharia,* Islamic law, which he did for nearly four years at the University of Jordan.

At this same university, a professor of religion, Abdullah Azzam, became the first to declare the rebellion in Afghanistan a Jihad and call Muslims to war. But Salameh didn't follow him. Instead, he left the university for store clerk jobs making thirty-five dinars a month—about fifty-three dollars. His father was a career army man, but that was another path Salameh didn't intend to follow.

In 1988, the year Azzam was meeting with Sheik Omar in the Pakistan training camps, Salameh got a typical five-year visa to America. He told his family he wanted to make money and escape Jordan's mandatory military service. Trained in no particular skill or profession, he found few jobs when he arrived. In Arabic communities in Brooklyn and Jersey City, Salameh said his prayers and shared rented rooms with other young Muslims. Most had never lived outside a Muslim society before. For this Western culture, God seemed no more important than sex and liquor. Women worked outside the home without permission. They seethed under the insult of it all.

"He never had a penny," a fellow mosque member said. Another had a harsh explanation for that: "He is stupid." He was an unlikely warrior for Jihad. "This man doesn't have the courage to kill an animal," another concluded. In his new home in America, people noticed he was always quick to get involved in Muslim causes. Whether he was following his political beliefs, or just filling up free time in between jobs, no one knew for certain.

Circumstances, probably more than religious devotion, landed Salameh in dangerous company in America. He was a follower, a man with no direction of his own, when he literally immigrated into the lap of terrorism. His first contacts in America were his cousin El-Gabrowny, and El-Gabrowny's cousin Nosair. Nosair was such a fanatic that he alienated many of his brethren at his Jersey City mosque and began praying at home with his circle of would-be martyrs. The impressionable Salameh became his disciple.

They bought guns, trained at suburban rifle ranges, and played soldier among the trees and meadows of local parks. Other Jihad cells were set up around the country, in cities in Texas, California, Illinois, and Michigan. In common, they had Sheik Omar for inspiration and Afghanistan as their training ground. It proved a profitable profession for Salameh. He would eventually make more money as a terrorist-in-training than he ever had sweating in a bakery or laboring on a construction site. He had purpose, comrades, and a chance to be a hero. "If you care about others, God will take care of you," said the Koran. Salameh taped this aphorism to the wall of his rented room.

The day Ramzi Yousef slipped into the country, Salameh celebrated his twenty-fifth birthday. With Nosair in prison, Salameh needed another inspiration. Yousef filled the role. That day, September 1, 1992, terrorism literally came to America.

When Pakistani International Airlines flight 703 rolled up to Kennedy Airport's international arrivals terminal, among the throng of bleary-eyed men and women who disembarked came two thin, bearded twenty-five-year-old men, Ramzi Yousef and Ahmad Ajaj.

Yousef was imported talent, a shadowy, Afghani-trained terrorist with twelve aliases who knew how to build and plant explosives. Ajaj, a Palestinian, had spent the past five months in Pakistani training camps, learning the art of guerrilla warfare. His mission in the United States was to assist Yousef and to make sure Yousef eluded the Immigration and Naturalization Service, even if it meant sacrificing himself.

At the INS counter, agent Cathy Bethom looked surprised when the swarthy, bearded Ajaj produced a Swedish passport. Yousef was in another line, lagging behind.

"My mother was Swedish," Ajaj told her. "My father was

Pakistani." Then he yelled at her, much too loudly, "If you don't believe me, check your computer."

In the next line, Yousef was getting closer to the counter. Ajaj watched the agent flip through his passport booklet. He knew what to expect. He'd traveled to the United States before. But he couldn't use his own name and passport this time. The Israeli national police had files on him. They had arrested him once for arms smuggling and knew he was connected to the terrorist groups Hamas and Fatah.

Agent Bethom was eyeing the passport photograph curiously. Something was wrong with it. It was too thick. She stuck a fingernail under the photo's corner and peeled it back, revealing the photograph of another man. Ajaj—or Khurram Khan, according to the passport, had simply pasted his photo over the original. She signaled for backup, and he was arrested.

Yousef, standing at the next counter, didn't betray even a flicker of interest. He presented a valid Iraqi passport. The only thing missing was a visa to enter the country. "I want political asylum," Yousef told INS agent Martha Morales.

He recited a story about being beaten by Iraqi soldiers who suspected him of being a member of a Kuwaiti guerrilla organization. He raised his right hand and swore that he risked persecution if he returned to Iraq. Morales decided there was something suspicious about Yousef and told her supervisor he should be detained. But she was overruled, and Yousef disappeared onto the streets of New York.

Along Atlantic Avenue, the main street of Brooklyn's Arabic community, Yousef called himself Rashed. He told people he was Iraqi, although his accent revealed a dialect of Pakistan. He told some people he'd grown up in Kuwait. Two other newcomers were seen on the streets with Rashed about the same time. One spoke Farsi, the language of Iran. Another had a Pakistani accent, like Rashed.

Abouhalima helped Rashed get a livery license so he'd have identification. Within two days of his arrival, he had moved in with Salameh. The two grew so close that Yousef even listed Salameh as his next of kin on medical records.

Yousef had been in America only a few weeks when the terrorists got a warning signal, courtesy of the FBI. Late in September 1992, agents suddenly appeared at the homes of Sheik Omar's followers. Two dozen were slapped with subpoenas. On a Monday morning, they showed up at 26 Federal Plaza in Manhattan and sat in a hallway outside FBI headquarters. No one ever saw a grand jury. Instead, they were led one by one into an office, where each was asked to allow himself to be fingerprinted, photographed, and questioned.

"Do you know Mahmud Abouhalima? Nosair? Sheik Omar? Shalabi?" agents asked. "Has anyone ever tried to recruit you to fight in Afghanistan?"

Ahmed Sattar, a Brooklyn postal worker, was asked about the Alkifah Center and the money it raised. "We're going to get them. Sooner or later, we will. John Gotti was put on trial two times and we got him," an agent told him, comparing the sheik to the crime boss the FBI had finally put away. At that point, Sattar stopped answering and began reading the Koran.

Another of the sheik's followers waited in the hallway, somewhat irked and amused, and talked loudly to the others about the insensitivity and audacity of the FBI. Emad Salem, dressed in his usual leather jacket, cap, and sunglasses, was the sheik's bodyguard and security adviser. The FBI offices were a familiar place to him; he even knew John Anticev, the special agent in charge of the questioning. Until two months earlier, the sheik's trusted bodyguard had been an FBI informant.

Their collaboration had ended bitterly. Salem had told the FBI that Nosair was organizing a terrorist campaign from his prison cell. The FBI wanted Salem to catch the plot on secret tape recordings and testify against Nosair and his cousin, El-Gabrowny, and anyone else they could catch. That wasn't the deal Salem had made when he became an informant. The FBI had promised him his double-dealing would never become public. After an angry confrontation, the FBI decided Salem had to testify or get lost. They had other informants; they'd investigate Nosair and the sheik's other cohorts without him.

The FBI subpoenaed him along with the others two months later, in part to keep his cover intact and in part to annoy him. The FBI had fingerprints from Nosair's car, found parked a few blocks from the hotel where Kahane was shot, and agents were trying to match them. Among those fingerprints were those of two men who would soon be known as the World Trade Center bombers. But the FBI subpoenaed only Egyptians, and these two men were of Palestinian descent. Neither was in the sheik's inner circle.

The Egyptian government had been putting pressure on the State

Department to take some action against the sheik. The Egyptians were convinced that Sheik Omar was sitting in New Jersey ordering the terrorist campaign in Egypt against the Mubarak government. A rumor was circulating that a plot was under way to assassinate the secretary-general of the United Nations, an Egyptian aligned with Mubarak. It was a legitimate reason to investigate the sheik's radicals.

The INS was preparing to deport the sheik, but he would probably just move to Afghanistan or the Sudan and continue his campaign. The FBI wanted to nail him. If they could bring charges against his inner circle, in the murder of either Kahane or Shalabi, the trail would lead back to him. That was, in fact, how they had convicted John Gotti. So they started with the Kahane killing, and they knew Abouhalima was Nosair's closest associate.

A press conference couldn't have gotten the warning back to Abouhalima faster. The news didn't come as a shock. "They suspected me a long time ago," the Red would say later. Salameh, the underachiever, would have to be responsible for organizing much of this new operation. Abouhalima was under surveillance again.

Salameh was living on Kensington Avenue in a diverse working-class neighborhood of Jersey City, the kind where as many as twenty men could crowd together in an apartment, sleeping on mattresses thrown on floors, without drawing much attention. He shared apartment 4 with the Yasin brothers, two American engineering students of Iraqi descent, and Bilal Alkaisi, a cabdriver from Jordan.

Jersey City, with its chemical companies and diverse populace, would be the center of the terrorists' operations. The Twin Towers of the World Trade Center beckoned from the other side of the river, just a quick drive through the Holland Tunnel. But first Salameh and Yousef needed a hideout. Kensington Avenue could too easily be traced to Salameh; the telephone had once been in his name.

Salameh had once shared a room with a quiet Egyptian student named Ashref Moneeb. Now Moneeb had a two-room apartment in a redbrick building on Virginia Avenue, about a mile away. He wanted to split the rent again. In October, Salameh and Rashed moved in. It was an ideal setup. Ashref lived in the living room; Salameh and Rashed shared the bedroom. They put a separate phone line in the bedroom, and Salameh and Yousef racked up thousands of dollars every month in overseas calls. Sometimes until dawn, they talked long and loudly with contacts in Yugoslavia, Pakistan, Jordan, Iran, Israel, Saudi Arabia, and Turkey. The phone eventually doomed their domestic arrangement. Most of their time was spent behind that closed door. Abouhalima was still being watched but managed to elude the FBI and meet his cohorts at the Virginia Avenue apartment. Aboud Yasin came to the meetings, and sometimes Aboud's older brother, Musab, would visit as well. Moneeb didn't mind the visitors as much as he tired of the phone calls.

Once Salameh had installed them safely in the hideout, it was time to set up their financial web. Bills were mounting with each overseas consultation. They had to pay rent, get cars, and eventually stock their bomb factory.

That's where the mild-mannered chemist came in.

Nidal Ayyad was a stereotypical American success story. Tall, slender, and handsome, Ayyad had a degree in chemical engineering from Rutgers University and a $35,000-a-year job. Born in Kuwait, he was a naturalized U.S. citizen, lived with his mother and two younger brothers in a suburban home, and was the sole support of his family. A marriage had been arranged for him with a Jordanian woman; he was about to start his own family in his adopted country.

He and Salameh were the same age, but that's where the similarities stopped. Ayyad was an achiever. Salameh couldn't get a job or a green card or a wife. Salameh was so lonely he had asked his father to send him a woman from Jordan who was willing to marry him. He had little to lose in his quest for heroism, but Ayyad had everything at stake.

Both had been born just months after the Six-Day War in 1967 ended with the Israelis occupying Palestine. Salameh was seven months old when his family moved from the West Bank and resettled in Jordan. Ayyad's father and pregnant mother had moved to Kuwait, where he was born. Two decades later, the two Palestinians met on the other side of the globe. They became friends, and co-conspirators. Salameh even carried a photograph of them both posing with Nosair between them, the Empire State Building and the Manhattan skyline as a backdrop. They shared one more link: it was their fingerprints the FBI found in Nosair's car.

Ayyad had another photograph of himself that he kept at his home. In it, he is sitting in a chair with the Palestinian flag draped over his shoulder, one hand gripping a hand grenade. His face is partially covered by a headdress, and under his robe he wears a red Rutgers sweatshirt. It wasn't a face he showed many people.

Ayyad was from a strict family. His father, a clothing salesman, believed deeply in law and government and America. His parents had divorced when he was twelve, his father had moved to America, and the rest of his family had followed him there six years later. Ayyad had enrolled in Rutgers and become a U.S. citizen. His father was proud. He didn't know his son's other face.

In October, Salameh and Ayyad opened a series of bank accounts, some individually, some jointly with each other and with Salameh's former roommate and fellow Jordanian, Alkaisi, as well. They used their own names, but gave the Jersey City Islamic Center as their mailing address. Over the next four months, more than $100,000 would pass through these accounts. Salameh had dutifully sent money home to Jordan every month, but he made the last of those transfers in August. This money was for Jihad.

The original source of this money would be impossible to trace. It was arranged through a network of sources and collected, in part, by the seventy-year-old Muslim Brotherhood, through Abouhalima's old associates in Munich. The FBI and CIA would be able to trace tens of thousands of dollars in wire transfers originating from Iran; other funds seemed to originate from throughout the Middle East. Transfers were traced to locations in Saudi Arabia, Kuwait, and other countries. But the most significant amounts were those sent from Iran. Government counterintelligence experts were split on what that meant exactly. Were the bombers a "self-propelled" group tapping overseas funding? Or was the bombing directed by Iran? If they ever learned the answer, it hasn't yet been revealed. Not a word about overseas finances would be mentioned at the bombers' trial.

When the money started coming in, Salameh bought a dark green Chevy Nova so he could transport the equipment and materials they needed to make their bomb. Then he went looking for a place to stockpile explosives. He found it conveniently located just a few blocks from their rented room on Virginia Avenue. The Space Station compound was perfect.

* * *

Abrahim Kamal was born on November 30, 1992. That day, Salameh withdrew $3,400 from his account in crisp, new hundred-dollar bills. Using the alias, he rented the ninety-dollar-a-month storage locker. The same day, Yousef used the same name and appeared at City Chemical, a local company. The alias was similar to the name of an Egyptian watchmaker who had been found dead in the trunk of his car in Kennedy Airport's parking lot a year before. He was Ibrahim Kamal. No connection was ever made between the body and the pseudonym.

The Kamal who showed up at City Chemical made a $3,615 order and plunked down fresh, new hundred-dollar bills in payment. Delivery was to be made to Kamal & Company at the Space Station. The shipment, the first of three from City Chemical, included one thousand pounds of urea, 105 gallons of nitric acid, and sixty gallons of sulfuric acid. Yousef had been very specific about the chemicals. He asked the salesman to check the nitrogen content of the urea crystals; it was high—46.65 percent. The sulfuric acid had to be ninety-three percent pure, the rest water.

It was delivered two days later. That frosty morning, Salameh and Yousef almost missed the truck. Al Diaz, the driver, rumbled up to the gate and waited for someone to open it. He got out, looked around, didn't see anyone, and was starting to pull away when two men came racing down the drive, shouting and waving at him.

The gate lifted and Salameh directed Diaz down the drive to the Space Station's center building. To his dismay, Diaz then discovered that the final resting place of the dozen heavy drums he was to unload was a room on the second floor. The elevator was supposed to lift one thousand pounds but had a notice posted on it: no more than two hundred pounds. Each load of chemicals weighed more than that.

Diaz opened the back of his truck. For the next hour he plopped a load of bottles and drums on his moving cart, dumped each load into the elevator, and sent it up while he hoisted the cart up the flight of stairs. On the second floor he loaded the stuff back on the cart and pushed it into the previously empty storage room. He repeated the process half a dozen times while Salameh and Yousef watched. When it was over, Diaz caught his breath and tried a little small talk. He was hoping to encourage a sizable tip.

"What are you going to do with all this stuff?" he asked. The two men just shrugged and smiled. He didn't get an answer—or a tip.

Ayyad took a sabbatical that month from his job and the terrorist plot to travel to Jordan to be married, while Yousef stockpiled an arsenal of chemicals. By the time Ayyad returned with his new bride, Salameh had started looking for a place where they could work on their bomb. It had to be private and easy to reach from the storage locker. He found it on Pamrapo Avenue, a few miles away, where a long, ramshackle garage had been converted into two apartments. Salameh told the landlord his name was Alaa Masrous and persuaded him to rent it without a lease, on a month-to-month basis. He gave the landlord $1,100—one month's rent and a month's security—on New Year's Day, 1993.

It would be their laboratory. Despite popular theory that anyone could make a bomb, an explosive powerful enough to blast furious damage into a skyscraper was not an undertaking for amateurs. It would require more than a thousand pounds of explosives, detonated by volatile nitrogylcerin. The most delicate and dangerous part of the operation was mixing the nitro.

They worked late into the night for the next month, stopping only for food, prayers, and daily telephone calls to their contacts in Pakistan and Iran. They also used the phone to scam a way to stay in contact with their jailed cohort, Ajaj, who was serving an eight-month sentence for immigration fraud. Ajaj used his phone privileges to call a contact in Texas at a fast-food joint called Big Five Hamburgers, in Mesquite outside Dallas. The contact then used Southwestern Bell's three-way calling feature to patch the calls through to the Pamrapo bomb factory. It allowed them to collaborate by phone, without leaving a trail to Pamrapo on the prison phone records.

Abouhalima and Aboud Yasin arrived with buckets of chemicals and bottles of acids from the storage locker. They transformed the 1,200 pounds of urea into an explosive. Then they mixed the nitroglyerin, and popped it into the freezer. Frozen nitro can be transported more easily, but it can explode if it freezes too fast. It turned their refrigerator into a giant pipe bomb.

Carl Butler and his dog had no idea what was going on downstairs. Butler always walked his dog at 11:00 P.M. and frequently saw the same two men—the tall, red-haired Mahmud and the beardless, shorter, and darker Aboud—carrying boxes and buckets into the downstairs apartment. Once he saw Abouhalima shouting out orders to other men in a language he didn't recognize. Butler never spoke to them and never thought they were particularly suspicious.

Despite their surveillance, the FBI never tracked Abouhalima to the bomb factory or the storage shed. By January their investigation had yielded little. The rumors of an assassination plot against the UN secretary-general, Boutros Boutros-Ghali, had been declared unfounded. They hadn't matched the fingerprints on Nosair's car. They had found two red, curly hairs clutched in the hand of the dead Shalabi, hairs that could have been Abouhalima's. But they didn't have enough evidence to compel him to give a hair sample.

Three months before the bombing, a man who worshiped at Al Salaam mosque in Jersey City, where the sheik now concentrated his efforts, telephoned an agent of Israeli intelligence, the Mossad. He had once worked with the agent, and told him he was alarmed because some fellow worshipers had asked him to help them buy explosives.

The Mossad agent called the FBI. "We've got it covered," he was told. The FBI was still watching Abouhalima, still monitoring the two dozen Egyptians subpoenaed in September. Other informants inside the mosque had been developed since Salem was dropped.

One of them was approached by mosque worshipers about getting explosives. Agents met all day, trying to decide what to do. They decided they had no choice but to pull him out of the mosque. The FBI couldn't risk allowing an informant to actually provide the explosives.

In both cases, the explosive was dynamite and the amounts small, apparently to be used in pipe bombs. As Anticev would later put it, "Not in our wildest dreams did we think it was a . . . fifteen-hundred-pound chemical bomb . . . we thought we were getting close to a pipe."

Despite both of those incidents, the FBI began the new year, 1993, with little evidence that any of the sheik's followers were about to engage in anything criminal. The threat against Boutros Boutros-Ghali gave the FBI an excuse to begin a preliminary investigation, but Abouhalima had never led them near the other conspirators. The FBI didn't have a clue about what was being brewed across the river on Pamrapo Avenue.

The Justice Department doesn't allow the FBI to keep an investigation ongoing unless some evidence is gathered in the preliminary stage to warrant it. Individuals have the right to be protected from domestic spying. So six weeks before the World Trade Center blast, the Justice Department closed the investigation.

About the same time, the bombers' plot stalled. On a gloomy Sunday afternoon, Salameh's prowess behind the steering wheel cost them Yousef's services for a week. On January 21, the two were driving on a rain-slick road not far from Mahmud's New Jersey home when Salameh lost control and the car skidded off the roadway. The Nova was totaled. It hit the curb so hard that the cops on the scene thought Salameh must have been drunk. He was thrown from the car; Yousef was so battered he was hospitalized for a week. He had to make calls to chemical companies from his hospital bed.

Salameh, of course, wasn't drunk. He was just a bad driver. He had received his driver's license only five months earlier—after flunking the test four times. He'd even flunked the vision test twice. Finally he gave up trying to get his driver's license in New Jersey. Using El-Gabrowny's Brooklyn address, he somehow got a New York license.

While Yousef recuperated, Salameh, Abouhalima, and two members of Abouhalima's paramilitary group drove deep into the Pennsylvania woods to test their concoction. It exploded. But they still needed the final touch—something to give their bomb more boom. Ayyad spent the next month trying to persuade someone to sell him a detonating explosive and compressed gas.

He tried to buy lead nitrate, a highly explosive substance used as a detonator by construction firms. But Allied Signal, the chemical company where he worked, didn't stock it. He tried City Chemical, where he told the saleswoman he was buying for his firm. But the sales manager couldn't find any record that Allied Signal had permits for the handling of explosives.

"But I'll pay in cash," Ayyad protested.

"The method of payment isn't the problem. I need a purchase order from the company for lead nitrate," the manager said.

He tried to buy compressed hydrogen gas, so commonly used in Middle Eastern terrorist bombings that it's considered their signature. He couldn't order it through his company. He called a Pennsylvania firm that did business with Allied Signal, but he was told the order would still have to be placed through the company stockroom.

Meanwhile, Abouhalima feared they couldn't wait much longer. He didn't know the FBI had dropped their investigation, and thought they might still be watching him. On January 30, when he ended his cab shift and reported back to the dispatch office, his boss, a fellow Muslim and neighbor, told him someone from a bank had called asking for his unlisted home number. The caller had said Abouhalima had applied for credit and the bank had to contact him.

Abouhalima was furious that his boss had given out his number.

He hadn't applied for a loan. "It's the FBI checking up on me again!" he told him angrily. Everyone close to the Red knew the FBI watched him. As the ranking member of the *gamaii,* Abouhalima was the facilitator among the bombers. He organized the consultations, made the decisions, and was in contact with all members of the group. But he had been careful not to make these calls from his home telephone; there would be no records if the FBI checked.

They had planned to detonate their holy war early in February, but they'd lost time when Yousef was hospitalized, and without the hydrogen they were stuck. Salameh's roommate Moneeb had suddenly evicted him and "Rashed"; the loud phone calls they made at all hours were disturbing him. So the two packed up and spent the final weeks living back on Kensington Avenue with Al-kaisi and the Yasin brothers.

In mid-February—two weeks before the bombing—Salameh took the eight-hour ride to the small town of Attica in western New York, a village presided over by the gray-walled, medieval-looking fortress of Attica prison. There, among New York State's most violent felons, Salameh visited his idol, Nosair, for the last time. Mahmud made the journey the following week. Just one year before, shortly after Nosair had been sentenced to Attica, he had telephoned Abouhalima and belittled him, accusing him of being too afraid of the FBI to work for Jihad. Now Abouhalima could redeem himself. The first stroke for Jihad and Nosair's freedom was just one week away.

As the plot was heading into its final hours, Ayyad took a few sick days off from work and rented a car. With Salameh behind the wheel, they went on a scouting mission into the Trade Center garage. Ayyad got out of the car and made a rough sketch of the garage floor plan. Then they drove back to Jersey City, and with Salameh's typical good luck, another driver crashed into their rented Olds. The terrorists spent the rest of the afternoon at the police station, filling out an accident report.

A week later, on Wednesday, February 24, Ayyad rented another car, this time a red Chevy Corsica. He drove Salameh down Kennedy Boulevard to a car dealership that also was the local Ryder truck representative.

"How do I go about renting a Ryder truck?" Salameh asked Patrick Galasso, the rental agent.

Galasso described the three trucks he had, and told the men how much they would cost. The smallest and cheapest was a ten-foot panel van. Salameh didn't know which one to take. He and Ayyad discussed it for a few minutes in Arabic, and then Salameh made a phone call. He hung up and said he'd take the panel van. He'd need it at least until Sunday.

The next morning, Salameh and Ayyad took the red Chevy on another scouting trip to the World Trade Center garage. Later, Aboud took Salameh on practice drives with the van. Ayyad, back at his desk at Allied Signal, finally reached a firm that would sell them compressed hydrogen. It was to be delivered the next day.

Late that Thursday afternoon, assistant manager Dave Robinson saw the yellow Ryder van, followed closely by a blue Lincoln, stop in the Space Station's drive. As each car pulled in, the driver punched in locker 4344's code to raise the security gate. Robinson looked around the building again and saw Salameh and some other men hoist the heavy gas tanks into the back of the van.

A few minutes later, Blessing Irgiri, the other clerk, saw the van drive past the office window and stop at the gate. He recognized the two men inside. It was Kamal and the man he'd met that morning, Salameh's friend from Israel. "What are you doing with a Jewish guy?" Irgiri had joked when introduced. Kamal had once told him he'd been born in Palestine but had been forced away to Jordan by the Israelis.

"He's a good Jewish guy," Salameh had replied. "Sometimes he loans me money."

Now the van moved through the gate with Kamal behind the wheel and his Israeli friend sitting beside him. The bombers had only a few tasks left to do: report the van stolen, and load the bomb into its cargo hold. Tens of thousands of people would die if their bomb could bring down just one of the World Trade Center's towers. The psyche of America would be crushed, the symbol of its greed and power shattered. Like the states of the Soviet Union, broken by their defeat in Afghanistan, the United States would begin to crumble and fall.

* * *

Dawn was still three hours away. The temperature had sunk into the low twenties, and snow clouds blocked whatever light the crescent of the new moon might have shed. Streetlights along Jersey City's Kennedy Boulevard cast the only pools of illumination. From one of these the yellow van emerged, moving slowly into the all-night gas station at the end of the street.

It stopped at a pump. A dark blue Lincoln pulled in behind it. Bringing up the rear of the caravan, a red Chevy stopped at another pump. The usually bustling intersection of Kennedy and Route 440 was mostly deserted; no other cars were in the station or at the shopping plaza across the street.

Willie Hernandez Moosh was working the midnight-to-eight shift as usual. He left the Plexiglas cubicle between the pumps in the center island and walked toward the customers. A quirk of New Jersey law prohibited self-serve gas stations in the state. It was an oddity of legislation that had preserved Moosh's job at that same Shell station for eleven years.

"What do you want?" he asked, stopping at the passenger window of the van.

"Fill it up," Ramzi Yousef told him.

Moosh twisted off the gas cap and stuck in the nozzle. The passenger door opened and Yousef slid out. Moosh looked curiously at him. He had a long, pointed face, Moosh thought. A horse face surrounded by beard. Horse-face ducked under the gas hose and began walking around the van, looking it all over as if he were inspecting it.

A block away, just around the corner at the Pamrapo garage apartment, the bombers had backed the van down the drive, behind the house, and up to the apartment door. Pamrapo was a quiet, out-of-the-way, two-block residential street. The garage was hidden from the street down a curving driveway—really just a path through weeds and junked cars—winding up to the porchless door. With fingers numb with cold, and as quietly as possible, they then packed the cargo hold with their lethal creation: a masterpiece of chemicals, bonding agent, fuse, and detonator.

It had been a work in progress for more than two months. With lab masks slapped over their mouths and noses to protect them from the fumes, they had mixed gallons of stinging nitric acid in big metal drums with the urea crystals until it formed a gel-like mass. Then the concoction had been mixed with old newspapers and the gooey mess shoved through a funnel into cardboard boxes and paper bags.

The nitro had been the most difficult exercise—a balance of sulfuric and nitric acids with glycerine. Acid splashed on their clothes, burned their skin, and corroded the floors and sink. The fumes were so strong that the door hinges rusted from the inside. An unexpected burst of chemicals left the white walls streaked with blue. Nitrates spattered the walls of the empty bedroom.

No one could see them as they loaded their accomplishment into the van. Four containers of home-brewed nitro were arranged among the boxes. Long fuses, threaded through surgical tubing, were rigged to blasting caps and boxes of gunpowder inserted into each of the nitro containers. The hydrogen tanks were hauled in last, propped upright behind the boxes, against the rear doors. They would explode into a fireball, boosting the blast into an inferno.

The fuses were packed in tubing to reduce the smoke and to make sure they burned slowly enough to give the bombers at least ten minutes to escape. No timing device would ignite them. Jihad would begin with the striking of a cigarette lighter.

The ten-foot Ford Econoline van could carry two thousand pounds and hold 295 cubic feet in the cargo area. The urea compound alone weighed more than 1,500 pounds and, combined with the heavy hydrogen tanks, the load strained the van's capacity. Now, at the gas station, Yousef circled it, looking for some suspicious giveaway sign. Moosh apparently didn't notice the van was riding low on its springs. While its twenty-two-gallon tank was filling, he walked back to the Lincoln and asked the driver what he wanted. Another man was sitting in the passenger seat.

"Fill it up," Abouhalima told him. Then Moosh pumped gas for the red car that had followed them in. The van's tank was finished first. Salameh, sitting in the driver's seat, told Moosh the man in the Lincoln would pay, so he finished pumping the Lincoln's gas and then went back to the driver's window. Mahmud gave him twenty-one dollars.

Horse-face got back into the passenger's seat and Moosh heard all three cars start their engines. He watched as they began to roll away. Suddenly they stopped. The van quickly swerved into a parking space behind the station's cinder-block office. A white Jersey City police car had become visible, cruising down Kennedy Boulevard.

Yousef jumped from the passenger seat again and quickly jerked open the van's hood. He called to Moosh to bring him some water. By the time Moosh brought him the container, Salameh had gotten out as well and the two stood there, talking in puffs of cold air, looking into the engine. They didn't use the water. Moosh noticed the police car was passing.

Six hours earlier, Salameh had been sitting in another Jersey City squad car, reporting the yellow Ryder van stolen. The conspirators had dropped him off at the Route 440 shopping plaza shortly before 9:00 P.M. He went into the Pathmark supermarket, bought a couple of bags of groceries, and then called the police. Officer Ron Badiak drove to the shopping plaza to take the report. Salameh told him his story and showed Badiak the time-stamped grocery receipt. He produced his New York driver's license, gave the Jersey City Islamic center as his address, and the Kensington Avenue telephone number.

He had rented the van for fifty-nine dollars a day and paid the deposit with four one-hundred-dollar bills. Repeatedly, he asked Officer Badiak how he could get his rental deposit back. Then he deliberately gave Badiak the wrong license plate number for the van. Badiak drove him to 34 Kensington—where Salameh waited for the others to pick him up again.

Call it clever subterfuge, or just plain luck. Maybe the bogus license plate number kept the stolen-van report from going out on the radio. Maybe a 4:00 A.M. van caravan just didn't look suspicious. Whatever the reason, the patrol car that morning passed the band of terrorists and their bomb without stopping.

Moosh saw the driver of the red car begin to motion to the others, pointing toward Route 440. Horse-face slammed the hood shut and got back into the cab. What followed is one of the great mysteries of modern crime: Salameh, the accident-prone novice driver, slipped back behind the van's wheel. The man with poor eyesight who had flunked his driving test four times steered the bomb seven miles through the Holland Tunnel and led them into holy war.

11

DEAL WITH
THE DEVIL

The cosmetic waterfall trickled and gurgled pleasantly in the living room of Emad Salem's Upper West Side apartment, but he didn't sound soothed. As he talked on the telephone, thin sunlight filtering through the shuttered windows sliced slats of light across the walls and the photographs of himself and Sheik Omar hanging there. An agent of the sheik's undeclared enemy—the FBI—was on the other end of the telephone line.

"What they are doing is, I guess, putting it back in your ballpark," Nancy Floyd's calm, Texas-tinged voice was explaining. "Saying that if you agree to supply them with information like you would before, it's like ... Say the scenario went down and they took out the bomb, whatever ... and they went to arrest the people. They would look to you to be one of the witnesses to finger these people."

"Uh-huh."

"Which would in effect blow you from being able to continue providing information."

"Of course," Salem said.

A month had passed since the World Trade Center bombing. As far as Salem was concerned, that blast proved he had been right all along. He had told the FBI that Nosair, serving seven years in prison for assault and attempted murder, was at the center of a terrorist cell. He had warned them that Nosair was planning a variety show of assassinations and bombings. The sheik was their inspiration, but Nosair was their leader. Watch Nosair and you'll find the others, he had said. They are serious, dangerous people.

Salem was certain that, had the FBI allowed him to remain undercover among Nosair and his pals, he himself would have been the expert the terrorists sought to build the bomb and would have been able to prevent it. He would have saved those people and America.

But the FBI blew it. FBI brass didn't trust Salem, didn't have faith in Nancy Floyd, his FBI handler, and didn't take the Muslim extremists seriously. They blew it rather than pay the informant $500 a week. They in effect fired Salem and then came knocking on his door again seven months later.

And the same battle of wills with the FBI had begun all over again, a tug-of-war over money and testimony. The FBI wanted him back, but only if he would agree to testify against the subjects of his spying.

"And of course you both know that next week, if I made the trip to the jail, Sayyid Nosair would ask me to blow another bomb or to kidnap another judge or whatever," Salem told her. "He will ask me to do something." He had told the FBI so many times before about Nosair. This time around, were they going to do anything about it?

"We all know that this guy was involved. We all know this guy was inspiring these people and instructing them," Floyd began. Salem's call-waiting clicked and he checked the other line. It was a reporter wanting an interview. Salem loved this charade: playing the role of Sheik Omar's trusted aide on one line while an FBI agent waited on another. Just the day before, he had stood next to Mahmud Abouhalima's lawyer as television cameras rolled after the Red's arraignment. Such was the life of a spy.

"I'm sorry, Nancy," Salem said, switching back.

"That's okay. I mean, I agree with you. You got no arguments with me," Floyd continued. Agents rarely contested anything their informants said; they agreed, and blamed disagreeable decisions on their bosses. Today, Salem was complaining that the FBI wasn't willing to let him work as an informant again unless he did everything their way. "But, unfortunately, the area that I work in and this area are just completely different," she told him.

"I know. But I just don't understand and I feel bad at the same time," he said.

"Well, me too. I feel really bad and I agree with you."

Salem had good reason to feel bad. If he ever had to testify against anyone he spied on, he'd be trading his comfortable life for a life in hiding and a string of aliases. In the six years since he'd left the Egyptian army and Cairo, he had acquired a pleasant suite of rooms in an uptown Manhattan residency hotel, a live-in girl-friend who ran a thriving jewelry design business, an ex-wife, and the intrigue of being an FBI informant. The Bureau had paid him, and he sold his services elsewhere as well. All this would be gone if he ever had to blow his cover as an informant.

Last time around, he wouldn't do it. He told the FBI to wiretap Nosair's cousin El-Gabrowny, follow around that other cousin, Salameh, watch who went to visit Nosair in prison, and bug them and follow them. They could have left him in deep cover and made the case another way.

Instead, they accused him of lying, of making up bogus bombing plots so he could keep getting paid. They attacked the way Floyd had handled him and the $500 a week and expenses she paid him, and the supervisors accused Floyd of being too close to Salem and manipulated by him.

All in all, it had been a bitter blow to Salem's ego. He forgot none of it as he negotiated the terms of his reunion with the FBI through Special Agent John Anticev of the Anti-Terrorist Task Force. Floyd's intelligence division officially wasn't involved, but Salem still called her often. He bounced his complaints off her; she commiserated. Sometimes, he fished for information.

Now he was battling with Anticev's same supervisor all over again. "He's trying to prove the point with the day he told you, 'I will get him to testify. I don't believe you when you say he won't testify.' . . . They want everything to play their way, and unfortunately . . . it's wrong," Salem told Floyd. "They play it their way and the World Trade Center gets bombed."

"I know, well, I agree," Floyd said, as usual.

Salem laughed. "What other way? The other way is my way. I'm not trying to play bossy here . . . I know that I'm not a regular agent . . . but listen, because you didn't listen before. It takes a bomb for you to listen, and you're not listening yet."

"Right. They're more worried about whether or not you'll testify than they are worried about whether or not they'll get good information. . . . Unfortunately, there isn't anything I can do," Floyd said.

Floyd—straightforward, private, committed to God and country and the Bureau—was a calming counterpoint to Salem's mercurial, bombastic personality. She had patience with him while his ego drove other agents nuts. He was theatrical; she was practical. He liked an audience; she listened to his accounts of his exploits. She also believed Salem was a valuable intelligence source; her supervisors thought he was an opportunist.

Floyd had in fact warned her superiors and the task force that the Colonel couldn't be bullied onto a witness stand. She knew career military men; her father was one. But the FBI was used to getting its way with informants, and some of the FBI's supervisors wondered who was handling whom when it came to the wily Colonel.

By Bureau standards, Floyd was young—only thirty-one years old. The Bureau's "old guard" suspected Floyd was too soft on the Colonel. Salem was manipulative, a clever talker and arrogant. In the days after the bombing, as the Bureau wrestled with the reality that they'd dropped an informant who was inside the bombers' terrorist cell, the scrutiny boomeranged back to Floyd.

"Emad," she told him once, giving his name her southern inflection, "it's me and you against everybody with them trying to make it look like, you know, we were doing something wrong."

Salem almost shouted, "Absolutely! That's what they try to—"

"Yeah, when we were the only ones that were doing anything!"

"Absolutely not! We were doing everything."

"And they're just trying to cover their butts."

"Yeah, yeah," Salem heartily agreed.

"I mean, they got caught with their pants down . . . and instead of admitting they'd screwed up and hadn't done what they'd wanted to do, they try to make it look like we're the bad guys. . . . Now it's all come out that, you know, in fact everything you said was right . . . and not only that, but they should have . . ." Even the usually calm Floyd was getting angry now. "They didn't even follow up properly on the stuff that you'd given 'em!"

Floyd, who was single and lived with her mother, even had to defend herself from accusations that she'd gotten romantically involved with the forty-three-year-old Salem.

"They're accusing us of everything under the sun," Floyd told Emad. But agents who knew Floyd scoffed at the idea that she would commit an FBI sin and romance her informant.

Others inside the Bureau thought it was ridiculous that an intelligence officer would be scapegoated for a botched terrorism investigation. The intelligence division gathered information, and its agents passed it on to supervisors. It didn't build cases or prosecutions. That was the domain of the criminal division, which was very much involved back then.

But Salem himself didn't do much to bolster his own credibility. His polygraph tests were inconclusive; the FBI knew he fed information to Egyptian army intelligence agents. He had done work for the INS and had been in contact with the CIA. The Colonel was a loose cannon the FBI believed had to be brought in line.

Salem's phone clicked again. Speak of the devil—it was FBI Special Agent John Anticev. "Okay, call back later," Floyd told him, and hung up.

Anticev had worked with Floyd and Salem during the Nosair trial. He knew Salem's ego. He had heard his litany of allegations about terrorism. He called with news: Salem's file as an informant had been reactivated, but things were going to be a little different from what they'd discussed a few weeks ago. The FBI would try to keep him out of court if possible—but no promises.

"Then go on with the investigation?" Salem asked.

"Yeah."

"You know, from what I heard, the witness protection program, it's not the greatest thing in the world," Salem told him.

"If you do want to testify, it's a way of getting out of the area and, you know, having some money and protection," said Anticev.

Salem was certain he was going to end up on the witness stand, and wanted to know what his reward would be. That kind of negotiation was beyond Anticev's purview. He would leave that to the U.S. Attorney. But he told Salem the FBI would not blow his cover—"bring him in," as they put it—just so he could testify against one minor player.

"I want to get the whole bunch," Anticev said.

"You cannot, John, you cannot get hold of all of them. You cannot. You can get another three or four guys."

"Okay," Anticev said. He wanted to go over their deal once more before they signed off. The FBI would attempt to investigate whatever information Salem gave them, without putting Salem on the witness stand. But if they had to act quickly and arrest people to prevent another bombing or some other terrorist act, then Salem might have to testify.

Anticev gave him an example. He mentioned a man who Salem said had once asked him to build twelve bombs. If Salem told the FBI this man was collecting explosives, then the FBI would "put surveillance around him, around the clock." They'd document whatever he was doing and build a case against the suspect without having to expose Salem. "If something happens and it has to happen so fast . . . and it's a danger to public safety . . . I mean, I'm talking about saving lives now—"

"Yes."

"We'll have no choice," Anticev said. If the FBI had to rush in and arrest the man, bust up the plot before they had a chance to build a case, then Salem would have to testify and go into protective custody. "So, okay, that's it."

"Okay . . ." Salem answered slowly. "I understand. . . . That's a little bit different from what I was insisting before. Before I say, 'No way, Jose . . .' "

"Right."

"But after the bombing of the WTC," Salem added.

"Yeah?"

"I am with a different mentality," Salem said.

"Okay," Anticev replied. "I'm glad you are."

Bingo, as Anticev was fond of saying. Salem would testify. This time, the informant was going to play the FBI way. When they ended their conversation, Salem hung up and switched off the device he used to record all his telephone calls. Agents knew that Salem recorded everything.

*   *   *

The day before that conversation, the FBI had brought Mahmud Abouhalima back from Egypt in chains, with great fanfare and motorcades. It was March 25, 1993, and news had leaked that the "mastermind" of the bombing had been captured in Egypt and was being returned. The FBI chartered a plane and flew it to Cairo. Abouhalima was delivered to them there on the tarmac; the agents never got off the plane. He was tired, battered, and bruised, and had little to say as he was flown back to an air force base in upstate New York.

The FBI looked like geniuses for cracking the Trade Center case so fast. They made two arrests in less than a week, hauling in Mohammad Salameh when he tried to get his van rental deposit back, and Nosair's cousin El-Gabrowny on the same day. The mild-mannered chemist Nidal Ayyad was arrested next, six days later. Even Salameh's old roommate, Bilal Alkaisi, turned himself in the day Abouhalima was flown out of Cairo.

There were a few things the public, so recently reassured, didn't know. Abouhalima, if he was indeed guilty, had built the bomb right under the watchful eye of the FBI. The public didn't know about the subpoenas and the investigation the previous September. Even Salem was surprised that the Red could have been involved.

How could he have been involved if the FBI was watching him? "You can't monitor somebody twenty-four hours a day," Anticev told Salem.

". . . The guy's innocent or the guy, you know, snaked behind your eyes and he did it," Salem said.

"Well, it's the second one," Anticev replied.

The public also didn't know about the Colonel, the informant the FBI had dumped after he'd warned them about the bomb. They didn't know about the second informant who was asked to buy dynamite just a month before the blast. Nor was the public informed about the bombers' connection to the Kahane killing and Nosair, who was quickly emerging at the center of a terrorist conspiracy, even after the FBI and the police had proclaimed years before that no conspiracy existed in the Kahane assassination. The day after Salameh's arrest, Nosair was slammed into solitary confinement at Attica. "If the devil leaders of this state think placing me in segregation will end the war, they are wrong," Nosair told the corrections lieutenant who led him away. "This is only the beginning. The war will not end until I am released!"

These bungles became dangerous information in the hands of the media-hungry Colonel. The FBI needed his silence as much as his help. The man one FBI supervisor had called a buffoon was going to save their collective butts.

Salem was thirty-eight years old when he left Cairo for America in 1987. He had retired, after eighteen years in the army, with the rank of lieutenant colonel, and rather abruptly left his Egyptian wife and two children behind. Eventually his grown son and daughter would join him, but in the meantime he got himself a new American wife. Handsome, muscular, meticulously well groomed, and quite the charming actor, he met Barbara Rogers in a martial-arts class just two days after he arrived. Six weeks later they were married. He got his green card. Three years later they would separate and divorce.

The newlyweds didn't have much money. Rogers worked for Avon Products, and Salem got a New York City taxi driver's license. At just under six feet tall and two hundred pounds, Salem was a martial-arts and wrestling expert and gun buff. But driving a taxi in New York City was a little too much street action to suit him. He gave it up and went to work as a security guard at the posh Bergdorf Goodman department store and with security firms. He was hired by a midtown residency hotel and given an apartment, where he and his wife lived until they separated in 1990. He moved in with a German-American jewelry designer in her Upper West Side apartment. In those clean, spacious rooms, they stripped the paint from the woodwork and installed the little waterfall in the corner of the living room—along with an array of home surveillance devices. Soon Salem would decorate the walls with photographs of himself and Sheik Omar Abdel-Rahman.

About that time, in late 1991, Salem began his relationship with the FBI. He was working security for a residency hotel and an FBI agent appeared one day inquiring about some of the guests. Salem volunteered to spy. Later that year, the Persian Gulf was heating up, Iraq had invaded Kuwait, and Muslim fundamentalists were squaring off with Jewish militants as the trial of Kahane's accused killer approached. The FBI recruited Salem to funnel information to agents as prosecutors prepared for Nosair's trial scheduled for November 1991. Salem told the FBI he was in touch with Egyptian army intelligence as well. Agents told him not to reveal his relationship to the FBI.

Salem managed to gain El-Gabrowny's trust through his younger brother, who was a former Egyptian army colonel as well. The brother still had contacts in the Egyptian army and checked out Salem. He was who he said he was, the brother concluded. It was a credit to his acting ability because Salem, with his leather bomber jackets, sunglasses, and cloak-and-dagger personality, seemed dramatically different from the devout brethren who rallied around Nosair.

Early in 1992, almost immediately after Nosair was shipped off to Attica, Salem reported what sounded like a wild tale. Nosair had telephoned El-Gabrowny from prison, angry that he "had done his part for Jihad" but that El-Gabrowny and the others were doing nothing to get him out of jail. At El-Gabrowny's request, Salem had visited the new Muslim martyr at Attica, and Nosair had asked Salem to build bombs, recruit others, kidnap his judge, take hostages, whatever it would take to spring him. It was an alarming story, but Salem told a lot of stories.

Salem liked to say he was in Egyptian president Anwar Sadat's personal guard and had been wounded during the assassination: "a bullet in the head and two in the belly," as Salem put it. He told his wife he hadn't really retired from the army, but had been sent to America undercover to look for five missing Egyptian officers. He told a neighbor he had been thrown in a prison cell on one trip to Egypt, had had to fight off snakes tossed in with him, and had escaped into the desert after cracking the cell's combination lock. Testifying against a drunken driver, he told a judge he had periods of amnesia. He told FBI agents that a great actor, the "Anthony Quinn of the Arab world," was a personal friend. He kept a photo album on his coffee table with snapshots of people being tortured. He would open it for reporters who sought interviews with him as he posed as the sheik's aide. Then, satisfied with their horrified looks, he would admonish them, with an expansive gesture, "Ask me no questions."

His braggadocio and ego made agents suspect that his allegations were figments of his imagination as well. The FBI was never too sure what was on Salem's agenda, or for whom he was spying. Agents had received a report that he had even tried to sell information to Kahane Chai, the murdered rabbi's militant group. The Feds had half a dozen other informants in the Egyptian community. Even Abouhalima's taxi dispatcher had informed for the FBI once—so if Salem couldn't be brought in line, they didn't need him. At least so they thought.

The showdown came in July. Early in June, El-Gabrowny had asked Salem to go with another member of their *gamaii* and visit Nosair again. On June 14 he made the long drive to Attica again, and again he reported back to the FBI that Nosair was plotting terrorism and escape. Nosair wanted Salem to rent safe houses where his cohorts could build bombs. He wanted outspoken Jewish state assemblyman Dov Hikind assassinated, and the judge who sentenced him killed as well. Nosair had given him the names of people who would help him. One of the people he named was Salameh. Nosair also said they should consult with Sheik Omar.

Two days later, according to what Salem told the FBI, he met with El-Gabrowny at his Brooklyn apartment and they talked about the plan. Salem bought some time by telling El-Gabrowny he'd have to buy a timer and detonator and other devices overseas and have them shipped.

Three days later, Salem met at Brooklyn's Abu Bakr mosque with the man Nosair called "Dr. Rashid," an African-American Muslim named Clement Rodney Hampton-El, who, Salem told the FBI, offered to provide the weapons. Salem said Dr. Rashid told him he could provide M-16 rifles, Uzis, even ready-assembled bombs for about $1,000 apiece.

On June 27, Salem met with El-Gabrowny again. He had visited his cousin Nosair in prison, and told Salem that Nosair was getting impatient; he wanted to know how their plan was progressing. Salem told the FBI that he stalled. He had bought a five-foot coil of fuse and a dynamite stick to convince El-Gabrowny he was serious. He said he told El-Gabrowny he was still waiting for the devices from overseas. "Can't we make them here?" Salem said El-Gabrowny asked him. Salem assured him they were too difficult to assemble.

Salem dutifully reported these developments to the task force agents he had been working with for the past nine months. But internally at the FBI, some things had changed. The supervisor in charge of the case had retired and the agents worked for months without one. Anticev became ill, and other agents replaced him. By July, there was a new supervisor running the show who had never even met Salem.

When they did meet, at a Manhattan hotel, Salem knew immediately the supervisor didn't like him. Worse, after working as an undercover for nine months, it was clear that FBI brass didn't believe him either. They were furious he'd been paid a regular stipend rather than per-information bonuses. They accused him of milking the system and shut off his payments. Then they put him on a polygraph for two and a half hours, but the test was inconclusive.

In the end, the FBI basically told the Colonel to put up or shut up. They wanted him to agree that he'd actually testify to the allegations he'd made. But that wasn't the deal Salem had made nine months earlier. He agreed to work only as an undercover. The FBI decided it wasn't going to pay him another dime.

The Colonel stalked away, convinced the FBI were fools. He extracted himself from Nosair's plot by telling El-Gabrowny the FBI had questioned him and he had to drop out of the plan or risk leading the FBI to them all. He threw away the fuse. And he was convinced that once he withdrew, the terrorists had gone looking for outside assistance—and found it in Afghanistan.

"You know what it was?" Nancy Floyd asked Salem once after the blast. "They didn't trust my instincts."

"They didn't trust you and they didn't trust me either," he replied.

"Well, it's instinctive not to trust you. But they should have trusted me and they wouldn't."

A few weeks after the World Trade Center bombing, one of Floyd's supervisors called her into his office and asked her bluntly what, in her opinion, went wrong back then. "I may be nailing my coffin lid down," she said. "But the bottom line comes to this . . . this thing was handled completely wrong from the very beginning. . . . All they wanted to do was have him testify . . . Emad had the information about the bombs and where they wanted to have them placed. If we had done what we were supposed to have done, we would have known about it . . . we would have used our heads and come up with a solution of trying to neutralize the situation."

Floyd had been the first to contact him after the single greatest act of terrorism on U.S. soil. "Since the bomb went off, I feel terrible. I feel bad. I feel here is people who don't listen," he told her.

"Hey, I mean, it wasn't like you didn't try and I didn't try," she consoled him.

Anticev called as well. "You were right," he said.

"I feel terrible," Salem told him, too. "I sit here and watch TV and I'm pulling my hair. If we was continuing what we was doing, this bomb would never go off."

"I know. But don't repeat that," Anticev had replied.

Salem himself took some of the blame. If he had agreed to testify back in July, he wouldn't have been asked to withdraw from the case. Every time he drove past the World Trade Center, he slowed down and looked at the huge towers, imagining what would have happened if the bombers had successfully brought them down.

"Fifty thousand people could have gotten killed because I am a coward person. I feel like shit," he told Anticev.

"Look, don't think that way about yourself," Anticev told him. The FBI had continued to monitor the fundamentalists without him. They had other informers who prayed at Sheik Omar's mosque in

Jersey City, Al Salaam. They were hearing things, reporting back, trying to get closer to the sheik's inner circle. "But we ran out of time," Anticev explained.

Salem then met at a neighborhood coffee shop with Anticev and Louis Napoli, a city detective assigned to the NYPD-FBI Anti-Terrorist Task Force. "You know, guys, you gotta know how these people think," he told them. "You thinking American, these people thinking Egyptian and Middle East. . . . That's not the last bomb."

"Hell, I know that," Napoli said.

Anticev and Napoli may have been humoring him, just to get him back into the fold and keep him quiet. When they brought him downtown to FBI headquarters, Salem was irked to find the FBI still didn't trust him. His photograph was tacked to the wall with those of the other suspects.

Anticev and Napoli drove him past the World Trade Center, through the barricaded and closed roads, past the bomb crater. As they passed, Salem contended he had warned them the Trade Center was going to be bombed. "I told you so, that this is one of their targets. You forgot. You have your papers. Go back to it. World Trade Center. Empire State Building. Grand Central. Times Square."

"I looked over my notes," Anticev said. "I didn't see anything about a target."

Napoli chimed in, "I was there also. I don't remember you saying a target."

So Salem played it cool, too. He remained noncommittal. "Ah, what are you going to do now, Emad?" Napoli asked him during one of those early meetings. "What do you wanna do? Tell us what you wanna do?"

"I don't want to do nothing," he said, and then described his reaction when he'd heard that Salameh had been arrested "The minute he said 'Salameh, Mohammad Salameh,' I just said, 'God. I said that guy before.' And of course, Salameh didn't do it by himself alone."

The day agents grabbed Salameh, El-Gabrowny's apartment was searched because Salameh had used his address on his driver's license. El-Gabrowny wrestled with a police officer in the doorway— and was promptly arrested. On him, agents found five phony Nicaraguan passports with the photos of Nosair and his family on them.

"Look, El-Gabrowny's not going anywhere," Anticev told him, happy to have him play it cool while he worked on a plan with his

FBI bosses. "Salameh's not going anywhere—except the bad guys are probably running away all over the place."

Anticev was right about that. By the time Salameh was busted—March 4, just six days after the blast—most of his accomplices had already made it out of the country. Salameh himself would have been on a Royal Jordanian Airlines flight March 5 if he hadn't been arrested the day before. Ramzi Yousef had jumped a flight to Pakistan the night of the bombing. Mahmud Abouhalima had left next, on March 2, to Saudi Arabia and then on to Egypt. Even Bilal Alkaisi, the taxi driver who had shared the Kensington Avenue apartment with Salameh and Aboud and Musab Yasin, was nowhere to be found.

At 34 Kensington Avenue in Jersey City, the FBI found the very cooperative Yasin brothers. Born in Indianapolis to parents of Iraqi descent, Aboud Yasin was a graduate student in engineering who, along with his older brother, Musab, seemed to have the bad luck to share an apartment with Salameh. Yasin was at 34 Kensington when the FBI arrived. He told agents that Salameh hadn't lived there in some time, and actually led them to the Pamrapo apartment where he said Salameh had been living. He even told agents he had taught Salameh how to drive a Ryder rental van just a few days before.

The agents were delighted. They wrote up his interview, classified him as a cooperating witness, and said good-bye. Yasin had an airline ticket to Jordan the entire time. He was gone the next day. Later, when the FBI realized they had let him slip away, brother Musab contacted him. He was in Iraq, living with relatives in Baghdad by then, and politely declined to return. He was indicted as a conspirator.

The day Salameh was arrested, the manager at the Space Station opened the locker that the pseudonymous Mr. Kamal had rented, and then called the FBI. The next day, agents descended on locker 4344 and found bank records and receipts for chemicals. The following day, three Arab men rushed to Kennedy Airport and asked a ticket clerk for the next flight anywhere off the North American continent. That afternoon, they flew to South Africa.

Agents found receipts at 34 Kensington that gave a clue to the flight the missing Iraqi Rashed had taken into the United States. It was issued in Karachi, and the next ticket in the sequence was issued to Ahmad Ajaj, who was serving six months in prison for attempting to enter the United States with a phony Swedish passport. The FBI decided to interview Ajaj, and discovered he had finished his sentence just a few days before. They found him at an INS center and slammed him back in jail. The next day, March 10, agents arrested Nidal Ayyad at his New Jersey home. Phone records showing calls to the Space Station, joint bank accounts with Salameh, and his inquiries into buying explosives provided enough probable cause to land him in a jail cell.

After Salameh's arrest, Anticev and Napoli had asked Salem to inquire innocently about Abouhalima's whereabouts. No one had seen him around, and he hadn't been to work since February 26, the day of the blast. Salem learned from Mahmud's younger brother, Mohammed, that the Red had left the country on March 2. He was on a religious pilgrimage, Mohammed told Salem. He'd gone to Saudi Arabia, but something had gone wrong. He couldn't stay there. His wife and children were meeting him at his father's house in Egypt—which was the last place Abouhalima should go.

Salem warned Anticev that if Abouhalima was arrested in Egypt, the Egyptians wouldn't tell the United States until they had finished with him. They would torture him and beat out of him whatever he could tell them about Sheik Omar. Then they'd kill him and bury his body in the sand. The FBI would never know what happened to their prime suspect.

The Egyptians had the Abouhalima family's home wiretapped and heard their conversations with their pilgrim son. They lay in wait and took the Red into custody. The distraught family called Mohammed in America. Mohammed called El-Gabrowny's brother Mohammed, the former army officer. His Egyptian army contacts confirmed it and Salem learned of it from him. Salem called Anticev and told him, "My advice . . . you must bring him back immediately before he is brainwashed. . . . He must not be tortured . . . they will be hanging him upside down right now. I know what I am talking about."

It turned out that dozens of people in the Muslim community heard within a matter of days that Abouhalima had been arrested in Egypt. Anticev got suspicious. He asked Salem if he was sure this wasn't a lie being spread to get the FBI off the Red's trail.

"No," Salem answered flatly.

"No?"

"No," Salem insisted.

"Okay, why?"

"Because everyone is hoping the Federal Bureau of Investigation [will go] pick up Mahmud from Egypt . . . to go as fast as they can to save him from Egyptian FBI," Salem explained.

"So they want us to pick him up to save his life?" Anticev didn't sound convinced. Days had passed since the State Department had formally made inquiries to the Egyptians and there was still no response. Anticev asked Salem if he could call his Egyptian intelligence contacts.

"A phone call? No. Nobody talks about things like that over the phone. . . . Over there, every phone bugged." His contacts, Salem explained, would think he had come to America and grown stupid.

It took ten days before the Egyptian government would confirm they had Abouhalima. It was ten days of typical interrogation: cattle prods and cigarettes applied to the genitalia. He was tied to a pole, cold and naked, and beaten. Napoli and FBI agents flew to Cairo in a chartered plane, and Abouhalima was delivered to them on the airport tarmac. Blindfolded, bruised, he settled into a seat.

The FBI was convinced that Abouhalima—through his contacts with extremist groups in Afghanistan—had planned the bombing. But there was no evidence against him, except his sudden departure. Agents who had been investigating Abouhalima since the Kahane killing once again couldn't connect him to the crime. Anticev once told Salem how the FBI had first linked Abouhalima to terrorism.

"We knew that he was a, you know, big guy, went back and forth to Afghanistan," Anticev told him. "Listen to this, this is funny."

Nosair's phone records showed he called one Brooklyn phone number over and over again. It was listed under "Weber" on Fifth Avenue in Brooklyn, so Anticev and Napoli decided to go and check this Weber guy out. They didn't know that Weber was Abouhalima's wife's maiden name; they just thought it odd that Nosair's most frequent contact had a German name.

"And we knock on the door," Anticev recounted, "and somebody, an American guy, answers on another floor, and we go, 'Who is this Weber?' And the guy goes, 'Him? I think this guy's a terrorist.' We go, 'Why?' 'Well, he has all these Arabs up there all the time, and this and that, uh, he has magazines about bombs and stuff like . . . his real name is, is Mahmud Abouhalima.'

"And I just looked at Louie, you know, and we said, 'Bingo.' "

The FBI had connected the Red to Nosair back then, and had

questioned him about the Kahane killing. Where were you that night, Mahmud? they asked him. Were you outside the hotel that night in your taxi? But the NYPD already had publicly announced that Nosair was a lone gun nan. There was no conspiracy.

The FBI knew about the paramilitary training camps, and agents learned about Nosair's connection to the radical sheik. They had boxes and boxes of propaganda they'd hauled out of Nosair's apartment, even what looked to be a "hit list" of prominent Jews. But they left most of Nosair's documents untranslated, sitting in an evidence room. Operation Desert Storm was beginning, and the FBI had Iraqi citizens to follow. It had hours of wiretaps from the Iraqi mission to translate. Meir Kahane was as villainous to most as the man who killed him, and the FBI decided to let his case rest in peace.

*   *   *

Mahmud Abouhalima was offered up as the mastermind. But, as far as the American public was concerned, Sheik Omar Abdel-Rahman was the devil behind it. The mysterious blind sheik fit the role of terrorist demon better than the big redheaded taxi driver.

Sheik Omar had once complained to a reporter that he wasn't well known. Overnight, he became an international villain. Among Americans who wanted a clear-cut and simple enemy, he replaced Iraq's Saddam Hussein as an object of hate. Congressmen, alarmed that some of his disciples were accused of the bombing, called for the sheik's arrest. Rocks shattered the window of his Jersey City mosque. But the only legal charge filed against him was immigration fraud.

The FBI, more practiced in combating domestic terrorism than threats from abroad, viewed the concept of a terrorist cell as if it were an organized crime family. The sheik, agents were sure, was the crime boss. The others were his mob crew. Sheik Omar might not have built the bomb, but the FBI was certain he had given it his approval, just as surely as John Gotti had approved his crew's mob hits. Put the mob boss away, and the crime family withers. Put the sheik away, and the mob crew has no direction.

The FBI and local police watched a terrorist cell organize on both sides of the Hudson River. They didn't recognize it, they didn't stop it from bombing the World Trade Center. But once the truth literally blew up in their faces, they were going to make sure it didn't happen again.

"Naturally, what I'm more interested in—I am, of course, interested in putting these people in jail—but the long-term effects of this type of group in this country," Anticev told Salem. "I mean, we can lock up ten people tomorrow, but that's not going to mean another one isn't gonna happen two years from now."

"Well, that's what I was saying since day one," Salem replied.

The media connected each arrest to the sheik. The FBI knew the evidence was not entirely that clear. It was widely known in the Muslim community that Abouhalima and Sheik Omar had split over the Alkifah's money and Shalabi's killing. Salameh had worshiped at the sheik's mosque, but had never been part of his inner circle. Ayyad wasn't a follower. The bombing purported to have strong Palestinian motives, and the sheik had never been an advocate of the Palestinian cause; it was too secular in nature to be worthy of Jihad. His obsession was Egypt and bringing down its president, Mubarak, replacing his Western-style state with an Iran-style theocracy.

Some of those around him thought the sheik and his inner circle seemed taken by surprise by the bombing. He was fighting deportation, and being linked to an act of terrorism was not going to help his cause. Salem had heard nothing that implicated him. As public hysteria over the sheik increased, even moderate Muslims who loathed him became alarmed that the *mufti* might be getting a bad rap. In Egypt, where extremist groups were bombing and killing daily, the sheik was considered a spiritual leader, but in no way a commander.

As a *mufti*, or religious adviser, Sheik Omar offered his interpretation of what was permissible under Islamic law. Unfortunately for Mubarak, one of the sheik's more nettlesome religious opinions followed a fourteenth-century doctrine which decreed that Muslims were duty-bound to kill Muslim leaders who did not rule by Islamic law. This opinion had gotten the *mufti* charged with Sadat's assassination a decade earlier. It was a charge that even Egypt's stringent criminal justice system couldn't prove.

Once, during Nosair's trial, Salem had told FBI agents that the sheik had called Mubarak a pig, and had asked Salem to kill him. If Salem could catch him on tape issuing such a *fatwah*, he could link Omar Abdel-Rahman to the terrorist cell as more than just a spiritual adviser. (A *fatwah* is a religious legal opinion, like the death sentence issued by the Ayatollah Khomeini against the writer Salman Rushdie.)

For such testimony the FBI would pay dearly. Agents told him that in a big case, the reward for testifying would be "at least in the six-figure range. It's at least $200,000."

"This is pennies," Salem retorted. In exchange for a life on the run, he wanted to be a millionaire.

After Salameh was arrested, the FBI tried to placate him with a peace offering because, as Anticev put it, his motives for coming back to work were so noble. "I sincerely believe [you] are doing it for your reasons . . . like you told me . . . from your heart and for the country and everything," Anticev said. So the FBI gave him $2,500 for just talking to them again.

By the time Salem was through negotiating, more than $1.5 million would be riding on his work and on his willingness to take the witness stand. Salem held the trump card. A month after the dust had settled at the bomb site, the FBI had no evidence against Sheik Omar.

Salem was willing to do whatever was necessary to get evidence on the sheik and his cohorts. He told Anticev he was willing to go into the Muslim community wired.

"You realize the situation with being wired?" Anticev asked him. The FBI had never let him wear a wire before. It was too dangerous; if you were searched, the game was over. And whatever was recorded wouldn't be admissible in court unless the wired person was there to testify.

"I know my life, the rest of my life and my children's life will be in jeopardy. . . . But at least the world should know [the sheik is a fraud]," Salem replied. "This guy, he is supposed to be leader in Islam. . . . As a good Muslim, you shouldn't lie."

"And meanwhile, he lies," Anticev interjected.

"He comes to the world and lies. That's bullshit. Excuse my language. That's really bullshit. And I don't [believe that's] Islam."

The bomb squad and the National Response Team had finished sifting through the site; agents and cops had interviewed everyone who had been anywhere near the World Trade Center that disastrous day. Six bodies had been buried, and four men arrested, but the worst that American jurisprudence could do to the man they believed was behind it all was deport him.

"So, right now we have nothing solid concrete on him?" Salem asked.

"No, he's a tough guy to get," Anticev replied.

He explained that they had to catch the sheik in an overt act to connect him to the conspiracy. It could be as simple as a conversation in which he encouraged the plan. If Salem could catch such a conversation on a hidden recorder, it would be evidence that the sheik had knowingly played a role. It was just about the only way to implicate him, short of one of the four defendants turning evidence against him. That didn't seem likely to happen.

"If Salameh comes back or Ayyad comes back to the sheik and says, 'Sheik, I bought the chemicals . . . to make the bomb,' and the sheik says, 'Uh-huh, very good.' Bingo," Anticev said. "The sheik is in the conspiracy. He's just as guilty as Salameh."

12

TRAPPING THE SHEIK

Where will the next bomb go off? As the FBI and the NYPD plodded through the evidence the World Trade Center bombers left behind—fingerprints, parking stubs, bank accounts, receipts, hunks of twisted metal, and bags of detritus—that constant anxiety overshadowed the investigation.

Four days after the explosion, *The New York Times* had received a letter claiming responsibility. The day agents arrested chemist Nidal Ayyad at his home, they went to his office at Allied Signal and seized his computer and electronically restored files he had deleted. In those files they found nearly identical drafts of that letter.

> The following letter from the LIBERATION ARMY regarding the operation conducted against the W.T.C.
>
> We, the fifth battalion in the LIBERATION ARMY, declare our responsibility for the explosion on the mentioned building. This action was done in response for the American political, economical, and military support to Israel the state of terrorism and to the rest of the dictator countries in the region.
>
> OUR DEMANDS ARE:
>
> 1—Stop all military, economical, and political aids to Israel.
>
> 2—All diplomatic relations with Israel must stop.
>
> 3—Not to interfere with any of the Middle East countries interior affairs.

If our demands are not met, all of our functional groups in
the army will continue to execute our missions against
military and civilian targets in and out of the United States.
This also will include some potential Nuclear targets. For
your own information, our army has more than hundred and
fifty suicidal soldiers ready to go ahead. The terrorism that
Israel practices (Which is supported by America) must be
faced with a similar one. The dictatorship and terrorism
(also supported by America) that some countries are practicing
against their own people must also be faced with
terrorism.

According to the Liberation Army, the American people were
responsible for their government's crimes, and therefore all world
revolutionaries should join in the fight against America.

When the *Times* made the letter public late in March, New York
FBI director James Fox hastened to assure the bomb-shocked citizens of the city that no evidence suggested there really were 150
suicidal soldiers ready to strike. But the citizenry was spared what
the alarming evidence did show: that at least ten fingerprints had
turned up at the storage locker and makeshift lab that didn't match
those of any of the known suspects. And Ayyad had a second letter
in his computer, one he didn't have the chance to send before his
arrest. It promised another blast:

"We are, the Liberation fifth battalion, again. . . . Unfortunately,
our calculations were not very accurate this time. However, we
promise you that the next time it will be very precise and WTC
will continue to be one of our targets. . . ."

Unlike the other suspects, Nidal Ayyad didn't have an airline
ticket in his pocket. He was sticking around. As the investigation
continued, the FBI suspected that the Rutgers alumnus was much
more than the mild-mannered chemist he seemed. Just one day
before he was arrested, he was already trying to get more chemicals
for explosives. This raised a queasy question: Since the other suspects were out of the country or in jail, who was Ayyad counting
on to build the bomb this time?

Terrorism experts privately warned the departments of State and
Justice that the Muslim extremists' victory over the Soviets in
Afghanistan had united fundamentalists in fresh fervor. Afghanistan

was just the start; passion for Jihad had produced a new and possibly more dangerous breed of terrorists—members of society with citizenship papers and seemingly a stake in the American dream. The new terrorists wouldn't necessarily be imported from overseas or be part of some state-sponsored terrorist organization. They could be your neighbors, an ad hoc group coming together for just one glorious act.

Former Egyptian army colonel Emad Salem, that master of double-talk and deception, had the best chance to find them. The FBI had little choice but to turn to the grandstanding double agent they had spurned. But this time, he was going to be directed and controlled. When he worked for Agent Nancy Floyd in the intelligence division, he mostly did what he wanted and came back and told the FBI what he'd seen or heard. Now they needed him to follow specific instructions about gathering evidence and building a case.

"In other words, you're gonna have to be directed more than you were," Anticev explained, " 'cause we, you know, I didn't know much about the community, the new fundamentalism was brand-new to me, brand-new to Nancy. . . ."

"Uh-huh."

"As far as, you know, the financial rewards, I don't know exactly what it is, but it's very good."

This time, Salem would wear hidden microphones and tape his Muslim brothers. He had one contact person who acted as the conduit to Anticev. Anticev had given some explanation for this, some sort of "Chinese wall" built around him so his information didn't have to be turned over to the defense lawyers.

Salem was still Sheik Omar's security guard and self-appointed spokesman for the fundamentalists. Nothing had happened to make Sheik Omar or El-Gabrowny suspicious of Salem. Muslims can't simply turn away their brethren for personal dislike; they all must work together to serve Allah. So Salem still frisked people at press conferences and swept the sheik's apartment for bugs. He gave reporters interviews, visited his friend Mahmud the Red in jail, and stayed close to Mahmud's younger brother.

But if the people in the sheik's circle knew much about the World Trade Center bombing, they weren't talking. Salem couldn't even trick the sheik into saying whether or not he knew Ayyad or Yousef. "I know thousands, and millions know me," he replied. In the wake of the bombing, Sheik Omar held press conferences in which he denied knowing any of the men accused.

In early April, Sheik Omar's nemesis, Egyptian president Mubarak, visited the White House and took the opportunity to tell the press that the United States could have prevented the World Trade Center bombing if it had listened to his warnings about the sheik. The following day, April 6, as Mubarak met with President Clinton, the sheik gave a memorable press conference in his Jersey City apartment. In it he denounced Mubarak and accused Egypt of spying on American citizens. At his side throughout his statement were three faithful aides: translators Siddig Ali and Abdo Haggag, and security officer Salem. Salem learned a great deal that month about his two colleagues.

Haggag, a young Egyptian, had expected Mubarak to travel to New York City after his White House visit. Salem gathered that Haggag had been involved in some sort of assassination plot. When Mubarak changed his plans and skipped New York, Haggag told Salem he feared the plan had been leaked. He wanted Salem to come to his apartment and sweep it for bugs.

The second translator, Siddig Ibrahim Siddig Ali, was up to something as well. Salem learned he had been conducting some sort of surveillance at Manhattan buildings. Siddig, a well-educated, charismatic Sudanese man, worked for a downtown security firm. Either he or Haggag, or both of them, could be among the unapprehended bombers, Salem told his pals at the FBI.

In any event, with the hated Egyptian president in the country, the sheik decided to receive the press in his bare, fourth-floor Jersey City apartment.

"You are all going to make some money today, eh?" said a man at the door. "The chance of a lifetime. Please, take off your shoes and leave them inside the doorway before you come to see the imam."

Soon, fifty-seven writers, photographers, and camera operators were occupying every inch of space. The sheik stood inside his bedroom, out of sight, while his aides buzzed around the room, looking for his hat. Finally, someone located his tasseled skullcap. Then the door was opened, and he emerged from the bedroom on the arm of a tall, thin man. The sheik himself was no more than five feet, seven inches tall, with untamed gray whiskers that sprang into a shrubby beard. He wore dark glasses.

After the sheik reached the sofa and was seated, Siddig Ali made a short statement: "Dr. Omar says that pictures will only be taken of him—no photographs of anyone else in the room, video or camera." Siddig Ali introduced himself as Dr. Hassad, the imam's translator. Then he pulled a white veil across his own face, saying, "These are his instructions."

The sheik started by making a nine-point statement about that dirtbag lying thief and scoundrel, the president of Egypt, who, by the way, had been entertained in Washington yesterday by the president of the United States, but could not last even one minute in his own country without martial law. Egypt was a land befouled with corruption, torture, sadism. He spoke in Arabic, occasionally spitting the name Mubarak contemptuously.

Now the sheik was ready for questions.

"How could the sheik go on TV and say that he didn't know the suspects in the World Trade Center bombing if one of them paid his salary at a mosque in Brooklyn and another drove him around and got him an apartment?" someone asked the translator.

"I go to most American mosques, I know thousands of Muslims, and I cannot tell you about all of them," the sheik began, Siddig Ali translating. "If I know a person yesterday, I may forget him today. I would not know every person that prayed behind me in that mosque."

Normally, to prevent the scandalous distortions of the press, the sheik permits interviews in live broadcasts only, and requires all print questions to be submitted in advance, and all his answers printed in their breathtaking entirety, without editing. Unfortunately for the sheik, he was live at 5:45 P.M. on the evening news. But he handled the barrage with poise, even with an out-of-control press corps in his living room.

"The direction of asking me questions about knowing a person or not knowing him is the wrong direction," he said. He smoothly twisted his answer back to the hated Hosni Mubarak, president of Egypt, a torturer who, Sheik Omar said, subjected his victims to "hungry mad dogs."

"And this kind of question is not known except for the interrogation in Egypt," said Sheik Omar. "In Egypt, they ask about your friends, your acquaintances, your relatives. And this is a wrong direction in interrogation and in all kinds of reporting."

Had he been in Pakistan or Afghanistan, and connected in any way with the CIA?

"My work as a preacher is according to God, Allah's paradigm. My work is not to gather people or send volunteers. My work is not to collect money. My work is to call on people to collect money for the mujahedeen and to go over there for Jihad. . . . My work is to show people what reward from Allah they will get from Jihad, so they can go over there, wherever it is called.

"And my work is not like what they claim, that I work with the CIA. This is not true."

He gently kidded with a reporter who asked him how he supported himself, and who had paid for the apartment. "Do you want to give me some money?" asked the sheik.

He condemned the bombing of the World Trade Center, the taking of lives, and attacks on all houses of worship. Then he was asked one more irritating question: Did he condemn the killing of the anti-Muslim Zionist Meir Kahane?

"Don't ask me this," said the sheik, curtly. "It was settled in front of the court. It is irrelevant." With that, the sheik declared his thanks to the reporters and to Allah the merciful, the beneficent. A reporter remarked to a colleague about the sheik's adeptness with the press, his charm, which was disturbed only when he snarled Hosni Mubarak's name.

"I don't know why he's so mad at Mubarak," said the other writer. "After all, he's the one who got him the job."

Born in 1938, he was blinded at the age of ten months, when diabetes robbed his vision and sentenced him to an alien childhood. The only relative with the will and patience to tend to the disabled boy was his uncle, a devout Muslim whom he would later call "my set of eyes." The uncle kept those eyes focused almost exclusively on the words of Allah. The boy was forced to rise before the early-morning prayer at 4:00 A.M., to memorize the Koran. During the searing heat or chilling rain of north Egypt, young Omar would sit on the mosque floor. His uncle refused to let the absence of vision deprive the boy of spiritual enlightenment, so he taught his nephew to read Braille. By age eleven, young Omar had memorized the entire scripture. His affinity for the scriptures made him a natural candidate for religious training. He excelled in religious schools and graduated in 1965, earning top honors. But he wasn't offered an appointment in a state-run university, a snub that left him embittered.

Instead of teaching, Abdel-Rahman was assigned to become imam, prayer leader, at Fayoum, a small village of about twenty-thousand people, situated along the Nile. Although his fiery style and energy helped revitalize the mosque and boost its attendance, he was disappointed by the community, stunned by the villagers' lax morals and their lukewarm adherence to the laws of Islam. He missed academe, and in 1967 he returned to Cairo University to study for an advanced degree. Cairo was a city in turmoil in those days, where Arabs were still trying to recover from their crushing defeat to Israel in the Six-Day War. Abdel-Rahman met many veterans of the humiliating battle, and their stories fortified his suspicion that the Arab world's secular leaders had again betrayed their people.

By the time he returned to Fayoum in 1968, the sheik's sermons had taken a decidedly political turn. He referred to Egypt's leader, Gamal Abdel Nasser, as "pharaoh" and "infidel." He bitterly criticized the country's privileged class and unequal distribution of wealth. Within months, his biting political commentary had captured the attention of the Egyptian security forces, and Abdel-Rahman found himself shadowed by officers. Within weeks, he was arrested for his criticism of Nasser. He was banned from preaching, by order of the military forces. His pay, cut in half, was barely enough to cover his rent. At the age of twenty-one, he had been effectively placed under military house arrest. The restrictions simply focused his anger. When Nasser died in 1970, Abdel-Rahman could not allow the occasion to pass without expressing his disgust for the Egyptian government. He went from door to door, calling on his followers to use Nasser's death as an opportunity to show Muslim solidarity. On October 15, 1970, as a crowd gathered at a memorial service, he walked up to the lectern and halted the mourning. "Do not pray for this infidel," he told the crowd. "He is not worthy of your prayers."

Abdel-Rahman was arrested again, and this time he served eight months in prison. But as words of his protest spread, more Egyptians were drawn to this brash, blind preacher. He returned to school, and immediately began preparing for his doctorate. He wrote his dissertation about the most crucial subject facing Islam, a topic that would consume him and his followers for decades: the Koran's teachings about political violence and whether the scriptures banned Jihad during the holy month of Ramadan. At the core of his beliefs was the teaching of a fourteenth-century scholar who ruled that Muslims have the duty to kill leaders who fail to rule by Islamic law. After graduation, those views won Abdel-Rahman a warm welcome in Menya, the southern Egyptian town where he was assigned to preach. Menya had one of the most radically fundamentalist populations in all of Egypt, and was the birthplace of the Gama al-Islamiya, the extremist group dedicated to the violent overthrow of the Egyptian government.

It was then, ironically, that Abdel-Rahman entered into a short-lived alliance with the Egyptian government, a partnership the nation's leaders would live to regret—or die regretting. Nasser's successor, Anwar Sadat, felt threatened by Egypt's surging communist movement, so he decided to court the Islamic fundamentalists on the far right of the political spectrum. Sadat allowed Saudi Arabia's King Faisal to bankroll a massive grassroots campaign against communism and atheism in Egypt. Faisal sent more than $100 million to the director of the fundamentalist Al-Azhar University, Sheik Abdel Halim Mahmoud, with the understanding that he undertake an Islamic revival movement. Mahmoud saw it as a way to spread the sacred Word of God—the same way that fervent Muslims, nearly two decades later, would see the United States's funding of a proxy war against the Soviet Union in Afghanistan. America might be funding a war against communism, but for the mujahedeen, it was only a small battle in the centuries-old Islamic Jihad.

So, too, did Faisal and Sadat see Islam as a way to snuff out the advances made by the communists. Mahmoud directed a far-flung campaign to convert the Egyptian masses, funding dozens of new books, pamphlets, and recordings. And Mahmoud also instructed one of his most impressive students, Omar Abdel-Rahman, to spearhead the campaign in Upper Egypt and the University of Asyut.

They also funded public works projects to build a long-term political base. The fundamentalists built mosques and hospitals, schools and poverty-relief organizations. In many Egyptian communities, the Islamic fundamentalists delivered the kind of social services the government failed to provide. While government officials drove their Mercedeses in Cairo, squandering millions in public funds on gambling debts, mansions, and other Western extravagances, the fundamentalist Muslims provided food and shelter to the poor and the elderly. While Sadat courted Israel, the United States, and the West in general—and allowed dissident Egyptians to be tortured in government jails—it was the fundamentalist Muslims who taught peasant children to read, who provided housing for their parents, and who tended to their impoverished communities. The words of the Koran were, like the holy scriptures of other religions, a source of comfort and strength to the oppressed. Now, thanks to Sadat's agreement with the Saudi Arabians, the fundamentalists in Upper Egypt had the means to care for their followers' physical needs as well.

Abdel-Rahman's popularity grew in Asyut, where he once again gravitated toward Islam's most extreme fringes. He became captivated by the teachings of Sayyid Qutb, a radical religious scholar who wrote extensively about the future of Islam shortly after World War II. Qutb professed that the world was divided into two opposing camps, the Society of Allah and the Society of Satan. It was the sacred duty of Allah's followers to convert or conquer the others, Qutb taught, by force if necessary. Most Egyptian Muslims considered Qutb a volatile fringe character with little credibility. His following was small during his lifetime, and he was executed in 1965, convicted of an attempt on Nasser's life. Abdel-Rahman revered Qutb as a genius and martyr, and taught his students to adopt Qutb's call to arms. Abdel-Rahman attracted an eclectic following of theology students and peasants, and was the most visible symbol of the Islamic revival in all of Upper Egypt. The sheik's growing militance and Sadat's shifting political concerns brought their truce to a speedy, decisive end. By 1977, Sadat felt a greater threat from the Islamists than from the communists, so he ordered a crackdown on the fundamentalists whom he'd sponsored seven years earlier.

The sheik, sensing that another prison term was imminent, fled to Saudi Arabia. The Saudis welcomed him, and the same affluent Muslims who had underwritten his revival campaign in Egypt now paid him handsomely to teach in Saudi Arabia. Because the sheik was blind, he was granted a position in a girl's school. He was also given ample time to travel extensively throughout the Middle East, and meet with other leading Islamic scholars and politicians. He used the experience shrewdly, making the high-level connections that would later prove instrumental to his crusade—including Dr. Hassan Al-Turabi, leader of Sudan's Islamic Front. But the sheik's focus, as always, was on Egypt. He returned there occasionally, and kept in constant contact with his followers in Gama al-Islamiya. In 1979, when Sadat went to Camp David and signed the treaty that made Egypt the first and only Arab country to make peace with Israel, nearly every radical Muslim, Omar Abdel-Rahman included, vowed to bring down his government. And when five of the sheik's followers were charged with assassinating Sadat, the sheik, too, faced a murder charge and a possible death penalty.

Government prosecutors knew there was no way to charge Sheik Omar directly with the brazen midday assassination, so they accused him of inciting it. In 1982, he, then in Egypt, was put on trial, charged with issuing a *fatwah*—sanctioning Sadat's assassination. It was clear from the testimony of the sheik's co-defendants that he had inspired and encouraged a war against the government. He had met with at least three of the suspects in the months before the assassination of the president. One Gama al-Islamiya member told the court that Abdel-Rahman had urged his followers to take donations, which had been gathered to build a new mosque, and use the cash to wage a Jihad. Another testified that the sheik had given his flock permission to fund their operations by robbing jewelry stores—but only if the owners were Christian.

"We chose him as our spiritual leader because he calls for holy war," the defendant testified.

One confessed assassin, Abud Zumor, testified that Sheik Omar had given his approval in principle, but had never known about the actual plan to murder the president. "[Sheik Omar said] it was to shed [Sadat's] blood, unless he obeys God's law," Zumor testified. "But as regards the assassination at the October 6 parade, the sheik's advice was not asked. We had lost touch with him."

As the trial dragged on, Sheik Omar laughed and chatted with several of the defendants who had carried out the shooting. When the sheik finally took the stand, he was unrepentant. He used the witness stand as a pulpit from which to preach his rigid interpretation of the Koran. But he was careful that in praising Sadat's death, he didn't implicate himself. It was a skill that would serve him well eleven years later, in the wake of the World Trade Center bombing, as Salem tried to gather evidence against him.

"Man-made laws are complete infidelity," the sheik bellowed from the witness stand. "It's either Islam or the state of ignorance. It's either faith or infidelity. Those who don't rule according to God's orders are infidels, oppressors, wrongdoers."

He blasted Sadat, saying the president had "attacked religion by normalizing relations with the most [abhorrent] to those who believe, by signing the two treaties at Camp David."

Five men were eventually executed for the killing. Abdel-Rahman was cleared of all charges and released. The notoriety of the trial made him a Muslim folk hero. Young Muslims wrote songs and poems about the plight of the blind preacher, and raised money to pay for his defense. The Egyptian government, embarrassed by his acquittal, began an intense operation to squelch the sheik's inflammatory message. He was again followed by guards and government agents. Between 1984 and 1989 he was arrested five times, and spent several more years under virtual house arrest. Ever the rebel, he taunted the government, and even feigned an attachment to his jail cell. "Cell 24—I loved it very much," he once said in court, "and I always asked to return to it."

Under house arrest, too, the sheik learned to toy with his government captors. An army jeep with a cadre of soldiers would stand guard on the dirt road outside his home. Abdel-Rahman would walk from his house to the mosque, weaving through traffic in the street. The jeep, in a desperate attempt to keep him under surveillance, would follow—blocking the cars, buses, bicycles, and camels moving down the village's narrow road.

People who watched the spectacle would rally to Sheik Omar's defense, shouting insults and taunts at the soldiers.

"Leave the old man alone!"

"He's a man of God!"

Sheik Omar would quiet the crowd, then begin his sermon with a message the soldiers had just helped reinforce. "The oppressor and his armies must know they cannot stand up to Allah."

Despite his defiance, the government's restrictions eventually succeeded in muting Sheik Omar's influence. A new, even more radical generation of fundamentalists was rising to capitalize on the frustrations of the Muslim masses. The sheik's hard-core supporters continued to surface in various plots and attacks against the government, Western tourists, and secular businessmen. But the sheik was fading from public view, and his dream of founding a religious government in Egypt remained a distant mirage. In 1987 he complained that Egyptian president Hosni Mubarak had effectively silenced him. "We have found no one who will listen or pay attention to us," he said.

Even within the fundamentalist right, Sheik Omar faced potentially deadly challenges. Gama al-Islamiya and the other Jihad organizations that he advised were splintering. One rival group in Fayoum, led by Shawki al-Sheikh and his *shawki'een* organization, publicly declared Sheik Omar an "infidel." When Shawki was killed in 1988, his despondent followers were reported to have placed Sheik Omar on a death list.

Once again, the sheik decided to renew himself outside of Egypt. He traveled to Peshawar, Pakistan, one of the emerging capitals of the Islamic universe. Ever since the Soviet Union attacked Afghanistan in 1979, Muslims from around the globe had rushed to Peshawar to raise money, run guns, and train soldiers for the Afghan resistance. By the time Sheik Omar arrived in 1988, the Soviets were already preparing to pull out, but the flow of arms and money continued until the beginning of 1991. He began a friendly alliance with Gulbadin Hekmatayar, the warlord who received nearly half the arms the CIA was funneling to the mujahedeen. The blind cleric was fascinated by the collection of high-tech hardware: shoulder-launched Stinger antiaircraft missiles, plastic explosives and mines, M-16 rifles. Even more astounding was the attitude of the Americans. Hekmatayar, the sheik, and the others would repeatedly blast the immorality of the West, and made no secret of their desire to topple all that the United States stood for. Yet the Americans continued sending weapons and military trainers. Moreover, the CIA quickly began using Sheik Omar as a middleman for the arms shipments. Afghanistan had earned itself the appellation "Jihad University."

When the war ended, the sheik decided to move to America. With some help from his Sudanese friend Toorabi, some good luck, and astounding incompetence by the Immigration and Naturalization Service, he managed to slip into the country. Abdel-Rahman had been under the State Department's watch since 1987, his role in the Sadat assassination and other violent demonstrations having earned him a place on the "undesirables" list. But on the day he left the Khartoum airport, an improbable series of breakdowns took place. First, a Sudanese employee of the U.S. Embassy failed to check the lookout list, because, it was later said, the computer had broken down. Sheik Omar was issued a visa. Had the employee checked, he would have seen that Egyptian officials had sent a cable earlier that year, warning of the sheik's violent history. Then the State Department waited four months before notifying the INS that the sheik had been improperly allowed into the States. Even after his name had been added to the updated lookout list, the INS repeatedly failed to detain him as he left and reentered the country.

Years later, the State Department acknowledged that the visa allowing Sheik Omar into the country had been stamped by the CIA—the same benefactor that had once funded the radical rabbi Meir Kahane.

The sheik adapted quickly to life in America, where his followers provided him with apartments, transportation, and a position preaching at several mosques. It was a perfect setup. He could live quite comfortably in the outskirts of New York, raising money, socializing with the other Afghani veterans, and winning converts for his mission back in Egypt. He could preach whenever and wherever he pleased, without a hostile government breathing down his neck. And when he was ready, he could try again to attain his ultimate goal: a religious government in Egypt.

* * *

When April ended without the FBI arresting anyone else, the sheik's circle began to unclench. It was time for Salem to wire himself for sound. He knew what that meant. Anticev had made it crystal clear that the FBI didn't want a repetition of what had happened last time. Salem wasn't going to come back to them with allegations and then refuse to testify, leaving the FBI hanging. "You get all this great evidence and then we turn around and say either you get out or you'll have to testify . . . then we get into a problem with each other . . . so we want to make everything perfectly clear," Anticev told him.

Salem stuck a body microphone in the zipper of his pants and set off to implicate the sheik's two aides.

His first meeting was with Siddig Ali. The two men had much to talk about. Like Salem, the thirty-two-year-old Siddig worked at security firms, took martial-arts training, and was a gun buff. He knew Mahmud and Nosair and, like Salem, he talked a lot. As with Salem, it was somewhat hard to discern boast from fact.

Salem described his military expertise and told Siddig Ali he was a trained explosives expert. He could build bombs. Salem reported back to the FBI that Siddig Ali had bragged that he had helped test the Trade Center bomb. Now, Siddig Ali told Salem, he had his own plan. He wanted to bomb the United Nations.

Later that week, Salem trudged up four flights of stairs to Haggag's apartment. Haggag, a computer operator with a Wall Street securities firm, was so devoted to Sheik Omar that he had moved into an apartment in Jersey City right next door to the sheik's. When Salem arrived there, he found Mohammed Abouhalima, Mahmud's younger brother, there with Haggag.

He caught Haggag and Mohammed on tape, talking about the plan to kill Mubarak. Haggag was worried about the FBI; agents had questioned him. He told the visiting FBI informant that he was sure there was an FBI leak. Haggag suspected he knew who it was. He accused Siddig Ali.

It was a good ploy, pointing the finger at Siddig Ali. The devout Haggag loathed Siddig Ali, who was a bigmouth with grandoise plans that could get them all killed. The Mubarak plan was a suicide mission. They were supposed to dress up in room-service uniforms and kill him in the Waldorf-Astoria Hotel. There certainly had been a leak. To accuse Siddig Ali could draw attention away from the real informant—Haggag himself. He had gone to the Egyptian consulate to warn them.

At the time, the FBI informant—Salem—and the Egyptians' informant—Haggag—didn't know how much they had in common. Haggag, in fact, decided he didn't like this braggard Salem any better than he liked Siddig Ali.

The day after meeting with Haggag, Salem, wearing his hidden microphone, met with Siddig Ali in his Jersey City apartment. As an act of good faith, he brought along a timing device he'd bought in Chinatown. "It works by batteries," he explained.

"Yeah?" Siddig Ali watched him.

"I am showing you a very professional operation," Salem said of the eighteen-dollar gizmo he had purchased on Canal Street. "Once we attach this key to the first and last key, and you make a click on, the volt will reach the timer. The timer, you start it on sixty. . . ."

Once Siddig Ali seemed duly impressed with Salem's technical ability, Salem moved on with the plan. Rent an apartment, a safe house someplace where the members of this mission can meet, he told Siddig Ali. And create some kind of verbal code to keep the plot secret. Siddig Ali said he didn't want too many people to know yet. Salem badly wanted to find out who else Siddig Ali was counting on.

"I have a question. Are Palestinians among these people?" Salem asked.

"Yes."

"Are there Iraqis among these people?"

"Yes."

"If there are some Egyptians, it is not a problem."

"Not too many. There is one or two."

"No problem," Salem agreed.

"Only one," Siddig Ali offered.

"Who is he?"

"No need to tell."

Salem persisted. "I am thinking about a particular person. If you tell me his name, I'll tell you 'no need for him.'"

Siddig Ali didn't bite. "You don't know him."

And Salem backed off. "As I don't know him, I have nothing to do with him."

"Some Sudanese," Siddig Ali volunteered.

Palestinians, Iraqis, a few Egyptians—it sounded like the composition of Siddig Ali's paramilitary training group. The soldiers for Allah went to a rifle range in Pennsylvania where they all learned to shoot. Most believed they were preparing to fight for the Muslims in Bosnia. But that mission could change at any time.

Salem let the topic rest for a moment while they talked about other incidentals of bomb-making and Salem continued to brag about his expertise. "I have a question," Salem asked suddenly. "Will Mohammed Abouhalima be involved in this operation?"

"Yes," Siddig Ali said, and Salem pretended he didn't want to know any more about the involvement of Mahmud's brother. Because the FBI was watching Mohammed, it was dangerous to know too much. Salem made it clear he was protective of Abouhalima's family and wanted no one to know anything about Mohammed. "Do not mention it and do not bring it up," Salem responded. "For my sake, Siddig. I trust in God. I am doing that for the sake of the Lord."

Siddig Ali assured him of his loyalty to Mahmud's brother. "Listen, I love him very much. He was a member of our group. He was very good in training, especially his shooting."

Salem suggested dynamite for the operation, although the amount needed for such a big job might be hard to handle. Big orders of dynamite would draw suspicion. "We need big quantity," he told Siddig Ali.

"A ton?" Siddig Ali asked.

"No, not a ton," Salem replied, and decided to go fishing for information about the Trade Center. "With a ton you can destroy a huge building, especially if you put it on the cornerstone. . . . You are talking to an expert. If these children had put the bomb on the cornerstone of the World Trade Center, it would have been totally demolished. But they are ignorant. They didn't know exactly where to put it. They put it in the basement."

If Siddig Ali knew anything about the bombing, he didn't reveal it. So Salem kept talking. "Now, what is the purpose from getting the United Nations?"

"This is the world's government . . . who governs the world today."

"That is okay. That's it," Salem agreed heartily. "Your idea about the United Nations is an excellent idea."

"Now, we don't want to mention it by name, let us agree on a code name."

"Okay," Salem agreed again. "Give it a name."

"Any name. For example, Persjani. Or another name. How about *Al-bait al-kabir*?"

"*Al-bait al-kabir*," Salem repeated. The Big House. "With God's blessing."

The tapes left little question about Salem's veracity. He couldn't be suspected of exaggerating this time. It sounded like another wild plan, a lot of bravado and talk. But so had bombing the World Trade Center. The United Nations had an underground parking garage available only to UN staff and diplomats. But only a permit or diplomatic plates were needed to breach the security. Grandiose as Siddig Ali's plot seemed, no one was laughing it off at FBI headquarters.

Foiling potential terrorists and bringing a successful case against them wasn't an exercise the FBI had practiced much. Terrorist activity in the United States had been mostly domestic in origin, from the Weathermen radicals of the 1970s to the Puerto Rican liberation groups of the 1980s. By the end of the decade, most of those groups had been dismantled. From 1982 through 1986, there were 127 criminal acts the FBI considered terrorist-related. From 1987 to 1992, that number dwindled to thirty-eight. The FBI successfully monitored, infiltrated, and then arrested the domestic groups' members—occasionally after their bombs had gone off. The investigations began as intelligence-gathering operations, like what Salem was doing when he worked for Nancy Floyd.

"Terrorism is a hybrid," Anticev had told him. "It's half counter-intelligence rules, half criminal. And how to apply one from the other is still a gray area in the government. . . . Things can happen when you're doing an intelligence case. All of a sudden it turns immediately into a criminal case . . . and it could jeopardize people like yourself."

Anticev had no idea how prophetic he was. "You can be going along happily, you know, gathering intelligence. Then one day, *boom*, six hundred pounds of TNT is in place and ready to go. Immediately, everything changes."

Salem talked with his FBI contact daily, sometimes twice a day, and schooled him on how to proceed. They had to determine whether Siddig Ali's plan was serious, or merely grandiose talk. Salem had to focus on him. He had to be careful not to play too big a role, but let Siddig Ali call the shots. The FBI didn't want to risk Salem entrapping the conspirators—assuming Siddig Ali was not all talk. Entrapment is a defense that basically means a government agent has encouraged or persuaded someone to commit a crime that the person wouldn't have committed otherwise. Salem had to be careful not to seem as if he was talking Siddig Ali into the plot.

As details of the bombing became legendary among radical Arabs, it was hard to tell who actually knew something and who was simply pretending to know. Everyone *seemed* to know something about the blast, mostly what they'd heard somewhere else. Three days after the Big House meeting with Siddig Ali, Salem offered four men a ride to a late meeting at Jersey City's Al Salaam mosque. It was after 2:00 A.M., and he didn't know the men well. They all began talking about Salameh. Salem switched on his hidden recorder.

"When the bomb, when this thing happened . . . when he drove the van, he was not able to drive anyhow," one man was saying. "To take it from Jersey to Manhattan. . . . That is why I am not convinced Mohammad was driving the van. He made an accident with a small car. What could he do with a heavy van?"

The consensus in the car was that Salameh couldn't have driven the van. Salem pulled over and parked on the street below the mosque. "He couldn't drive, why did he drive a car?" Salem asked as he slammed the car door.

"I don't really know," the man continued. "He didn't have a car . . . he is not working, he has no money, he doesn't have a single penny. . . . When he said that he is going to rent a van, I was not convinced. I told them that Mohammad is not able to drive."

After the meeting, Salem walked to his car with the man and pressed him for more details. "Then you know how all this began?" The man nodded, but would say nothing else.

Late the next night, Salem wore his wire again when he met with the would-be bomber Siddig Ali in an apartment in the Crown Heights section of Brooklyn, above a karate school that Siddig Ali attended. They could meet secretly there. Salem brought with him several impressive-looking devices for detecting bugs on phone lines.

Siddig Ali was delighted with an apparatus Salem attached to the phone. It had a little green light that went on when the receiver was lifted, and if the green light went off, it meant the call was being tapped.

"What brand is it?" Siddig Ali asked.

"It is made in Germany."

"I'll take it. How much is it?"

"What are you talking about?"

"I mean, its price?"

"What price? There is no God but Allah," Salem said graciously.
"That's okay."

"There is no God but Allah," Salem persisted.

"Please!" Siddig Ali and he argued back and forth about his gift.
"We have a proverb in the Sudan," Siddig Ali told him. "It says,
'Eat like brothers, but you must settle the accounts like
merchants.' "

"Okay, no problem," said Salem, who billed the FBI for his expenses. "We don't settle any accounts because there is no account
between us."

Siddig Ali finally accepted. "In the name of God the Merciful, I
thank you."

Salem intended to find out if he was thankful enough to reveal
the name of the mysterious Egyptian and more of the UN plot.
While Siddig Ali served coffee, they talked about getting gunpowder and bullets. Siddig Ali said he had spoken that morning to a
man who would procure them. Salem said he had found them a
safe house in Queens, a house with a garage that they could rent
for one thousand dollars a month.

"I was able to make an arrangement with the man to avoid paying security. I told him, 'I'll stay one month with you and I'll leave.
I have no wife, no children. I don't know him and I don't want to
know him.' I didn't go to him like this, I disguised myself. I put on
a mustache and eyebrows and a wig, pair of glasses. . . . The way
I do my makeup is the same way I'll do when we go to the big
operation, which is the Big House."

"Is it a long or short trip?" Siddig Ali asked, returning to the
house.

"About forty-five minutes walking."

"Is it a quiet neighborhood?"

"Yes, very quiet. . . . We put our stuff there and we conduct our
meetings here."

"We'll learn what we're about to do. I want you to tell the brothers. Of course all the names will be changed. You assign each one
a different task. My task is to build the device."

They talked about the political dispute between Salem's homeland, Egypt, and Siddig Ali's Sudan; and they both cursed Mubarak. Mubarak had accused the Sudan's pure Islamic state of harboring terrorists and aiding the fundamentalists who were fighting to bring his government down.

"I would like to ask a question. Is Abdo Haggag one of us?" Salem asked.

"In this operation? No. He was trained in a similar operation. Everyone has different capacities. I am not talking physical strength."

"The strength of faith," Salem said.

"The strength, the courage, and the readiness to face death before life, and the love of God and his prophet Muhammad," Siddig Ali replied.

"For my sake, tell me who is the Egyptian man who is with us. You've told me before that most of us are Sudanese except one Egyptian. I fear this Egyptian."

"No, don't worry."

Salem pressed again. "I thought it is Mohammed Abouhalima, but no. I thought it was Abdo Haggag. You told me no. So who is he?"

"Don't worry."

"Okay." Salem gave up.

"This Egyptian—he is ready to fight and execute operations even if it takes his life. He is ready to be a martyr. We need an operation with the least number of losses, and this is very dangerous. . . . We need people who obey us blindly and without many questions."

"You're the prince," Salem said, acknowledging Siddig Ali's leadership. He apparently wasn't going to pry any names out of him.

"These things don't need consultation," Siddig Ali told him. That was Mahmud the Red's mistake, Siddig explained. He consulted with too many people on everything. "No one should know about this operation, not even him. And not Mohammed Abouhalima. Nobody. . . . In time, the people that I will choose will know, in time."

They agreed that each of them would come up with five hundred dollars to rent the Queens house. Siddig Ali said he wanted to time the Big House bombing with Mubarak's next visit to the United Nations, scheduled for September 1993, the same month the trial of Abouhalima and the other World Trade Center bombers was to start. "Although it's a long time from now," Siddig Ali added.

"Better to do it before the trial," Salem suggested.

Then Siddig Ali revealed he had a second operation in mind, an easier one, which they could pull off faster. "The defense association upstate," he said, referring to a gun range outside the city, operated by the Jewish Defense League.

"There are lots of Jews there?" Salem asked. "Sons of bitches, it will be the armed battle!"

Salem's enthusiasm must have encouraged Siddig Ali. "You know what else?" he offered.

"Snipers?" Salem suggested.

"Not there . . . in Manhattan." The target, he told Salem, was state assemblyman Dov Hikind, a Jew known for his vocal support of Israel and other Jewish causes.

"Dov Hikind," Salem repeated. Sayyid Nosair had targeted Hikind as well. "This was Sheik Sayyid's wish long ago."

Within days of that meeting, even before Salem's tape was translated from Arabic, the FBI notified the NYPD that it had received information that Dov Hikind could be in danger. Siddig Ali's grandiose plans were incredible, but the FBI wasn't taking any chances. Nosair's plot from his prison cell had sounded ludicrous, too—until his friends bombed the World Trade Center.

City detectives told Hikind and his wife on May 17 ,that they needed protection, and a squadron of bodyguards was placed around the frightened family. To protect the undercover operation, Hikind was officially told only that there had been reports of death threats; unofficially, law-enforcement sources told him it was connected to the World Trade Center bombing defendants.

The next evening, May 19, Salem and his wire were back at Siddig Ali's apartment, where they said their evening prayers together and shared a meal. Between praying and eating, Siddig Ali told Salem of yet another plan. He wanted an assault on 26 Federal Plaza in lower Manhattan, the headquarters of the FBI and the U.S. Attorney. He called it "the Center" and proposed that they kill the agents and take higher officials hostage to trade for the release of the defendants in the Trade Center case.

To prove it could be done, Siddig Ali had somehow gotten detailed diagrams of the building. To finance all his operations, Siddig Ali said he had a contact who could provide counterfeit money through sources in the Persian Gulf. Millions of counterfeit dollars were available, he explained.

"Okay, how much he wants to sell the million?" Salem asked.

"For one hundred and fifty thousand dollars."

"That is reasonable." Salem didn't ask where the terrorists, who were struggling to put together one thousand dollars just to rent the safe house, were going to get $150,000.

Siddig Ali seemed to anticipate his question. "Now we are finding that man who has the money," he told Salem. "He is a good guy."

"Is he a good Muslim?"

"He's as good as you are."

"Of course," Salem replied.

Siddig also said he had solved the dilemma of how to get the car bomb into the Big House. He had contacts at the Sudanese mission to the UN, he hinted. He could get his hands on a car with diplomatic plates.

"You're a dangerous man," Salem complimented him, laughing. He turned the subject to the sheik. "Did you ask Sheik Omar about the Big House operation?"

"Yes."

"What did he say?"

"He said it is a duty, it is a must."

"Okay, then I'll begin," Salem said, promising to start assembling the bomb components.

"But don't tell him anything," Siddig Ali quickly added.

"No, no, I won't even open the subject with him."

Salem had been trying unsuccessfully for weeks to get the sheik to incriminate himself on his tapes. Siddig Ali's admonishment against consulting him was going to be an obstacle. Salem would have to find a way around it if he was going to trap the sheik. Siddig Ali's talk alone wasn't enough.

As they ate dinner, Salem brought up the Trade Center bombing again. "I learned they originally wanted to bomb the Big House, and then it was changed to the World Trade Center."

"Yes, exactly."

"Why the World Trade Center?"

"The operation is to make them lose millions, and that is what happened. This is a message. We want to tell them that you are not far from us. We can get you anytime."

Siddig Ali explained that the Koran condoned violence in the holy war for Islam. "Victims from both sides, the enemy and the Muslims, is a must. The enemy, when they die, it is a good deed, and the Muslim, when he dies, it is the way to Heaven. He becomes a martyr. A Muslim will never go to hell by killing an infidel."

Salem wasn't there to debate Islamic theology. Many times he had told his FBI associates that he felt he had a duty to Islam to work against extremists who distorted his faith's true meaning. He could have pointed out to Siddig Ali that, so far, no Muslim martyrs had been made—or that many more Muslims interpreted the Koran as a message of peace that forbids the taking of innocent life. He had lashed out before against the "hypocrites" of Islam. Instead, he just finished dinner.

The next day, Siddig Ali gave Salem three hundred dollars to rent the safe house, and they made plans to visit their heroic comrade, Nosair, at Attica on Friday, their holy day. On this visit, Salem would be wearing a microphone. It was a difficult decision to make. The FBI had to advise the prison officials, risking the absolute secrecy they'd maintained so far. But they couldn't risk having Salem frisked and the wire discovered while Siddig Ali was standing by.

This time Salem wanted to wear the wire. He wanted to break this case. He tried to help the FBI understand the terrorists' frame of mind, why they were so committed to committing acts against the country where they had made their homes.

"They think that they assassinate the American nation by bombing American symbols. They think they are heroes," he explained. "The United States of America is the head of the snake. The Arab world is the tail of the snake. Israel is the tail. . . . Of course, they have a certain grudge against Egypt. But the main concern is the United States of America."

Salem wanted to be a hero, too. That Friday, Salem, Siddig Ali, and other associates of Nosair made the long drive to western New York, where Salem asked Nosair for guidance in their new operations. Nosair told him to trust in God and seek *istikharah*—spiritual consultation. Salem left Attica for the long ride back, with Nosair's directive that he consult the sheik.

The timing was becoming critical, though Salem didn't know it. The FBI, in its effort to protect Dov Hikind's safety, had traded off the safety of their informant. That weekend, reporters noticed the assemblyman's bodyguards. Hikind revealed that he was the target of an assassination plot, and that the plot was somehow linked to the World Trade Center bombers. When it hit the newspapers the following week, Salem's cover—and, he believed, his life—was in jeopardy.

A shaken Salem had breakfast with his ex-wife, Barbara Rogers, one morning, a few days after the news of Hikind's assassination threat hit the newspapers. The night before, he told her, he was sure he was a dead man. Siddig Ali heard the story on the news. He lined up Salem and several other men who knew about his plans for Hikind against a wall and put a revolver to each man's head. "Allah is going to tell us who the traitor is," Salem quoted Siddig.

Nobody confessed, and Siddig seemed willing to believe it was coincidence and not a leak. But Salem was furious at the FBI and considered dropping out.

It was early, just hours after midnight on Sunday morning, when Siddig Ali and Salem got an audience with the sheik in his apartment. They talked with the blind cleric about the plan to assassinate Mubarak, and told him that someone had leaked the plot. They also talked about Haggag; by now, Siddig Ali knew Haggag was accusing him. Salem told the sheik he needed consultation. During his Attica visit, Nosair had advised him to seek guidance on whether another matter was *haram,* or forbidden under Islamic law:

"With all due respect to Sheik Sayyid, I felt that God's blessings have greeted me and are with you, and I am struggling with this issue. Do we consider the United Nations to be a house of the devil because its actions result in destruction and not just obfuscation?

"We shall prepare a big thing," Salem continued. "A big thing, God willing, and let her have its fate. Is this action permitted by the Islamic fate we believe in, or is it *haram*?"

"It would not be *haram,* but it will muddy the waters for Muslims," the sheik replied.

"Do we do it or—"

"No," the sheik said flatly.

"We don't?"

"Find a pl . . . find a plan," the sheik began.

"Ah," Salem acknowledged.

"To inflict damage on the army, the American army, because the United Nations would harm Muslims, harm them tremendously."

"Then we don't do the United Nations?" Salem repeated.

"No."

"Something to the military?" Salem asked.

"Yes. Let it, let it—think of something else, because the United Nations will be considered as a center for peace."

"What about 26 Federal Plaza?"

"Well, a little bit later. We'll talk about this."

Salem told him that plans to strike FBI headquarters were already under way.

"It doesn't matter. Slow down. Slow down a little bit. The one who killed Kennedy was trained for three years. We don't want to do anything in haste."

Bingo, as Anticev would say.

"God bless you, Sheik," Salem answered. "God bless you, Sheik."

13

WITCHES' BREW

This time the FBI took Emad Salem seriously. Before the World Trade Center bombing, FBI supervisors had doubted his words, discarded him, and brushed aside his warnings that a terrorist attack was imminent. It was a deadly mistake, one that the government couldn't afford to make again. Now Salem was reporting that terrorists were planning another assault—this one far more shocking, brazen, and violent than the two-second blast that gutted the Trade Center. It would be a massive, devastating sneak attack on an unsuspecting American public—radical Islam's Pearl Harbor.

The plan Salem began reporting to the FBI in March and April 1993 called for a series of bombs, intended to blast various targets across the city, knock out transportation links, destroy crucial government office buildings and high-profile symbolic landmarks. In quick succession, the bombs would cripple major sections of New York's infrastructure and inflict casualties numbering in the hundreds or thousands.

One bomb would be planted on the George Washington Bridge, the engineering marvel that spans the Hudson River between New Jersey and upper Manhattan. If all went as planned, the blast would rip through the asphalt, steel girders, and cables, sending cars, pavement, and innocent commuters plunging into the river, more than one hundred feet below.

Two more would take out the Holland and Lincoln tunnels, which burrow beneath the Hudson River to connect lower Manhattan to New Jersey. Engineers say the underwater structures are built to withstand such a blast. But the bombers were counting on the explosives to smash through concrete walls. They hoped that the cracks in the tunnel would allow a torrent of Hudson River water into the structure, sweeping away civilians in a tidal wave of smoke, flames, and toxic fumes. Those three bombs, aimed at Manhattan Island's busiest links to the mainland, would isolate New York's nucleus. But the worst, bloodiest assaults were reserved for the city streets and skyscrapers.

The bombers had scouted out FBI headquarters in Federal Plaza and the United Nations building, the diplomatic community's global headquarters. Both would be blown up during business hours, when they were jammed with office workers and government officials. The bombers also planned to blow up symbolic targets, such as the Statue of Liberty, the world's most recognizable emblem of American liberty.

To settle an old score with their Israeli adversaries, the bombers also had saved one massive explosion for New York's midtown Diamond District, which is run and populated mainly by Hasidic Jews.

"Boom! Broken glass, dead Jews in the street," one of the bombers bragged.

Jihad's first major assault on U.S. soil would be a sweeping apocalyptic vision, surpassing Hollywood's most extravagant disaster films. If all went according to plan, the bombs would paralyze Manhattan, inflict a massive loss of human life, and exact a significant toll on the American psyche. Americans, who had for so long ignored the pleas of Islam's radical advocates, would now know that their complacency was a debt to be paid with blood. Even after the World Trade Center bombing, many Americans shrugged off the danger of terrorist assaults in the United States, and wrote off the attack as a fluke. The bombers had managed to kill six people, but they hadn't knocked down the building as planned. And the fact that Salameh was arrested while haggling for his four-hundred-dollar deposit made the bombers seem almost comical, a Middle Eastern Gang That Couldn't Bomb Straight.

This time the bombers aimed to erase any doubts about the radical Muslims' determination and capabilities. The television images of ravaged buildings, battered bodies, and weeping survivors would be broadcast around the globe. New York, the smug, mighty Mecca of Western power, would be hobbled by bomb craters and humbled by Jihad's wrath. America and all the world would instantly know the terrifying message the bombers were trying to send: We can get you any time.

Although FBI agents were startled by the brazen scope of the plot, this time they didn't hesitate to begin a full-scale sting operation. Salem was ordered to continue listening, gathering information and winning the trust of Siddig Ali and his assistants. When the plotters decided it was time to build their explosives, the agents instructed Salem to volunteer to find a suitable safe house and bomb factory. In late April, Salem led Siddig Ali and the others to a rundown neighborhood of Jamaica, Queens. He showed them a large building, somewhere between a big garage and a small warehouse, at 131-09 90th Avenue. And it was private, located on a block of abandoned buildings and industrial storage facilities.

The building also had a unique feature that Salem neglected to mention: it was wired. Unknown to the bomb builders, FBI agents had prepared the site by installing a hidden television camera. The camera, nestled in the rafters of the garage's ceiling, would provide agents with twenty-four-hour surveillance of the site, so the explosives would—literally—never leave the FBI's sight.

Siddig Ali and his crew leased the site beginning in mid-May, and began the work of assembling the explosives. The chemicals used in the Trade Center explosion had been difficult to obtain and dangerous to mix, so the second round of bombings would use a simple mixture of fuel oil and fertilizer. This type of explosive, known as ANFO, is a time-tested terrorists' recipe, and is even described in the radical instruction manual known as *The Anarchist's Cookbook,* first published in the early 1970s. All it requires is that pellets of fertilizer be mixed with the proper ratio of high-quality fuel oil, then ignited with a blasting cap or similar charge. It was less complex than the Trade Center explosives and, pound for pound, less powerful. But the ingredients were so easy to get that the bombers could build a greater number of bombs to make up for their lower firepower.

FBI agents watched patiently, allowing more and more of the sheik's followers to draw themselves into a web.

Siddig Ali and the second team of bomb makers also had learned an important lesson from the Trade Center bombers' mistakes. Salameh had been tracked down through a vehicle identification number. This time the bombers decided to use stolen cars to transport their explosives, and contracted with an experienced car thief, Victor Alvarez, to provide them with wheels. Alvarez, who was Latino, was an odd addition to the collection of Middle Eastern émigrés running the operation, so he was given a whimsical code name, "Mohammed the Spanish."

They contacted Clement Rodney Hampton-El, an African-American Muslim from Brooklyn, who had fought in Afghanistan and injured his leg by stepping on a land mine. Hampton, who worked in the kidney dialysis unit of a local hospital, said his mujahedeen connections could provide hand grenades, Uzis, and fully assembled bombs, according to what Salem told the FBI. Salem offered to produce a timing device, as a show of good faith, and provided Siddig Ali with a timer given to him by the FBI. But by late May, the FBI agents grew worried about the timer, and their jitters nearly derailed the entire investigation. After the World Trade Center disaster, FBI officials were wary of allowing the bombers access to a timer, even one under the watch of twenty-four-hour television surveillance. What if the plotters somehow managed to sneak it out and detonate a bomb? FBI officials decided to play it safe. They replaced the functioning timer with an inoperative decoy. That way, even if the bombers did somehow elude the Bureau, their bombs wouldn't blow.

The trouble was, their decoy didn't match the original timer, and the difference was visible to the naked eye. Salem saw the new timer on May 29, and was furious. If Siddig Ali or the other bombers detected the switch, they might suspect that Salem had changed it, and if that happened, Salem would be a deceased informant. He blasted John Anticev for allowing the switch. Anticev explained that the agents had to keep the device safe, and suggested that Salem tell Siddig Ali that he'd switched the timer himself. Salem grew indignant.

"I cannot," he said.

"Why not?" Anticev asked.

"Because if he gets mad at me and he feels I'm playing games behind his back, I'm the one who will be killed."

Salem had called Anticev a few hours before he was scheduled to meet Siddig and four other plotters at the safe house. He demanded that the FBI replace the timer; if they didn't, Salem said he'd tell Siddig Ali he was being followed by government agents and drop out of the plot.

"It's under the camera twenty-four hours. It's under your own eyes," Salem said, dismissing Anticev's worries about the timer. He stopped, cleared his throat, then continued, "If you don't trust your own agents, that's a different story."

After two months inside the cell, Salem had no doubt about the bombers' willingness to kill. He had heard Siddig Ali talk about suicide missions and murders and nonchalantly describe bombs that had wiped out hundreds of innocent bystanders. There was no way Emad Salem was going to do anything to raise his suspicions.

"If this guy is talking with that mentality, he can do me in a split second," Salem said. "And then you will charge him with a homicide, but I will be in a casket."

Anticev paused.

"All right. Let me get hold of Louie, and I'll see if I can get it for today's meeting."

A few minutes later, Anti-Terrorist Task Force agent Louis Napoli called back. Napoli offered to send an agent to return the timer, but he needed to know where to put it. Salem told him to lay it flat on the table, to the extreme right.

"It's on its way," Napoli said.

"Thank you very much," Salem replied.

"Okay. Lots of luck," Napoli said as he hung up.

As the plot progressed, Salem grew increasingly aware of how much the FBI depended on him, and he decided it was time to use his leverage. Before the Trade Center bombing, agents had tried to penny-pinch him. If Salem was to reap any reward for putting his life on the line for the FBI, he knew he'd better negotiate it soon. On June 11, when Napoli asked Salem to meet with Assistant U.S. Attorney Gil Childers, Salem decided it was time to cut himself a deal, and force the FBI to commit itself to a firm dollar figure.

"It's getting too much to me! It is no work anymore. It is finished!" Salem said, again threatening to leave the investigation and doom the FBI's case.

"Why do you keep saying these things?" Napoli said, trying to calm him. "Emad, trust us. Believe me, we're not hanging you out to dry."

Salem exploded. "No! I don't want to meet with anybody! I'm not selling potatoes here."

"I know. You're selling your life here, mister."

"I'm sorry, Louie, I'm sorry to be screaming."

"I know what you're going through. Let me call. This way if they do go into negotiations, you wind up with what you want anyway."

Salem wasn't about to let the FBI off that easily. He gave Napoli a not-so-subtle reminder of his fragile health, to let the agent imagine what the case would be like without Salem's help.

"I feel a pain in my chest. I'm not feeling well right now," Salem said.

"All right, listen. Do you want me to go to a million five? And then, if there's a negotiation, you can bring it down?"

"No. There is no negotiation."

"All right. Do you want me to just give them a total and tell them there's no negotiating it?"

"Absolutely," Salem said, his heart palpitations having apparently subsided.

"All right. That's just what I'll do."

Less than a year after FBI officials had balked at Salem's price tag of five hundred dollars a week, they now agreed to pay him $1.5 million. What a difference a bomb makes.

Unlike the World Trade Center investigation, which was a desperate attempt to recover from the FBI's grievous early miscalculations, the second investigation ran so smoothly it almost seemed choreographed. Expensive though he might be, Salem had burrowed so deep into the cell that when it came time for the actual arrests, the scene seemed more like a dress rehearsal than an actual police raid.

It was early on the morning of June 23. Inside the safe house, twelve of the plotters were mixing the fuel and fertilizer, wearing white coveralls and stirring the chemicals with long wooden spatulas. Dozens of FBI agents surrounded the garage, wearing windbreakers and bulletproof vests. Sharpshooters were stationed on rooftops and behind cars to provide cover. When the agents decided to move, there was no need to kick down the door, because Salem had left it unlocked. There was no need to track the plotters across the globe because they were standing there, spatulas in hand, on videotape, mixing the explosives. A line of agents filed silently in the door, stood next to the bombers, and handcuffed them without a struggle. Siddig Ali and Haggag were directing the operation, as three other men dutifully helped to mix the witches' brew.

The raid went so smoothly that it raised a troubling question: Why hadn't the World Trade Center bombing investigation ended this way? If FBI agents had listened to Salem the first time, maybe they could have set up the safe house, the video cameras, and the arrests. If FBI agents had paid more attention to the evidence seized at Nosair's home in 1990—if they had translated the bomb formulas and sermons and threats to blow up American buildings—maybe they would have realized the deadly seriousness of their plans. And maybe, then, the World Trade Center bombers would have been arrested this easily, before their explosion took six lives.

Despite his repeated requests to Anticev and Napoli, Salem was also handcuffed by the agents who filled the garage. Instead of being taken to prison with the rest of the bombers, however, he was taken to the hospital because he felt ill, short of breath, and faint. Emad Salem, Egyptian commando turned macho bodyguard and fearless informant, was suffering a panic attack.

After a few hours in the hospital, Salem was released, and FBI agents prepared to place him in the Federal Witness Protection Program. He would be given a false identity and moved to a guarded, secret location, so no one could harm him before he had a chance to testify. Salem asked for one last visit to his Upper West Side apartment, to gather a few things before he went into hiding. Somehow, without his FBI escorts noticing, Salem managed to call Egypt and leave a message for a contact in the Egyptian intelligence community. He told them about the arrests, and that he was now headed underground. The Egyptians' biggest concern, Sheik Omar Abdel-Rahman, was still at large, but Salem advised his contact that the circle was closing.

"The matter is under research to arrest Sheik Omar Abdel-Rahman," Salem said. "I don't know when I'll be able to call you again, but I'll do my best."

* * *

Ed Smith no longer could remember what happened to him in the days and weeks after Monica had died. The swarms of people at the wake, the return to Ecuador—it had fled from his mind. He had brought home from Ecuador a statue of the Virgin of Montserrat and created a little shrine with the icon and Monica's picture. He burned candles. Every night, she had prayed to the Virgin, who had protected sailors from a dangerous voyage out of port. The still photographs from the sonogram of their developing son were on the mirror in the bedroom, where Monica had taped them. He had plans to go to Ecuador, to visit the Rodriguez family and Monica's grave. She was buried in an aboveground vault. Every day, her father went to the site, polishing the stone, tending the plot.

"You're putting all this money into it—for what?" someone had asked Monica's dad about his lavishment on the tomb.

"If I could do it in gold, I would do it—it's my daughter," he said.

They were retired people, and Ed was thirty-one years old, and as much as he was with them in spirit, he could not build his life around a marker in a cemetery. He returned to Long Island and went back to work, and found that people who barely knew him went out of their way to offer him an evening out. He hit the road, viciously. Anything to avoid the empty house. The nature of sales is that you know a lot of people and a little personal information about each of them. Not much information. Not close. Inevitably, people who hadn't seen him for a few months would ask: Hey, when's the baby coming?

One of his customers reached him on the phone in a rage.

"I been calling you for a month, you didn't call me back, what's the matter with you?" he asked Smith.

"To tell you the truth, I took the last month or so off," said Ed. "I'm really sorry, I'll take care of you now."

"There's no excuse, Jesus Christ, I've got a business to run, and you're letting me down—you can't do that to people," said the customer.

"I know, I know," said Ed, quietly. "I'm sorry."

"It is unacceptable," said the customer. "By the way, why did you take that month off?"

"My wife passed away."

"Oh," said the customer. "I'm sorry. What happened?"

Ed explained about Monica working in the basement of the Trade Center.

"I feel terrible," said the customer. He paused. "But that's still no excuse!"

That night, Ed came home, shaking his head in amusement at such world-class boorishness. He switched on the news. The police and the FBI were announcing that they had foiled another plot by Muslim fundamentalists to bomb the tunnels around New York City, the Statue of Liberty, and the George Washington Bridge.

Ed catapulted back into the haze from which he had been rising. The next morning, he did not go to work. It wasn't a decision. When the sun came up, he just didn't leave the house. He stayed inside for the weekend.

Trying to get their point across for Allah. Bullshit. Someone was paying them, and they were hiding behind the robe. What God would want people to die?

14

MARTYRS IN WAITING

Inside the Abu Bakr mosque in Brooklyn, Sheik Omar's faithful were preparing to become martyrs. The mosque, a muscular brick row house, was surrounded by dozens of FBI investigators, police detectives, and immigration agents—all heavily armed—who had come to arrest the sheik. Behind the wooden police barricades, which read POLICE LINE DO NOT CROSS, nearly a dozen TV crews circulated among the throng of neighborhood residents who'd turned out to marvel at the commotion. Several crowds of Hasidim came to revel in Sheik Omar's downfall, chanting "Go to hell!" and "We come to see Satan!" At the door of the mosque, twenty Muslims stood guard, with the foreboding posture of men concealing sidearms.

The siege had brought life on Foster Avenue to a standstill on July 2, 1993. After wrangling over legalities for weeks, federal officials had finally decided to arrest Sheik Omar, Islam's most visible leader since Iran's Ayatollah Khomeini. Now the world waited to see whether the blind cleric would surrender peacefully or try to resist the overwhelming fire-power amassed outside.

Sheik Omar wasn't the type of fellow to go down easily. By late June, press accounts and increased FBI presence in the Egyptian community made it clear that the law was closing in. He took sanctuary in Abu Bakr late on July 1, knowing that the Feds would be reluctant to barge into a house of worship. Then, early the next morning, as dozens of INS agents surrounded the mosque, a burgundy-colored minivan pulled up. Out of the mosque walked a bearded man wearing a white robe and the sheik's signature red cap. A Muslim guided the man to the van, opened the front passenger-side door, and helped him into the seat. Before the van could pull away, more than a dozen INS agents dashed toward the vehicle, guns drawn, and ordered the man out of the vehicle. They ordered him up against the van, so they could frisk him. As the bearded man stood and placed his hands up against the van's side panel, the agents knew they'd been fooled. On the man's arm was a digital watch, an accessory that would have little place on the wrist of a blind man.

Unfortunately for the sheik and his followers, they'd used the old "decoy sheik" trick one time too many. It had worked several months earlier, when Abdel-Rahman managed to slip the FBI surveillance team that had been following him. This time the mosque was surrounded by so many cops, detectives, and agents that he could send out twenty phony sheiks, and there'd still be a small army waiting to take the authentic imam into custody. So the standoff at Abu Bakr dragged through the morning, and with each passing hour the mood inside the mosque grew more desperate. About forty of Sheik Omar's closest followers were gathered inside to stand by their leader in his most trying hour. The sheik spent the morning upstairs, huddling with his lawyer and several advisers. At about 3:30 P.M., they broke to say afternoon prayers.

Now, at 4:00 P.M., it was clear that prayer alone would not resolve the situation, so the sheik's devotees offered a more tangible sacrifice: their lives.

"If they come in, we must fight to the death," said Usama Toobi, an adviser at the mosque. "They have no right to come into our holy place. We cannot allow them to desecrate Islam any further. We will fight them to the death."

Michael Warren—the Muslim attorney who had defended Sayyid Nosair in the Kahane shooting—was summoned to advise the sheik. The lawyer could feel the situation taking on its own momentum, hurtling out of control. Warren had been through standoffs with civil rights protesters and various Muslim organizations, but never had he felt such a sense of imminent bloodshed. As he looked around the room, he was startled by the anger and determination of his brother Muslims. They viewed their lives as an uninterrupted series of slights—from Middle Eastern governments, the American government, the Western media—yet nothing had prepared them for the indignities of the past six months. Ever since the bombing, it seemed that all of Islam was on trial. Muslims on the street were jeered by the public, questioned repeatedly by FBI agents, and harassed by the local police. The mosque was their only refuge, and the thought of federal agents invading this last stronghold stoked an irrational streak of protectiveness. Warren knew the mosque would be tense, but he hadn't expected this kind of despondency. "This smells like death," he thought to himself.

"Brothers, brothers, please," Warren pleaded. "Let us think carefully before we act. I understand your feelings. Your anger. Your outrage. And you're right—we *are* doing Allah's work. But don't let them draw us into a battle when they're prepared. Let us choose the time and place to fight. We can strike when *we're* prepared."

The commotion died down momentarily, but one of the worshipers now challenged Warren.

"How can you say that?" asked a man by the sheik's side, his voice growing angry. "Are you saying we should just stand by while they destroy our holy place? The Koran says we should fight to protect Allah's messengers, and that anyone who dies in this fight will immediately be accepted into the arms of Allah. Is this not the time for such a fight? If this does not meet the standards for such a fight, then tell me, brother, what does? What else possibly could?"

"Yes, yes, you're right," Warren said, thinking of the federal sharpshooters he had seen across Foster Avenue, with their high-powered rifles and precision scope sights. There might be a weapon or two in the mosque, but it would take the Prophet Muhammad himself, leading a squadron of fully armed mujahedeen, to tangle with the forces outside. "But if we fight now, some of us won't be around to fight another day. We will need you. Every one of you. We haven't got a single life to spare."

Sheik Omar stood to speak. The mosque grew so silent that the men could hear the faint chatter of police radios outside.

"There will be time," he said. "But, my dear friends, it is not here quite yet."

Omar was quite comfortable living in the crosshairs of hostile government gunmen. He had been there for most of his adult life.

But in the days after the Trade Center bombing arrests, the U.S. government began pressuring Sheik Omar, too, placing him and his followers under surveillance. Two of the main suspects—Salameh and the Red—were devoted followers of the sheik, and this roused the FBI. There was no evidence linking the sheik to the bombing. Still, agents followed him for weeks. Then, in late June, federal agents raided a garage in Queens, where men were mixing a witch's brew of explosives to bomb an assortment of New York City bridges, tunnels, and landmarks. This time the suspects included some of the sheik's closest advisers—even Abdo Haggag, his driver, cook, and interpreter.

Federal prosecutors searched desperately for evidence that would allow them to charge Sheik Omar. Once again, the sheik kept close enough to inspire the plotters, but just far enough away that he didn't leave fingerprints. He was the mufti, or spiritual adviser, not a terrorist organizer. So when the plotters, and government informant Emad Salem, asked Sheik Omar's approval for the plan, he replied with mystical generalities—a spiritual leader guiding his followers through difficult dilemmas of conscience.

The FBI agents were convinced they had enough to make a case, but the lawyers weren't so sure. A dispassionate reading of the facts left Justice Department officials frustrated. The tapes contained a lot of suspicious statements by Sheik Omar, but no "smoking guns." To average Americans watching CNN in their living rooms, the case was already infuriatingly clear. You didn't have to read very far between the lines to see what he and his friends were referring to. Why was the government waiting? These guys were caught mixing up explosives, and videotaped talking about their attacks, and the sheik told them it was permissible—why didn't the FBI just hurry up and arrest him? Public sentiment intensified after the discovery of the Queens garage, as the scope of the plot made Americans feel threatened and edgy. So it didn't take long for the politicians to rush to the front of the parade.

Elizabeth Holtzman, the New York City comptroller, wrote to the Justice Department, demanding that Sheik Omar be taken immediately into custody. Never mind that the allegations against the sheik had absolutely nothing to do with Holtzman's job, which is to balance the city's books. For days, mainstream politicians seemed unable to make it through a speech without invoking the word *pogrom,* and accusing Abdel-Rahman of a genocidal crusade against Jews. Republican senator Alfonse D'Amato was particularly shrill. He seemed to represent the vast audiences of talk radio, indulging whatever streetcorner bandwagon of bias and wisdom came his way and seemed sturdy enough for him to climb atop. D'Amato couldn't let an issue this emotional pass without turning it into a public crusade. He held press conferences, met with other legislators, and ferociously lobbied U.S. Attorney General Janet Reno to arrest the sheik. If nothing else, he could be detained for entering the country under false pretenses: the sheik had not revealed that he had been twice married under circumstances that suggest bigamy, and he had also bounced checks from time to time. His failure to disclose these facts to the border police wasn't exactly the biggest crime in the world, but it was something.

Even the Egyptians were pushing the United States to collar the sheik. Egypt wanted to retry him on a 1989 charge of leading a violent antigovernment demonstration. Egyptian foreign minister Amr Moussa met with U.S. Ambassador Robert Pelletreau, and asked that Abdel-Rahman be detained—even though the only extradition treaty between the two countries dated back to the Ottoman Empire and had never been tested.

The FBI, however, wanted the sheik to remain free. FBI director Jim Fox argued with Justice Department officials that the sheik was a "magnet" who attracted Muslims with evil intentions. His blindness made it impossible for him to build or plant any bombs himself. Why not leave him on the street, then, under intense surveillance, so that agents could watch the unsavory characters who came to him for guidance? The newspapers had forced FBI officials to arrest Salameh and company prematurely, Fox argued, so please don't let the politicians do it to us this time.

But Reno had pressures of her own. From the day she took office, the Attorney General had been watched by an army of critics just waiting for her to falter. Republicans had controlled Washington for twelve years before Bill Clinton took office in January 1993, so they were not pleased to watch him and his wife bring a whole generation of liberal Democrats into the Cabinet. The media and the Washington establishment suspected Reno was too soft, too inexperienced, and too liberal to run Justice, so the law-enforcement old boys' network wasn't about to give her any breaks.

To make matters worse, Reno had stumbled badly in April, with her handling of an armed standoff with an unusual religious cult in Waco, Texas. The cult leader, David Koresh, had holed up in a compound with his followers for a month, after shooting it out with agents from the Bureau of Alcohol, Tobacco and Firearms. When Reno ordered the FBI to move in with tanks, Koresh and his followers set the compound afire, killing 79 people. Reno faced brutal criticism for approving the raid. She also won acclaim for accepting the blame for the deadly fiasco. Now she was besieged by politicians and the public at large, people who wanted only one thing: Sheik Omar Abdel-Rahman behind bars.

Legally, it was a close call. Some of the tapes, secretly recorded by Emad Salem, suggested that Sheik Omar might have guided the plotters as they decided what to attack. He obliquely suggested that military targets would be a wiser choice than public places, because an attack that killed civilians would turn public opinion against Muslims. Was he steering them, or was he merely trying to stall the hotheads long enough for them to cool down?

It was clear that the sheik knew these men were planning some act of devastating violence, but he did nothing to stop them. His words could be read as offering encouragement. But the law said he could only be charged as a co-conspirator if he committed an "overt act," and his words appeared to fall considerably short of that standard. Sheik Omar hadn't driven the trucks or scouted the buildings. He hadn't told his followers to bomb anything. He was merely a spiritual adviser tending to his flock.

What if a group of Dubliners came to ask a Catholic bishop if it was ethical to support the IRA? How would Christians react if the bishop were locked up? But abstract concepts like due process and freedom of worship can't always survive a political firestorm. Eventually, Reno caved in. Maybe there wasn't enough evidence to charge Sheik Omar as a conspirator, but there was nothing to prevent the government from using a different law. Reno's staff attorneys found an arcane statute that would allow them to charge him with nothing less than sedition—advocating the overthrow of the government of the United States. The law had been written in 1866, to prosecute renegade Confederate soldiers who fought on after the end of the Civil War. The government had succeeded in winning sedition cases only once in five attempts. The sedition law didn't require evidence that Sheik Omar ever handled nitroglycerin, or had even a supervisory role. It was enough that he had spoken belligerently against the government of the United States, and that he had called for its overthrow. Many legal scholars felt that sedition was, at its most basic, a thought crime. But it was enough to allow Reno to arrest Sheik Omar, put the public at ease, and stop Al D'Amato from pestering her.

After refusing for weeks to indict the sheik, Reno announced on July 1 that investigators had uncovered "additional evidence" against him and that she had ordered his arrest. Now all they had to do was get him into custody, preferably without spilling blood in Abu Bakr mosque.

So, as the standoff on Foster Avenue dragged into the afternoon of July 2, Michael Warren managed to calm the sheik's followers and spur negotiations for the sheik's surrender. Speaking to the federal agents by telephone, Warren had convinced them that the sheik wanted to be accompanied by his lawyer and taken to an INS detention center in New Jersey, near his friends and relatives. Warren also wanted assurances that the angry mobs of Hasidim wouldn't be allowed anywhere near the sheik.

"Those people want him dead," Warren said. "If the government lets them near my client, the consequences for everyone will be grave."

At about 4:30 P.M., the agents agreed to cordon off part of the street to keep the crowd away from Sheik Omar.

"All right," Warren told them. "Just give us a few minutes."

The sheik sat quietly for several moments when he heard that a deal had been struck. Then he walked slowly downstairs to the room where his followers were waiting.

"We are ready to fight for you!" came a shout.

"No, no," he said. "Not yet. That is not what is necessary now."

He led the men in a short prayer, and several worshipers broke into tears. When the prayer ended, the sheik held up his hand and bade them farewell.

"My friends, I might not stand before you again," he said. "Allah Akhbar! God is great!"

With that, Sheik Omar opened the door. A cry rose from the crowd.

"Go to hell! Go to hell! Go to hell!" chanted a group of Hasidim, shaking their fists wildly at the sheik.

"God is great! God is great! God is great!" screamed the Muslims, as they formed a human shield to protect the sheik.

"Drop dead! Drop dead!" yelled the Hasidim, as Sheik Omar walked down the steps of the mosque and made his way down the street. "God is merciful! God is merciful!" the Muslims screamed as they watched their leader seated in an FBI van, then driven off through the Brooklyn streets.

PART THREE
JUDGMENT

15

PRISON BLUES

For all his fierce appearance, it was Mahmud Abouhalima who came the closest of all the bombers to cracking once he was arrested. Hard-core guerrilla warrior, yes. Blabbermouth? Absolutely. While he was incarcerated, Abouhalima talked about the bombing itself, as well as about his own worries and schemes. A picture of a terrorist emerges from statements he made under duress to Egyptian interrogators, then in the company of a surprisingly companionable New York City detective, later to two cellmates, and finally to the attorneys to whom he entrusted his case. While the jury and the public heard virtually none of his accounts, Abouhalima's discussions about the case provide the first glimpse inside the bomb plot—and, to a lesser degree, inside the mind of a bomber.

*   *   *

It was an oppressively humid August day, and the emotions inside the Nine South cell block were as turbulent as the clouds churning across the sky outside the barred window of Abouhalima's cell. For Abouhalima and the rest of his gamaii the television news blaring through the common area of the top-security wing was devastating. Sheik Omar, their spiritual leader, who had been jailed last month on immigration charges, had been indicted for sedition. He was accused of providing the spiritual incentive to commit acts of terrorism. Not only that, but Nosair, Mahmud's idol and friend, had been charged with actually guiding the conspiracy to blow up the United Nations.

Abouhalima quietly closed the door to his eight-by-eight-foot cell, but he couldn't block out the monotonous voice of the television newsman. While he sat on the dingy pink metal desk that was bolted to the cinder-block wall, guards watched as Abouhalima buried his face in his hands. How could his plans have gone so badly awry? He had fallen out with the sheik, but he'd never wanted to see the blind holy man jailed. The Trade Center bombing, the television reporter was saying, was listed as an underlying act in the charge against Nosair. Abouhalima had wanted to help Nosair, not mire him in a terrorist conspiracy.

At that moment the claustrophobia of Nine South—the ninth-floor unit at the Metropolitan Correctional Center reserved for the most notorious prisoners—was unbearable. Unlike other federal prisons and detention centers, which tend to be built in remote areas where land and labor are cheap, MCC was constructed in lower Manhattan, one of the most densely populated areas in the country. As a consequence, instead of a sprawling compound, the Bureau of Prisons commissioned a thirteen-story high-rise—a building without a common eating room and no grassy recreation yard where inmates could exercise or just simply stand with an unobstructed view of the sky. The only concession to the human spirit at all is a fenced-in basketball court on the roof. And after an attempted breakout in 1988, when a team of drug dealers bearing automatic weapons and wire-cutters tried to liberate their jailed leader by landing a helicopter on it, the building was strung with orange anti-helicopter devices. Being at MCC is more like being confined to a hospital than to a prison. Except that no one gets better at MCC. The best a prisoner can hope for is an acquittal.

Abouhalima stared out his slender window. He had been so hopeful when he arrived here. After Egypt, MCC had looked like a country club to him. He cocked his head and tried to block out the blaring television and the noises of other men on the tier. He could hear Salameh beginning to wail from the tier below him. He must have just heard the news about the sheik and Nosair.

Abouhalima still had family in Egypt. The news of the sheik's indictment would certainly mean more bloodshed there. Since the blind cleric had been taken into custody, fellow militants had grown bold in their proclamations, promising that the West would pay if any harm befell Sheik Omar. Now the U.S. government wasn't simply threatening to deport him; he had been charged with sedition—a little-used provision in the law that did not require the government to prove that Sheik Omar had participated in a bombing but that he had merely helped the revolutionary effort in any way. The penalty, if he was found guilty, could be life in prison. Surely this news would lead to riots in the streets of Cairo.

Abouhalima had told men on his tier all about what he had confessed to the Egyptians. He admitted to them that he felt bad about talking, but after all, he pointed out repeatedly, who among them could withstand torture? He couldn't remember everything he had said, but now, he told the others, he was worried that some small admission he might have made to end the blinding pain had caused the sheik and Nosair to be indicted.

At dawn on March 14, Abouhalima had been sleeping in his father's house in Kafr-el-Diwar, on the Nile Delta, when the military secret police surrounded the modest building. They'd pulled him out of bed, handcuffed him, and pulled a sack over his head before throwing him into a waiting jeep. They'd driven him to a military facility about twenty-five miles away. For Abouhalima, the facility became the House of Pain.

What happened to him next was standard treatment of Muslim extremists by the Egyptian military authorities. But unlike other prisoners, Abouhalima was wanted by the Americans. And that fact ultimately saved his life.

His captors tied a rag around his eyes, and stripped him naked. He was questioned and beaten, but Abouhalima would tell them nothing. He was a tough one, but his captors knew from experience what made strong men weak. They left him alone in a steel cell, naked, blindfolded, and without sanitary facilities, for over twenty-four hours. They left him alone to battle all the horrors his imagination could conjure. Then they began round two.

His interrogators beat his hands and feet with clubs and boards.

The plot to blow up the Trade Center, Abouhalima told them, had been conceived and planned by Islamic extremists. Two men who'd identified themselves as Iranian intelligence had shown up in a Pakistani city near the Afghan border, Peshawar, to approve the plan. They wanted to punish the United States for interfering in Middle Eastern affairs.

The Egyptian security goons strung wires from a hand-cranked generator to his genitals and blasted him with electricity.

Two men who spoke Farsi, the Iranian language, had come to New York a few months before the bombing to organize the plot, Abouhalima told them. Mohammad Salameh was one of the men they'd recruited. Later, two Iraqi men had shown up. All four had fled the United States following the explosion. Then Abouhalima blacked out.

Ignoring the second-degree burns on his genitals from the electricity, his interrogators revived him by putting cigarettes out on this sensitive area. The largest of his interrogators threatened to rape him.

Abouhalima confessed to being a member of Gama al-Islamiya, the outlawed organization dedicated to the overthrow of Hosni Mubarak's secular government. The money for the World Trade Center bomb, Abouhalima said, came from funds that Gama al-Islamiya had collected from wealthy Iranian industrialists and fundamentalist expatriates living in Europe. The money had been wired through Munich, Abouhalima told them, by a handful of sympathetic members of the Muslim Brotherhood, a seventy-year-old international organization known for sponsoring schools, clinics, and youth organizations.

Filthy and caked with blood and excrement, Abouhalima had his hands and feet tied to a board, and he was left to hang, like a slab of meat, until his tendons stretched and burned and he begged for relief. He wept for his fallen friend Shalabi, who had died, he said, at the sheik's insistence. His tormentors were unimpressed with reports of the sheik's squalid murders, and warned him that Egyptian soldiers were setting out for Kafr-el-Diwar to kill his brother and father and rape his wife, unless he revealed to them the role Sheik Omar had played in the bombing. Over and over, Abouhalima repeated that he could not tell them what he did not know. Instead, hoping to play on his captors' anti-Israeli sentiments, he described his own role in the slaying of Meir Kahane.

Unmoved, his interrogators beat him again, hitting him in the head with boards; weeping and weary, Abouhalima could tell them nothing else. The information he'd given, gathered over ten days of torture, was passed along to intelligence experts who fanned out through the Middle East, checking the accuracy of Abouhalima's confession.

All of what he'd told them was basically true, they concluded. Torture does have a way of cutting through lies. Abouhalima, still blindfolded and naked in his cell, shivered and prayed to God that the people he had implicated were smart enough to have gone into hiding when they heard that he had been arrested. He prayed to God that he could withstand more pain.

Then, unexpectedly, the torture stopped.

Exhausted, hurting, blindfolded, and chained at the wrists and ankles, Abouhalima was taken from his dark, filthy cell and thrown on the floor of a windowless jeep. Two goons from the Egyptian military police, the same ones who had jeered as he screamed, climbed into the jeep behind him. Abouhalima feared the worst. It was March 23, but he had no way of knowing it. After all the beatings, the cigarette burns, the hanging, and the threats, this is the way it ends, he thought, as the jeep bumped along the dirt road.

He imagined his desiccated corpse being discovered months from now, still handcuffed, on the side of some rarely traveled path. He would join the thousands and thousands of other opponents of Hosni Mubarak who had been silenced by a bullet. He began a wordless prayer to Allah. He tried to put his fear behind him and rejoice. He was about to become a martyr.

Those men of influence who had helped him with his glorious plan would know what he had done. They would count him among the true believers, the ones who had died so that Jihad could be victorious. His sons, seven-year-old Abdallah, two-year-old Khaled, and little Ibrahim, would grow up singing his praises. Their sons and his grandsons would take strength from the fact that they came from the mighty Abouhalima line, that their veins flowed with Mahmud's Crusader blood.

He tried to take a deep breath, but his captors had stuffed gauze into his nose. He hoped his fellow soldiers would never learn about his confession. He hoped the Egyptian army would kill him before he had to face the men he had given up after more than a week of unending pain.

He felt the jeep stop, and his heart began to race. This is where it all ends, he thought, over and over. He squinted his eyes under the bandage that covered his head, trying to hear the sound of a gun safety being released.

But instead the two goons lifted him by his bruised arms and threw him onto the heat-softened tarmac. He heard other voices arguing. What were they saying? The airplane? Maybe he was on a runway. Where was he going? Could it be that he was being returned to the United States?

The goons half-carried, half-dragged him up a ramp. He stumbled over a shin-high threshold. It *was* an airplane! Then he heard two men speaking clear, nasal New York English. He was going back to America! The engines started and began to whine as the plane started down the runway.

Once they were safely in the air, Abouhalima felt the manacles on his ankles being released. Then he felt hands, not punching and hitting and twisting his ears and testicles, but carefully unwinding the filthy gauze that covered his head. Abouhalima was afraid to move until the sleep mask that had been placed over his eyes as a blindfold was lifted. As soon as his eyes adjusted to the light, he saw the familiar drooping features of Louis Napoli, a detective from the Anti-Terrorist Task Force, the same man who had questioned him after the Kahane killing in 1990. Behind him stood three other men—FBI agents. Napoli surveyed Abouhalima's swollen face and cracked lips.

"You want a cigarette?" he asked. Abouhalima was so grateful for a kind word after spending ten days in an Egyptian torture chamber that he almost wept with gratitude. He accepted the cigarette, a vice he had valiantly kept hidden from his Muslim brothers. Smoking violates the prohibitions of the Koran. But today, every inhalation was a simple reminder that he was alive.

The two men smoked in silence.

"You have the right to remain silent," Napoli murmured in a monotone. "You have the right to an attorney."

When he finished, Napoli showed Abouhalima where to rest, and then sat down a few seats away. For a few moments he simply stared at Abouhalima. He didn't rush to fill the silence. He was a patient, deliberate man, and experience had taught him that the best way to extract information is to be ready to listen. Abouhalima asked for food, and Napoli directed one of the crew members to produce a tray. It was standard airline fare, but Abouhalima ate it as if it were a feast especially prepared for him.

"Tell me," said Napoli, as they enjoyed a post-dinner cigarette, "what do you know about Panrapo?" He made the Indian name sound like an Italian entree.

Abouhalima, feeling expansive from his first good meal in over a week, set the detective straight.

"*Pam*-rapo," said Abouhalima, correcting Napoli's pronunciation.

Napoli didn't react. Abouhalima had made his first mistake. He had admitted knowledge of the location of the bomb factory. He tried to recover. "I mean in Bainbridge," he said, making up a fictitious location on the spot to try to throw the detective off the scent.

Again, Napoli said nothing.

"Do you know a Rashed?" Abouhalima blurted out, using Ramzi

Yousef's street name. He couldn't stop himself. He had to know how much the FBI knew about the plot.

Napoli looked at him curiously.

"You mean Rashed?" he repeated carefully, and to make sure he understood Abouhalima, he spelled it out: "R-A-S-H-E-D?"

"No," said Abouhalima, suddenly flustered. "R-A-S-H-I-I-D." He realized he had made his second mistake. Unbalanced from his ordeal and starved for information, Abouhalima had unwittingly linked himself to the bomb factory and another bomber.

Abouhalima felt faint.

"I think I would like to lie down."

Napoli pressed him with a few more questions, but Abouhalima, horrified at the damage he might have done, waved the detective off.

He leaned his head back against the seat and closed his eyes. He was very tired, but as soon as he closed his eyes, he was back in the Egyptian prison. His eyes flew open and he swallowed back a scream. He closed his eyes again. Pretending to doze under the watchful eye of Louis Napoli and the three other agents, Abouhalima felt miserable and ashamed. He had broken down and given the enemies of Islam, the Egyptian security police, a statement rather than going silently to his grave.

But as he listened to the roar of the airplane engines whisking him away from his homeland, he felt his mood lifting. In the short days he had spent with his family in Kafr-el-Diwar, the news about Jihad in Egypt had not been encouraging. In the last year and a half, the undeclared war between Gama al-Islamiya and the government had reached a crescendo of violence. The militants had recently carried out a series of bombings and assassinations aimed at police, Coptic Christians, and tourists. More than 180 people had died so far in the strife, and Egypt's thriving tourist industry, which brought over $2 billion a year into the cash-starved nation, had slowed to a trickle.

In retaliation, government soldiers had conducted dawn raids, rounding up militants wholesale and shooting scores of them on the spot. From his town alone, a teeming center of the state-owned textile industry, police had carted off five hundred men as part of their crackdown on extremists. Thousands of others were detained in prisons without access to adequate health care or even decent food. When and if they were brought to trial, the proceedings were conducted in special military courts, and the detainees were frequently given death sentences.

And Mubarak was ready and willing to carry out those sentences. Already a handful of militants had been killed, and more executions were planned. A hangman waited for Abouhalima, too. But instead he was heading back to the United States, the place that both fascinated and disgusted him. He tried to remember what he had learned during Nosair's trial from that Jewish lawyer, William Kunstler. American-style justice was very different from what he was used to. He wasn't positive, but he didn't think an American judicial system, with all its pretensions to justice for the people by the people, could accept statements made under torture. Hadn't Napoli recited that little poem which began, "You have the right to . . ." as a way to remind him that he was in the hands of the Americans again? Abouhalima leaned back and listened to the soft talk of the FBI agents. Once the plane landed, he had to get himself a copy of the Koran and a good lawyer.

* * *

Since the afternoon of March 24, when the chartered FBI plane carrying Abouhalima touched down at the far end of the runway at Stewart International Airport in Newburgh, New York, the four telephone lines in the law offices of William Kunstler and Ron Kuby had not stopped ringing. It was just like the old days of the 1960s when the seriousness of the clashes between the protesters and the police throughout the country could be gauged by who was calling Kunstler on the telephone. But this time the callers weren't newly minted revolutionaries culled from suburban America; they were soldiers in a holy war. The first calls came from members of the Egyptian community who recognized the names and faces of the men being arrested for the bombing. Could Kunstler help these men, the callers wanted to know. Could he help them the way he had helped Nosair?

The second set of calls came from Ayyad's family. On March 10, hours before Abouhalima arrived at his father's house, the FBI had burst into Ayyad's middle-class home in Maplewood, New Jersey, interrupting the lavish meal his mother had prepared to break the day's fast. It was Ramadan, the most holy time of the year, but the agents couldn't have cared less if they were arresting Santa Claus on Christmas Eve. They handcuffed Ayyad and his entire family, including his mother, his pregnant wife, and his young brothers and sisters, and then proceeded to search Ayyad's home.

"I'll talk," Ayyad told the FBI agent who led him away in handcuffs. "It gets complicated."

The third set of calls came from Abouhalima. It was natural that the Red should telephone Kunstler. He revered the elderly attorney. After all, hadn't Kunstler managed to get Nosair acquitted on all but the gun charge? Not many lawyers could have done that. Abouhalima himself had hoisted Kunstler on his shoulders and carried him down the steps of the State Supreme Court in Manhattan.

From his brownstone office in Greenwich Village, Kunstler considered Abouhalima's problems. Once a person is arrested and charged with a crime of this magnitude, the first decision he makes as a defendant—choosing a lawyer to represent his interests before the court—is critical. Not only did Abouhalima need a good lawyer—he needed a squad of good lawyers. The government was putting together a conspiracy case that would have multiple defendants. Abouhalima needed a lawyer who would be part of a strong defense team. The first man arrested, Mohammad Salameh, seemed to be satisfied with a court-appointed lawyer. Ayyad had already met with a lawyer named Steve Sommerstein, but later called Kunstler and asked him for another recommendation. Sommerstein had become famous representing Joe Doherty, an IRA gunman who had spent eight years at MCC, fighting extradition to England. Through Sommerstein, Doherty's legal battle was so passionate and hardfought that the city actually renamed the street outside MCC "Joe Doherty Place" in honor of the man who claimed he was being held a political prisoner inside. Nevertheless, Sommerstein and the young chemist could not get along, so Kunstler had recommended Leonard Wineglass, one of Kunstler's old partners from the Chicago Seven trial.

As he listened to Abouhalima talk from MCC, Kunstler's eyes traveled absently over the odd decor hung on his walls: a framed picture of that sixties icon, Che Guevara; a snapshot of Kunstler arm-in-arm with actor Marlon Brando; nearly a full wall of civil rights awards; a poster for the Irish Republican Army; and a sketch of Ronald Kuby's late pet dog, Rufus. Oblivious to these mementoes of a long and contentious career, Kunstler was trying to advise the man who could turn out to be the most famous revolutionary of his day.

At the end of the conversation, Kunstler recommended that Abouhalima call Jesse Berman, one of the left-leaning lawyers commonly found defending high-profile, politically sensitive cases. In

1986, Berman had defended a member of the so-called Ohio Seven—white revolutionaries charged with bombing military installations and government offices in 1983. His spirited and irreverent defense got his client acquitted of some of the bombings but also got Berman thrown off the federal panel of court-appointed lawyers in Brooklyn.

Abouhalima thanked him and hung up the telephone.

*   *   *

As word of Abouhalima's forcible return to the United States spread, Egyptian extremists found a popular cause to rally around. The Western press, quoting law-enforcement sources, was reporting that Abouhalima had provided Egyptian authorities with a full and detailed confession, and that the confession had already been turned over to the FBI. Had Egyptian president Hosni Mubarak and his armed security police sunk so low that they were happy to act as strongmen for their wealthier Western patron? Criticism of Mubarak rang out from mosques all over the Middle East. From a remote town in Southern Egypt, a leader of Gama al-Islamiya, Hosni Nagdi, risked his life and came out of hiding to give an interview to a reporter from the Associated Press. His purpose? To attack Mubarak for acting as a puppet of the United States, and turning over Abouhalima to the FBI.

"The Egyptian regime is totally submissive to the U.S.," said Nagdi. "It surrendered him immediately, without even caring how the Egyptian people feel about it."

In retaliation, security police were put on heightened alert, and a curfew was put into effect in major cities. Additional manpower was recruited into the Egyptian police in order to handle the increased number of fundamentalists being rounded up each day. Police stormed a Muslim extremist hideout in Abu Tig, near Assiut, about twenty-two miles south of Cairo. But tempers were running high, and militants wouldn't give up without a fight. In the resulting shootout, a militant was killed and two policemen were wounded. The next day, about ten thousand extremists turned out to bury the dead militant. All day long they marched through the dusty streets, shouting anti-government slogans. Security police, alarmed at this display, fired guns in the air, trying to get the crowd to disperse. In the streets of Cairo, two words were being whispered: *civil war.*

Mubarak suspected that Omar Abdel-Rahman was the driving force behind much of this unrest. For years he had been stirring the passions of impressionable young men, exhorting them to bloodshed. Although the Egyptian government had charged Sheik Omar, in absentia, with terrorism, there was not much they could do. He always seemed to dance out of their grasp. Even now, some frustrating technical legal point was preventing the United States government from throwing the sheik out. It irked Mubarak that the sheik could live free in Jersey City, with full access to modern technology like computers and fax machines, spreading his gospel. And since the bombings, the sheik's reputation had grown exponentially. He could command a full contingent of the international press corps by simply agreeing to appear in a room and answer questions. Just a fortnight ago, Mubarak had watched him being interviewed on the TV news magazine "PrimeTime Live."

Mubarak tried his best to calm his citizens and deflect charges that he was putting American interests before Egyptian ones. The Egyptian interior minister issued a statement claiming Abouhalima had not been simply handed over to the Americans, but had asked to leave Egypt so that he could return to the United States to clear his name. Abouhalima had been confronted with evidence of his involvement gathered by the FBI, according to the statement, "but faced with this, he [had] denied his role in the incident."

This improbable statement did little to quiet the violence in the streets, or the growing fear that Egypt might tear itself apart. Sheik Omar lost no time adding his voice to the chorus of critics. Speaking from the pulpit in a mosque in Jersey City, he squared off with his mortal enemy. First he denied any involvement with the bombers; then he criticized Mubarak for serving up Abouhalima, saying the action proved that the Egyptian president could not stand firm in the face of the satanic secular West.

It was too much for Mubarak.

On April 2, one day before he was to meet with President Bill Clinton in Washington, Mubarak gave an interview to the London-based *Al-Hayat* newspaper. Abouhalima did make a "sensational confession," Mubarak bragged. The Red had described "how the operation was carried out and those who carried it out." Then he denied pointedly that he had turned Abouhalima over to the FBI in exchange for the extradition of Sheik Omar back to Egypt to stand trial on terrorism charges.

But, Mubarak said, barely veiling his threat, Egyptian authorities had learned a great deal about the sheik from Abouhalima, his old disciple.

Had Abouhalima implicated the sheik in the bombing? Mubarak was asked.

It was the chance he had been waiting for. Although his ministers would recast Mubarak's answer slightly the next day, Mubarak struck back at his expatriated adversary.

"It seems so," said Mubarak coolly. "I don't want to go further than that. [I'm] not at liberty to discuss these confessions now because the U.S. investigation into the bombing is still under way."

* * *

For the first month behind the tan walls of MCC, Mahmud Abouhalima was happier than he had been in years. He had his friend, El-Gabrowny, on the same locked tier. And he could communicate with Ayyad and Salameh by shouting or in quiet conference during their one-hour recreation period on the roof. But in addition to his fellow Arabs, Abouhalima found Nine South to be a haven of kindred spirits. It was like the old days when he had hung out with the Black Panthers in Munich. Every man Abouhalima met had a story, an ideological ax to grind against the government. Every one of them, Abouhalima thought, was a potential soldier in the war against the United States. And every day brought fresh faces as federal prisoners were brought into the Southern District Court to attend to the minutiae of their cases.

He was starting to relax a little after that horrendous ordeal in Egypt. He made friends with an overweight killer named Theodore Williams, who had once been a henchman of the legendary heroin trafficker Nicky Barnes. Williams was as anxious to learn about Islam as Abouhalima was to learn this great American sport of basketball. Williams was also teaching Abouhalima about another American pastime, smoking marijuana, which was smuggled in with the help of greedy guards.

To be sure, Abouhalima still had tense moments. It was difficult for him to control Salameh, who often screamed for hours on end, trying to get the attention of the guards. And it was hard to keep track of some of the loose ends of his *gamaii*. He had a scare when Ajaj was arrested. Word traveled quickly to Abouhalima's tier that another bomber was being placed in the segregated wing.

Abouhalima became agitated. He had no idea what kind of shape

Ajaj would be in. He was afraid Ajaj might give up Yousef and the others before Abouhalima could line him up with a decent lawyer.

He waited until he heard the locked door of the reception area on Nine South swing open.

"Don't say a word," Abouhalima shouted in Arabic. Then he listened. Ajaj didn't reply.

"Don't tell them anything until we have a chance to speak during recreation hour."

Abouhalima had been alarmed over nothing. After a few calls to William Kunstler, Ajaj was visited by the formidable Lynne Stewart, the lawyer who had become a legend in her no-holds-barred defense of the accused cop-shooter Larry Davis.

In fact, Abouhalima was proud to note that the entire defense team was shaping up nicely. Ajaj had Stewart, and at Kunstler's and Kuby's suggestion, Abouhalima had hired Jesse Berman. Ayyad was represented by Leonard Wineglass. Only Salameh was stuck with his court-appointed lawyer, an earnest-looking fellow named Robert Precht. But that couldn't be helped. So far, Salameh and Precht hadn't embarrassed the others too much. During one court appearance, Salameh had mugged for the court artists, and Precht had relayed his message to the artists: "Draw me like I am a human being, not a terrorist."

In group defense meetings on the third-floor prisoner-attorney conference room, Precht could hold his own.

By comparison, the prosecution team, lead by two clean-cut young men, J. Gilmore Childers and Henry DePippo, showed up at the pretrial hearings looking wiped out. Despite their white pressed shirts and expensive suits, they seemed to be fumbling.

They admitted that the FBI was still combing through the evidence pulled from the crater, and didn't expect to be finished before July. Of the four tons of twisted metal pulled from the whole, a full ton and a half was being brushed and the residue examined under a high-powered microscope.

And the prosecutors were furious when the defense team began hinting to reporters that the government's evidence would never stand up under cross-examination. The judge presiding over the case, Kevin Duffy, was also unnerved by the defense's show of press savvy.

Known for his rigorous treatment of lawyers and his folksy, approachable style, Duffy, a twenty-one-year veteran of the bench, wanted to maintain full control of the lawyers appearing before him. He had every right to be concerned. In 1983 he had presided over the trial of six defendants accused of committing a $1.6 million Brinks Truck robbery—a caper that had left three people, including a police officer, dead.

That case became a circus. The defendants claimed they wanted to start an independent black nation, which they called New Afrika, to be located in five Southern states. The lawyer for one of the lead defendants in the case was none other than Jesse Berman. The relationship between the judge and the defense team became so contentious and politically overheated that one of the lawyers, who screamed out that Duffy was a "racist dog," was eventually found guilty of contempt of court.

One case like that in a career was quite enough for Duffy. Without hearings or requests from either side, Duffy issued a gag order, barring both the defense and the prosecutors from talking to the press. The fine for the first offense would be two hundred dollars, and it would rise exponentially after that. The fine for the fourth offense would be $25.6 million, payable by working in the prison system at seventy cents a day.

The gag order brought the lawyers under Duffy's control, but it was also outrageously unfair to the defendants. The FBI had spent more than two months anonymously disseminating as much damaging information as they could about the bombers to television and print reporters. Anyone who picked up a newspaper in New York City could tell you that the redheaded bomber was the mastermind. Now, if the defense tried to counter, heaping public scorn on the prosecutor's contentions, they would land in jail.

Duffy also moved to ease Berman out of the case. Stewart, Ajaj's lawyer, had already been replaced by the seasoned defender Austin Campriello, a lawyer whose self-effacing style cloaked the mind of a razor-sharp strategist. In mid-April, Berman told Duffy that Abouhalima didn't have enough money to pay his fees. He asked Duffy for a three-week continuance while his client tried to come up with additional funds. Duffy denied the request and volunteered that he would not designate Berman as Abouhalima's court-appointed lawyer, which would have entitled him to the standard seventy-dollar-an-hour rate.

"He pressured me out of the case," Berman said. Wineglass followed.

Suddenly the trim defense team Kunstler had helped Abouhalima put together was toppling.

Instead of demanding that Berman represent Abouhalima in a caretaking role until the Red could find another lawyer, Duffy left Abouhalima without an active lawyer.

The sharks from the FBI smelled blood in the water. The transcript of Abouhalima's Egyptian confession had whetted their appetites. They knew that the prosecutors couldn't use a word of it against him in court; civil libertarians would have a field day if they even hinted at statements made under physical torture. But it gave them the full measure of the man they had hunted for so long. They knew full well what a powerful witness Abouhalima could be against the other bombers and against Nosair. Now that Abouhalima was without a lawyer engaged in his defense, this was the time to make their move. They began visiting Abouhalima, having the guards pull him out of the monotonous daily routine of prison and take him to a special room for questioning. They whispered promises, asked him to look to the future. Think of his young sons growing up without a father. Think of your friend Shalabi, his body desecrated at the hands of so many of the sheik's disciples.

In a panic, Abouhalima began to telephone Duffy's chambers, asking to speak to the judge. He also called newspaper reporters, denying his involvement in the bombing.

"No. No. No. No way. I'm absolutely innocent," Abouhalima told a reporter. "This [bombing] is something crazy, something absolutely stupid."

But at the same time he was claiming his innocence, Abouhalima was regaling his cellmate, Theodore Williams, with his exploits. The goal of the bombing, he told Williams, had been to force the government to free Nosair from Attica. The next target, he insisted, was the Statue of Liberty.

"How did you and five guys expect to blow up the whole thing?" Williams asked him.

"It's not just us," Abouhalima replied. "It's three hundred men across the country who would do anything to hurt the United States."

Williams, who had once beaten a man to death with a baseball bat, said later that he was shocked at his new friend's lack of human empathy when he talked about the bombing. After all, thousands upon thousands of people could have been killed, washed into the river, or torched like kindling in a 107-story inferno.

"Why didn't you blow up the Trade Center at night?" Williams asked, thinking of the pictures he'd seen on television of old ladies being carried down flights of stairs and a pregnant woman being airlifted off the top of the Trade Center by helicopter.

Abouhalima said it was too difficult to get into the garage at night. They had tried, he claimed, to bomb the garage early in the morning, before people reported to work, but "something went wrong."

Every day, Williams watched the FBI lead Abouhalima from his cell and counted the hours on his watch until he returned. He saw that his friend, who had seemed so happy and confident a few weeks ago, had fallen into a depression. He urged Abouhalima to make a deal with the prosecutors.

"Go for it, man," said Williams, with the confidence of a man who had spent more of his life behind bars than on the street. "Don't waste your life in here."

Abouhalima heeded Williams's words. One day when the FBI agents came by for one of their talks, Abouhalima told them he was tired of playing games with lowly agents. He wanted to speak to the men in suits, the leaders of the FBI's *gamaii*, the U.S. Attorneys.

That meeting was swiftly arranged. On a cool morning in May, Abouhalima finally sat across a buffed oak table from Childers and DePippo. When the marshal had unhooked his handcuffs and left the room, he nodded to the two men. The U.S. Attorneys formally introduced themselves. The small, dark-eyed man was Henry DePippo. The tall, balding one who couldn't seem to stop blushing was J. Gilmore Childers. Abouhalima smiled and looked Childers full in the eye. He wasn't deceived by Childers's schoolboy looks. Childers was one of their leaders. Hadn't his name come up when federal agents began investigating the Kahane shooting after Nosair was acquitted? And just recently, in the months before the bombing, Childers had subpoenaed scores of Egyptians living in Brooklyn and questioned them about Abouhalima. His name had traveled back to Abouhalima faster than if Childers had called him directly on the telephone. They had much to talk about.

Before a defendant becomes a cooperating government witness, he must go through a procedure called a "proffer." In a series of interviews he must truthfully confess all of his criminal deeds and the criminal deeds of his friends. In exchange, the prosecutors can't use the evidence he confesses against him. If the information provided is useful enough to the U.S. Attorney, he can ask the defendant to testify for the prosecution. In exchange for his testimony, his sentence can be reduced or even eliminated. There is a catch, however.

If the defendant is caught in a lie, the government will immediately kill the deal.

Abouhalima, like thousands of defendants before him, thought he could get the better of the government. Two years before, Sammy "the Bull" Gravano, the Gambino family's second-in-command, had made himself a legend at MCC by rolling over on mob boss John Gotti. Gravano sent Gotti away for life, earning himself hundreds of thousands of dollars in the process and shaving decades off his jail sentence; the FBI's New York director even gave Gravano a small gold pin in appreciation of his superb work as a witness. Abouhalima wanted the Gravano treatment. He knew how badly the U.S. government wanted to get the sheik. He sat down with Childers and DePippo to establish his terms. If he could make a deal, Abouhalima knew he would never return to that dingy cell at MCC.

First, he told them, he wanted his sentence reduced to time served. Second, he wanted money, lots of money, for the information he was about to supply. Third, his German wife, Marianna Weber, and their four children were facing deportation; he wanted the government to grant her citizenship in the United States, where the Muslim community would take care of her. Abouhalima carefully laid out his demands. Childers never flinched, but he never put a word of their agreement in writing. Abouhalima began his proffer.

A week later, they were still talking. Childers and DePippo advised Duffy that Abouhalima was engaged in discussions with the prosecutors. Duffy was suddenly made aware that the lead defendant in the most closely watched trial of the decade was talking to prosecutors without benefit of a vigorous defense lawyer. The talks ground to a halt.

The prosecution was stymied. And Abouhalima was in an awkward position. It wasn't the best-kept secret in MCC that he was talking to prosecutors about rolling over. Now he had to live among the very people he was about to sell out. His happy days at MCC were over. Abouhalima began to fear for his life. In a state of turmoil, he hired a lawyer, this time Hassen Ibn Abdellah, an African-American Muslim lawyer from North Elizabeth, New Jersey.

Although the Southern District of New York covers a large area, the number of defense lawyers who practice out of the Manhattan federal court is actually quite small. Many newcomers complain that it is a closed and unfriendly club. It is also a homogeneous one, made up almost entirely of white men who are either Catholic, Protestant, or Jewish. For the most part, they graduated from good law schools and spent a few years as federal prosecutors or stepped into a comfortable living earning seventy-five dollars an hour as a court-appointed defense lawyer. Abdellah would never be part of this club. Raised in the notorious Pioneer Homes housing project in Elizabeth, Hassen Ibn Abdellah had escaped poverty by getting a football scholarship to Bucknell University. He'd earned a law degree from Seton Hall University in 1983, and had worked for six years in the Union County, New Jersey, prosecutor's office, developing his skills as a trial lawyer. In 1989 he hung out his own shingle, handling state criminal work out of a converted dentist's office in a well-to-do section of North Elizabeth. His office was a busy one; Abdellah had a family to support, and had made it his mission to take part in social programs for inner-city youth. But he was never too busy to pray. Five times a day, he and his co-counsel on the case, Clarence Faines, grabbed their prayer rugs, walked into an unadorned room at the back of Abdellah's office, and prayed to Allah.

For a small-town lawyer to get offered a case of this stature was a once-in-a-lifetime proposition—a shot at the big time. It was also, Abdellah often marveled, a chance to be a witness to history. He took the case without hesitation, guessing, correctly, that his fees would never get paid.

Although Abouhalima bragged that he got along best with black Americans, and could only really trust another Muslim, Abouhalima was sending mixed messages to Abdellah. One day he told Abdellah he was going to flip. The next day he insisted that Abdellah begin working on his defense.

Abdellah felt sympathy for the man. He had been tortured, then locked away in prison. Abdellah could see that he was disoriented. And the tension between Abouhalima and the other defendants was starting to break him down. In early June, Salameh, always the weakest mentally of the bunch, frantically telephoned a friend, asking him to tell the world that Abouhalima, the great warrior for Jihad, was about to change sides.

His friend, Ahmed Sattar, an Egyptian-born postal worker who had been interviewed by the FBI in September, before the bombing, got in touch with *The New York Times,* one of the only papers that had a long enough reach to bring the news back to Abouhalima's hometown in Egypt.

"Abouhalima was making a deal," he told the reporter. Salameh had told him that "the officers are talking about it and some of the prisoners are talking about it. And the way Abouhalima is trying to avoid him, [Salameh is] sure about it."

Abdellah, Abouhalima's new lawyer, was mystified. His client was so mercurial that Abdellah had to read the newspapers first thing every morning to see if he still worked for him. "It's his decision," said Abdellah, exasperated. "But what can they give him? He's looking at life. They could give him fifty years. What's the difference?"

Abouhalima, fearful that the prosecutors would not meet his demands, wrote a letter to Duffy asking for a more experienced lawyer. He had met with Lawrence Vogelman, a professor at the Cardozo School of Law, and decided to hire him. But on June 16, when Duffy summoned Abdellah, Faines, and Vogelman to his courtroom, Abouhalima backed down and meekly told Duffy he would stick with Abdellah.

Sometime in July, Abouhalima, who had once wanted to work with the government, decided to fight them instead.

From then on, the government did its best to make sure Abouhalima's life got worse. Police rounded up the so-called second conspirators, including his comrade Rodney Hampton-El, and then, caving to political pressure, arrested the sheik. Ayyad, outraged that Abouhalima might turn on him to save himself, had begun meeting with FBI agents to discuss a deal. His new lawyer, Atiq Ahmed, said the prosecutors had offered Ayyad a chance to become a government witness. But Ayyad couldn't deliver the sheik as Abouhalima might have been able to. The best deal they could offer him was a comfortable cell at the minimum-security section of Allenwood Penitentiary—Club Fed, as it is called—for the rest of his natural life.

Ayyad agreed to those terms. "He's going from one extreme to the other every day," Ahmed said. "I've seen him at both ends. He's just concerned, he had a career that was beginning and a pregnant wife."

When Abouhalima got wind of Ayyad's deal, he lost no time in confronting him. He waited until they were standing next to each other on the central elevator, waiting to be taken to the MCC basketball court on the roof.

"If anyone should turn," Abouhalima hissed, "it will be me."
Ayyad decided not to turn.

*   *   *

Alone in his cell on an August night, Abouhalima, dressed in bright orange coveralls, got down on his hands and knees. While guards looked on he turned his face toward Mecca. His commandos were gnawing on each other like hungry dogs. There was no order left, no sense of honor or purpose. Abouhalima had lain on his thin mattress last night, trying to figure a way out of this mess. In six short weeks he would be on trial for his life, and his new defense lawyers hadn't yet gotten around to grappling with the meat of the case. He had closed his eyes last night asking God for guidance. Then he'd awakened to find that his hero, Nosair, and his spiritual guide, Omar Abdel-Rahman, had been indicted as terrorists. "God is merciful," he murmured, trying to believe his own words. "God is great."

16

THE TRIAL

Six weeks before the opening of the World Trade Center bombing trial, the new lawyers for the bombers opened up their morning newspaper and started to smile.

The paper, *New York Newsday*, is the only city newspaper that runs color pictures in its news section. For decades, Long Islanders have been raised on its older country cousin, *Newsday*, and in 1984 the paper started a sharp-edged New York version. Like every tabloid, *New York Newsday* is printed on simple wood pulp and, minus car advertisements, weighs less than a pound on an average news day. The news it carried this morning was devoured by the bombers' legal defense team.

Austin Campriello, Hassen Ibn Abdellah, Robert Precht, and Atiq Ahmed read that the informant in the bombing and assassination case, Emad Salem, had clandestinely taped every conversation he ever had with his FBI handlers. After the mass arrest in Queens in June, Salem had gone into hiding. The FBI swept through his Upper West Side apartment, picking up the tapes he made of the conspirators and hurriedly packing up his personal effects for his new life as a protected witness. Along with the tapes of the sheik, Siddig Ali, and Rodney Hampton-El, went cassette after cassette of Salem's conversations with FBI agents John Anticev and Nancy Floyd.

It wasn't until weeks later, when FBI agents sat down to identify and catalog the tapes in the evidence bags that federal agents realized what Salem had done. He had recorded every word, every casual, affectionate, sarcastic, and acrimonious exchange between him and his handlers. That much wouldn't have been a problem. But when the agents swept through his apartment, they inadvertently put those tapes into evidence bags. Now whatever Anticev and Floyd had said to Salem, and whatever Salem had said to them, would have to be transcribed and handed over to defense lawyers.

By the end of the day, word of the tapes had swept the FBI office in downtown Manhattan, and supervisors began to sweat. The relationship between informants and agents is complicated and the one among Floyd, Anticev, and Salem was even more so. Not even J. Edgar Hoover could have been happily cross-examined on the little in-between things an agent said to keep an informant happy and working. The agents could have made embarrassing admissions. They could have cursed the FBI. They could show a side of the agency that federal officials didn't want the defense lawyers—or the public—ever to know about. Worse than that, they could supply a blueprint of the FBI's own investigation. They could have spoken about hunches and suspicions that never made it into official reports. The tapes could damage and potentially sink not just this trial but the sheik's as well.

The tapes were an FBI nightmare. They were a defense lawyer's dream.

At the very best, Salem might have told his FBI handlers that someone else from the radical Muslim community had threatened to bomb the World Trade Center. That would be exculpatory evidence that could help the defense prove the innocence of the four men. But the defense lawyers would be almost as happy if Salem had warned the FBI that Abouhalima and his crew were about to blow the Trade Center up. It would run directly contrary to the story the FBI was putting out about their Herculean investigation. If the defense had evidence that the FBI had suspected Abouhalima all along, the prosecution would have a credibility problem the size of Nebraska.

Even tacit acknowledgment that the FBI knew what Abouhalima and his crew were up to would help the defense case. If the FBI had been warned about Abouhalima's plan, why hadn't it marshaled its considerable manpower to stop him? The Bureau would have to acknowledge that it had heard Abouhalima was plotting an explosion, but that it hadn't considered him a real threat.

Any defense lawyer in the country would give up a week's pay for a chance to cross-examine Salem's handlers: "Is it true, agent, that you didn't follow up on Salem's information because you didn't believe it? You didn't believe that Abouhalima was capable of committing a crime?"

For the defense, the news couldn't have come at a better time. Jury selection was beginning in less than six weeks, and it was already clear that the lawyers were not going to be acting as a team.

Abouhalima's new counselors, Hassen Ibn Abdellah and Clarence Faines, were as green as law students when it came to practicing in the Southern District. The courthouse is a country unto itself, with its own customs and its own sense of decorum. The judges greet the defense lawyers, depending on their moods, like old friends or annoying neighbors. Many a young prosecutor has felt his heart sink when the judge hailed the defendant's lawyer by his first name and they began reminiscing.

Ayyad's new lawyer was Atiq Ahmed, a portly Muslim who practiced law in Silver Springs, Maryland. Courtly and polite, Ahmed, who was born in India and spoke with a thick accent, was solid and dependable, handling small-time civil cases and the legal matters generated by a handful of Muslim centers in Maryland and Washington.

Their early excursions to Manhattan federal court had been jarring. Abdellah and Faines strolled jauntily into the courtroom, visibly scowled and bristled at decisions that went against their client, and hinted at elaborate conspiracies between the press, the prosecutors, and the FBI. Their behavior seemed to charm Ahmed, who became their constant companion, but it alienated Precht and Campriello.

Robert Precht, a grandson of the TV impresario Ed Sullivan, was a competent, thoughtful lawyer, but inexperienced at trial work. He recruited his boss, John Byrnes, a florid veteran barrister, to help him with the case. Ajaj's lawyer, the diminutive, genial Austin Campriello, was the most experienced of the defense group, and the most optimistic about his client's future. The case against Ajaj was the weakest of the four, since he had been in jail at the time of the bombing. Campriello had a good chance of convincing a jury that Ajaj couldn't be involved.

If the relationship among the defense lawyers was troublesome, the relationships between the lawyers and their clients were even rockier. Complicated, multidefendant cases require enormous amounts of preparation. There were literally stacks of boxes filled with discovery material: FBI reports had to be studied, and witnesses' statements analyzed. The lawyers had to visit and photograph locations that the prosecutors would be talking about: the Space Station, the bomb factory at Pamrapo, the cramped apartment at Kensington Avenue. Most difficult of all, the defense needed to help the defendants establish alibis. They needed to talk to friends, collect credit-card receipts, airline tickets, anything at all that would demonstrate that their clients could not have taken part in the plot.

Instead, the lawyers found large chunks of their pretrial meetings taken up with petty complaints about prison life. It was partially a result of stress. The hopes that Abouhalima and the others harbored for an easy acquittal had faded. And the Red had made himself unpopular with the people who could save him—the FBI—by agreeing to make a deal and then failing to deliver the goods. Apprehensive, overwrought, and locked in a dim cinder-block cage with nothing to do but worry, Abouhalima had become overwhelmed with irksome details of his prison life. The officials, with their stupid rules, wouldn't allow him access to the few pathetic diversions other prisoners enjoyed. When the World Trade Center defendants wanted to go to the prison library, the small room of mobile stacks had to be cleared of other prisoners. The guards wouldn't even uncuff them to do laundry; the defendants stood at the washroom sink in the Nine South wing of MCC, their wrists manacled, dunking standard-issue white gym socks in soapy water. The bombers asked the prison doctor for special Muslim meals, only to be told that the request must be approved by the prison chaplain, a Protestant. Meanwhile, the Muslim extremists were served pork at least twice a week.

Salameh became more and more agitated; this was, he complained, an orchestrated effort to push them to the brink. The guards taunted them, pressuring them to become government informants. He was convinced that these slights were occurring because he opposed the United States. It was political, he said over and over.

The lawyers were nonplussed by their complaints. "Try to concentrate on your case," Campriello told Ajaj soothingly. "If you lose, you'll have your whole life to take on the Bureau of Prisons."

But their clients were relentless. The lawyers wrote letters to Judge Duffy and prison authorities, trying to get kosher meals and an Arabic-language Koran for the bombers.

They attempted to sort through the discovery material on their own, preparing as best they could for the start of the trial. But on the eve of September 14, 1993, with jury selection due to start in less than twelve hours, the four defendants and their lawyers had never once sat down to plan their strategy as a group.

* * *

The first day of jury selection started shortly after dawn for almost every cast member of the vast, unwieldy drama. The significance of the day could not be underestimated. The panel of people who would decide the fate of the bombers would be winnowed from the citizens who showed up for jury duty that day. The law-enforcement community was ready. Federal agents and police, some of whom had been at the bomb site on February 26 and others who had only read about it in the newspapers, arrived especially early. They had been briefed by a security team who flew up from Washington, D.C., four weeks before. The message the experts brought was daunting. Always remember, the experts warned, that extremists believe that dying in the name of Allah is a holy act. Always remember, terrorists can be anywhere. What more flamboyant show of defiance than an attack in the majestic courthouse itself? The international press corps would be there. The Trade Center bombers would be inside, waiting to be freed.

But securing the massive, neoclassical courthouse was no easy matter. For starters, it sits less than a block away from the Brooklyn Bridge. Every day an average of 125,600 cars and trucks go across the bridge. Many of them pass through Foley Square, directly in front of the courthouse. Any one of those vehicles could be carrying a powerful bomb.

The building's height presented another problem. It was completed in 1936 from designs by the renowned architect Cass Gilbert, who almost thirty years before had built the breathtaking, seven-story U.S. Custom House in downtown Manhattan. By the time Gilbert took on his masterwork for the federal government, successful design didn't simply have to look good from the sidewalk, it had to redefine the Manhattan skyline. The last big building Gilbert had designed in New York was the Woolworth Building, literally a neo-Gothic cathedral to commerce, which, from 1913 to 1931, was the tallest building in the world. In the Woolworth Building lobby are two small sculptures—one of Gilbert holding a model of the building, and the other of his structural engineer measuring a girder. Cass Gilbert brought none of that sense of frivolity to the courthouse project. It is a stern, imposing, granite and marble building that reaches thirty stories into the sky. Almost invisible from the street but unmistakable from the other side of the East River is a golden pyramid on top, punctuating the clouds above Foley Square. It was an invitation to an airborne attack. The security experts posted sharpshooters on the roof of the Manhattan Criminal Court and the Municipal Building and arranged for a helicopter to fly overhead.

The security teams nailed down the wide, old-style windows. They cordoned off stairways that curled through the building. They erected X-ray machines and set up areas for crowd control. The proceedings were moved to the third floor, where the walkway from MCC enters the federal courthouse. The closer the bombers stayed to their jail cells, the happier the security teams would be. For two weeks before the start of the trial, surveillance teams had prowled around Foley Square, which extends for about half a city block west and north of the courthouse. Once a polluted swamp, then a dangerous slum, the pocket of concrete and trees got its name from "Big Tom" Foley, a sheriff, saloonkeeper, alderman, and Tammany Hall district leader. Foley's last saloon had been leveled to make way for the government buildings around the square. Now it was part of the "frozen zone." Every couple on their way to the Municipal Building to get married, every illegal immigrant on his way to file papers at INS, every scabby bum begging for dimes was scrutinized by agents, who carefully noted the regular comings and goings of the area.

On the first day of jury selection, blue barricades had been set up round the square. Uniformed police officers, wearing baby blue riot helmets and bulky bulletproof vests, stood shoulder to shoulder on the nineteen granite steps. Phalanxes of mounted police officers were stationed on either side of the block. Bomb-sniffing dogs and their keepers roamed the sidewalks. Around the back, agents armed with rifles guarded the entranceway to the underground garage.

The press corps stood obediently behind the police barricades, their television cameras and equipment set up in a cluster like a voracious electric octopus, beaming images of the bomb-sniffing dogs from Los Angeles to New Delhi. A few reporters grumbled that the security measures were a sham. No one from the jury pool could take lunch outside the courtroom without being inconvenienced by the security measures. No one in America could watch television that night and not understand that the government thought these men were extremely dangerous.

If the government really believed the bombers had friends willing to end their lives to free them, they grumbled, wouldn't a few more have shown up at their trial? Unlike El Sayyid Nosair's trial for the shooting of Rabbi Kahane, which threatened to break into a riot every day, only three quiet Muslim men showed up in court, friends of Salameh's from the Jersey City mosque. They granted no interviews, and sat unobtrusively in the back row.

The World Trade Center trial may have been as much a microcosm of the Middle East tensions as Nosair's trial. Less than twenty-four hours before jury selection started, Israeli prime minister Yitzhak Rabin and PLO chairman Yasir Arafat had endured an uncomfortable handshake on the steps of the White House. It was a gesture that caused a sharp intake of breath all over the Middle East. Suddenly the polarity that had divided that region of the world for more than a generation had diminished in force. Israelis and Palestinians were just waiting to see if the peace would hold.

The prosecutors had been in their offices, connected by a walkway to the courthouse, since just after dawn. Despite their endless preparation, Henry DePippo and Gil Childers were nervous. The defense lawyers seemed almost eager by comparison. As they fought their way through the crowd and into the oak-paneled courtroom, they issued little opening jabs.

"There is no evidence in this case that establishes a link between Abouhalima and Salameh, except they are both Muslims," Abdellah said to the press. "They are both from Arab countries and they went to the same mosque." Abouhalima's fate, he said, would rest on the fairness of the jury. "Whether he walks or not is not up to us," Abdellah said. "That's up to the jury. We guaranteed he would be well represented. We didn't sell him any dreams."

In fact, Abouhalima said later, the jury selection was the beginning of his nightmare.

The Southern District covers Manhattan, the Bronx, and Queens, and reaches out into the suburbs and the exurbs of Rockland, Orange, and Sullivan counties. From these communities, twelve jurors and six alternates had to be chosen. Fearing that average citizens would try to avoid serving on such a notorious case, the court sent summonses out to five thousand people, nearly three times the normal jury pool. It was the largest group ever assembled for a federal trial, and Judge Kevin Duffy used a firm hand in keeping the process running smoothly.

Instead of allowing the usual voir dire, in which prosecutors and defense lawyers question potential jurors to sniff out prejudices or preconceptions, Duffy decided to handle the preliminary screening himself. The prosecutors asked Duffy to inquire whether jury candidates had opinions about people from the Middle East. Precht and Campriello submitted questions aimed at digging out signs of prejudice against Arabs, Muslims, Israelis, or of opposition to U.S. policies in the Middle East. Abdellah and Faines wanted Duffy to ask prospective jurors what the Holy City was for Muslims—Mecca, Medina, Detroit, or Jersey City.

Duffy reviewed their questions and then, without further comment, set them aside. He began his own rambling, folksy introduction to the trial.

"The first thing to do is relax," he told them. "I'm serious about that."

He admitted that it would be difficult to find a jury who hadn't heard of the case: "I don't think if I went to a monastery I would be able to get that." He said he was looking for "jurors who recognize that cases are tried not in the newspaper or television but here in the courtroom."

But finding those jurors was not easy. One by one, the dutiful citizens of the Southern District made excuses:

"I don't feel well. Whenever I come down here, I get the runs, I get bad headaches. I get chest pains."

"One of the deceased in the bombing was a onetime neighbor of mine. Came from the same town and everything."

"I just retired, and my plans are that I am moving out of New York as of October."

"I don't speak English well enough."

"I was in a building that exploded and I was buried in rubble and I lost two and a half years of my life being in and out of hospitals. I still have a trauma with this sort of thing."

"I was a former partner of [U.S. Attorney] Mary Jo White."

"I have been dealing with agoraphobia."

"I am a Rastafarian. It is totally against my religious background to be judgmental in any way."

The jurors were all promised anonymity—each was identified by a number instead of a name—and told they would not be sequestered, but the excuses kept rolling in. After six arduous days of questioning, a smaller pool of potential jurors was isolated. Then the lawyers had their say. A retired publishing executive was seen talking to himself. Childers used one of his ten challenges to get that juror dismissed for fear that, he said jokingly, the jury would be deadlocked eleven to two.

The defense team had more trouble exercising their six challenges. They dismissed potential jurors who said the defendants were guilty. They seemed to favor African-Americans, and challenged several jurors who were pro-Israel. But it is always hard to gauge when a potential juror is skewing his or her answers in order to serve on the jury.

After one particularly rigorous round of questioning, the defense team joined the defendants in the cramped holding cell on the third floor, and began arguing whether specific jurors should be dismissed. Knee to knee, the lawyers shouted at each other until even the defendants began to look alarmed. Then one of the lawyers moved to settle the argument by suggesting that the defense team ask Allah for guidance. As the federal marshal in attendance shifted uneasily from foot to foot, the defendants and the lawyers dropped their heads and began to pray.

*　　*　　*

Finally, after eight days of selection, the jury was in place. The forewoman, Anita, was a young, college-educated African-American woman from Westchester. She was married, without children, and like her husband, she worked in telecommunications.

She dressed carefully and well, and she seemed comfortable around lawyers and judges. But courtrooms weren't unfamiliar to her. She had been a juror before, in a cross-burning case in Queens. She had found the defendant in that case guilty.

The jurors were either Catholic or Protestant. Seven had been to college; three others had completed high school. One of the women said her son had been murdered fifteen years ago. One of the men said he was a member of the National Rifle Association.

On October 4, the day of opening statements, they sat in the oak-paneled jury box like expectant schoolchildren waiting for class to begin.

Childers stood up from the defense table where Henry DePippo and two junior U.S. attorneys, Michael Garcia and Lev Dassin, also sat. Looking like a rough-hewn preacher, he faced the packed courtroom, silently acknowledging the members of the audience who had come to support him: the head of the FBI in New York, James Fox; Monica Smith's husband, Eddie; the U.S. Attorney, Mary Jo

White; and a handful of firefighters who had carried victims down 107 smoky flights of stairs.

Then he faced the jurors and began.

"It was lunchtime on Friday, February 26, 1993. In many ways it was like any other lunchtime at the World Trade Center," Childers told the hushed courtroom. "Tens of thousands of business employees in their offices, at their desks, going to and from their noontime meals. Visitors to the restaurants and to the observation deck filled the elevators. Everyone going about their routines, all minding their own business. All of these people, unaware that one minute later, at 12:18, their lives would be changed forever. For February 26, 1993, would become a day that would mark for all time the single most destructive act of terrorism ever committed here in the United States. From that point forward, Americans knew that 'this can happen to me, here in the United States.' "

The first witness the government called was Charles Maikish, director of the Trade Center complex. The prosecutors couldn't have asked for a more presentable spokesman. Maikish looked calm and intelligent as he took the stand and politely began to answer Childers's questions.

He said he had been sitting on the thirty-fifth floor of Tower One, signing leases, when he heard a sound.

"I felt a heaving in the tower itself," he said, then he walked to the elevator and saw that the cars, functioning under emergency control, were retracting to the basement.

"I knew we had a very major event."

Prodded by Childers, Maikish described taking the elevator to the lobby. "The smoke had literally filled the lobby to a point above my head," Maikish said, and went on to describe how he had set up a command center on the street. He had dispatched emergency workers into the smoky building to see if the tower was in danger of falling over, and sent a police car to pick up plans from a consulting engineer's office. Then a worker had arrived and told him that four employees had been killed.

As he spoke, Maikish's controlled expression began to crumble. Unashamed and with great dignity, he wept.

Over the next week, the prosecutors put on one witness after another, trying to impress upon the jury the fear, anguish, death, and destruction the bombers had brought to the city.

Port Authority police lieutenant Michael Podolak described how he ripped open a hole at the top of an elevator with his bare hands.

Inside he found a group of trembling five-year-olds who had been stranded near the forty-second floor. After lifting out a dozen of the kindergarteners, he was standing on the top of the elevator with child number thirteen when the elevator suddenly lurched and began to descend into the black, smoke-filled shaft. He and the boy clung to each other.

"I looked up and all I could see was that little bit of light that was the hole and somebody looking down at me, saying, 'Where are you going?' And I'm thinking to myself, 'Gee, I don't know where I'm going.' "

Firefighter William Duffy described breaking open an elevator door and finding it filled with barely conscious people.

"I just saw people lying from head to toe. . . . It was like opening up a tomb."

Joaquin Villafuerta, an elevator operator in the Trade Center for fifteen years, told the jury about the last time he had seen Wilfredo Mercado, the Windows on the World purchasing agent, alive.

"He was like a brother to me," he said, wiping his red-rimmed eyes. "We made a lot of plans together."

Over the strenuous objections of the defense, the prosecution showed the jurors morgue photographs of the victims of the explosion. When the picture of Monica Smith was passed around, the forewoman, Anita, began to cry and another juror shuddered and looked away.

Timothy Lang, the former stock trader who had been waiting for a parking spot when the building exploded, provided some of the most graphic testimony. "I felt a wall that was about two feet high of stone and I crawled over it, fell over a chair, felt a person. . . . Now I became very frightened." He described how he crawled to the edge of a pit: "I looked inside the pit and it looked very, very deep and at the base, I saw a yellow glow, but the stuff spewing out of the pit was hot, very smoky. I could almost see the particles and taste them. I had to move away from the pit very, very quickly. I just sensed a great danger there. I started to hear screams in the garage. The screams didn't last very long."

He described arriving in the hospital with a concussion and a broken nose, suffering from smoke inhalation.

Next the prosecutors had to present evidence pulled from the center of the crater. In their office complex at 1 St. Andrews Plaza, Childers and DePippo had filled three full rooms with fragments, each one tagged and inventoried. A fourth room was filled with

Econoline van parts. Every morning the prosecutors brought pieces to the courtroom. Every day, during the testimony, FBI agents identified the pieces and pointed out on the scale model where each one was found.

It was mind-numbing testimony, but it gave the prosecutors a chance to prepare for the meat of the case. They had come a long way since the early days after the explosion. As a rule, federal cases are an orderly affair, with a prolonged investigation resulting in a series of neatly executed arrests. This case was just the opposite. The defendants were taken into custody more quickly than anyone could have anticipated. No sooner did the prosecutors receive lab reports than they began presenting them to a grand jury. If the lawyers weren't reviewing grand jury minutes, they were bearing down on legal motions and discovery. The pace left little time for the studied, careful decisions that were Childers's trademark. By July 1, when Abouhalima decided not to be a witness for the government, the focus of the case began to shift. They could not make a deal with Abouhalima. They would not have him describing to the jury the inner workings of their terrorist cell. He would not point the finger at the sheik and tell the twelve men and women that the blind cleric had been the spiritual adviser for the whole bloody operation. Abouhalima would not give up Omar Abdel-Rahman. Nor would he turn against his old friend Nosair. This would not be a case about Middle Eastern politics; it would be a case against four men accused of a heinous crime. For now, that was enough.

Logistically, it was almost too much. Every bit of evidence had to be logged and charted. Every witness had to be debriefed, the statements recorded and turned over to the defense by early July. The two junior U.S. attorneys, Michael Garcia and Lev Dassin, were working night and day, making sense out of telephone records and translating recorded conversations.

By the end of July, there were still gaping holes in the case. At least two principal players, Ramzi Yousef and Abdul Yasin, were still fugitives, but that could be used by the prosecution as well as the defense. The defense would blame all the criminal activity attributed to their clients on Yousef. The prosecution would say that Yousef was the mortar that held this conspiracy together. There was no chance that Yousef would show up to contradict either one.

More troubling to the prosecution were the weak links in the chain of physical evidence. The FBI was still looking through thousands of parking tickets taken from the World Trade Center garage. But so far they hadn't been able to come up with evidence proving the bombers had ever visited the site. Even the chemical analysis had let them down. Bits of twisted metal were still being scraped and the shavings analyzed for chemical residue. So far, the results had been dispiriting. They were looking for a perfect crystal of nitroglycerin that could be chemically matched to what was left behind in the bomb factory. But the chemicals in the bomb had been almost completely consumed in the heat of the explosion. What remained were traces of nitrites, ammonium nitrate, and urea. Those were by-products of a urea-nitrate bomb, but they were also chemicals that saturated the remains of the parking garage. Ordinary car exhaust deposited nitrites. Fire extinguishers used to douse spot fires left ammonium nitrate residue. Before the explosion and during the rescue operation, maintenance workers had blanketed the area with a urea-based deicer. Because ruptured sewer pipes had soaked nearly every floor, urea from the wastewater was not hard to find.

While the case against Ayyad and Salameh was strong, the evidence linking Ajaj and Abouhalima to the blast was thin.

Ajaj, who had come into the country with Yousef, was in prison during the explosion. But Assistant U.S. Attorney Lev Dassin had hit a gold mine. After translating tapes routinely recorded at Raybrook, where Ajaj was serving his sentence, Dassin found that Ajaj had a friend in Dallas who had patched calls through to Yousef at Pamrapo. Those telephone calls would make it difficult for Campriello to argue that Ajaj was just Ramzi's innocent traveling companion.

Abouhalima was another matter. Until August, the only major evidence the prosecutors had against him was a gas-station attendant named Willie Hernandez Moosh. He had seen Abouhalima, Yousef, and Salameh making their way by deadly convoy to the mouth of the Holland Tunnel. What he said came damned close to proving beyond a reasonable doubt that those three men had been involved. But getting him to say it on the stand was another matter. Willie Hernandez Moosh was a simple man of simple habits. For eleven years he had worked at the Shell station at the corner of Kennedy Boulevard and Route 440. Even after it became clear that Moosh held the key to the entire trial, and he and his wife were relocated, kept under constant FBI watch, and given $4,500 for expenses, Moosh kept wandering back to the gas station for a smoke and to chat with his former colleagues about baseball. The only other witness who could place Abouhalima at the bomb factory was Carl Butler. The prosecutors needed one more piece. In early August the FBI executed yet another search warrant on Abouhalima's Woodbridge home. They had ransacked his house before, but this time it was different. The agents were not making general seizures; they were looking for clothing. They had taken nitroglycerin-stained clothing in Salameh's size out of the bomb factory, and they wanted to find Abouhalima's bomb-making clothes. They broke open closets and pawed through drawers. They looked in the hampers and in the garbage cans. Finally, as they were scouring the basement, they found a pair of broken-down black work boots. Over the big toe was a sulfuric-acid stain about the diameter of a quarter. The boots were Abouhalima's size. The prosecutors had found their link.

Back in the courtroom, Childers was running Joseph Hanlin, the ATF agent who had found the VIN number, through his testimony. Outwardly relaxed and conversational from years of testifying in court, Hanlin told the jury he had been an explosives enforcement officer with ATF since 1990. He said he was happy to have discovered two van parts: an internal section of a gear assembly and a covering. "When I saw these parts," he said, the Midwestern twang creeping into his voice, "I knew they had to be right at the point of the explosion."

Later he described finding the frame section with the VIN number punched into it.

"We couldn't read all the numbers," he said, "but we knew they were numbers and could be used to trace the vehicle. My opinion was that this came from [a] vehicle that had contained some type of explosive."

The testimony set off a flurry of cross-examinations, but Hanlin, coolly facing the jury when he answered the defense lawyers' questions, could not be shaken.

*   *   *

As the trial began to pick up speed, the defense team fell apart. Abouhalima learned that Kunstler was holding group strategy meetings for Siddig Ali and Hampton-El and the ten defendants and lawyers in the other case. He demanded that the lawyers in the Trade Center case do the same.

The first meeting was a disaster. To the dismay of the bombers, the lawyers couldn't even agree on a definition of a group defense.

Abdellah, Faines, and Ahmed thought that as a group they should concede nothing and make the government prove there was a bomb in the first place. Campriello, Byrnes, and Precht retorted that the strategy was a joke. Everyone in the country knew it was a bomb.

Abdellah scoffed. "If you guys are going to concede everything, I don't know why I even came."

They tried to accommodate each other, but at the end of the meeting, they agreed to disagree. They developed a kind of crude credo: If your guy isn't affected, shut up.

Campriello rarely attended subsequent meetings. In the tense weeks of the trial, the schism was widened by racial and religious elements until, by Thanksgiving, the two warring factions refused to eat lunch together. In court, Abdellah, who sometimes fingered prayer beads or chewed on a stick of licorice root to settle his stomach, was civil, but out of court he could barely hide his frustration.

The bombers' lives had gone from bad to worse. Every morning they were roused from sleep and dressed quickly in their orange coveralls. Handcuffed, they stuffed their prayer rugs in legal folders and were led to the third-floor processing room. Shivering in the dawn chill, they were given civilian clothes and waited, sometimes without eating, until the marshals led them up the nineteen steps to the walkway that joined MCC to the courthouse. The men missed breakfast and sometimes weren't returned to their cells until after the evening meal. Salameh became so distraught that he refused to come to court one day. Abouhalima complained to Judge Duffy that the prison psychologist had repeatedly told him to prove his innocence by "telling the government what they wanted to know."

"There are extremely high psychological pressures being placed on me," said Abouhalima. "An enormous pressure from within and without MCC."

Adding to his stress was news he had received from Egypt. Mubarak was once again taking aim at his old nemesis, Sheik Omar. Apparently annoyed with the deliberate pace of American justice, Mubarak announced to the world that the Egyptian government would try the sheik in absentia for sparking an antigovernment riot five years previously outside a mosque in Fayoum, a city sixty-five miles south of Cairo. The announcement was absurd. Sheik Omar had been tried for these offenses—which ranged from illegal demonstration to trying to kill a police officer—three years before and had been acquitted for lack of evidence. But Mubarak wouldn't be stopped. He had never formally approved the acquittal, a requirement under Egyptian law, and so they would be tried again.

Still, the sheik was better off than Abouhalima; he was in a hospital wing in Otisville prison in upstate New York, and had recently fired his lawyer. Now the blind imam was insisting that he be represented by William Kunstler.

Abouhalima tried not to worry. His lawyer, Abdellah, said their luck could change once the tapes Salem had secretly recorded were finally handed over to the defense lawyers.

On the morning of October 28, the defense lawyers awoke again to find their lives being played out in the headlines.

New York Newsday and *The New York Times* had gotten hold of the tapes. Both papers ran front-page stories. They quoted Salem chastising FBI agent John Anticev: "I told you the World Trade Center [was among the planned targets] but nobody listened."

The political fallout began almost immediately. The FBI announced it was conducting an immediate internal review of the way Salem was handled. During a press conference she had called to discuss violence on television, Attorney General Janet Reno was pestered by questions about Salem: What did the FBI know, and when had they first known it? Representative Charles Schumer, the chairman of the House Subcommittee on Crime and Criminal Justice, dispatched a letter to FBI director Louis Freeh, demanding he testify at a hearing on the handling of the World Trade Center bombing.

But for all the political grandstanding, the tapes said nothing that would slow the relentless progress of the prosecution. If Salem knew anything about the bombing, it was only in the vaguest terms. Nothing in the tapes would help the four men. The tapes were not the deliverance for which the defendants had prayed.

17

THE DAY OF RECKONING

By early December, the jury had heard most of the case against Ayyad and Salameh. And although their lawyers, Atiq Ahmed and Robert Precht, pretended to be unimpressed, there was an avalanche of evidence against their two clients.

In the hierarchy of the plotters, Ayyad and Salameh had been the expendable stooges who had convinced themselves that Allah had made them invincible. They had done little to cover their tracks. The jury had heard how Ayyad purchased chemicals, ordered hydrogen tanks; they had seen the hydrogen tank fragment after it was pulled from the blast. They had heard how Ayyad had discussed bomb formulas with colleagues, how he had telephoned and written news organizations, taking credit for the blast. He'd even licked the envelope and left a healthy sampling of his DNA all over it. He had used his computer at Allied Signal to draft another letter, warning that more bombings would follow. The day after the blast, when the bodies of the dead were being claimed at the morgue by grieving relatives, Ayyad was arranging to buy chemicals for another bomb.

Childers handed the jury a photograph of Ayyad. It wasn't a picture of a promising Rutgers graduate, a newly minted American citizen with a good job, a new wife, and a baby on the way. It was a picture of a man bent on destruction—his head draped in a kaffiyeh, clutching a grenade in one hand.

Even Ayyad's own father, Raymond, who attended the trial sporadically, was bewildered and heartbroken. During the course of the trial he had learned that his son, the success story, had lived a secret life as a terrorist. It was hard for a father to accept. "If he did this, he is a bastard," said Raymond. "But he is still my son."

The case against Salameh seemed equally as secure. Perhaps believing he would be given money to flee the country after the bombing, Salameh had done nothing to hide his identity, aside from occasionally using the alias Kamal Ibrahim. Along with Ayyad, he had stockpiled chemicals at a rented Jersey City storage shed. He had also rented the yellow Econoline van. Using a car rented by Ayyad, he had made a reconnaissance trip to the World Trade Center two weeks before the bombing to examine the garage. He had lived for a time at the bomb factory at Pamrapo Road in Jersey City, mixing the chemicals that would create the fiery inferno. It was more than enough evidence to prove the two men were involved in a terrorist conspiracy.

The case against Ajaj, though not as airtight as Ayyad's and Salameh's, as a whole looked more substantial than its parts. The jury heard how Ajaj had bought a ticket in Pakistan with Yousef, how they had traveled halfway across the world together and then split up on the airplane and pretended, as they approached U.S. Customs, that they didn't know each other. Ajaj carried a host of false passports, identifications, and bank letterheads—a terrorist kit, the prosecutor said, so that Ajaj could change his identity again and again. The jury saw that Ajaj had carried in his tattered black suitcase a wealth of bombing manuals and instruction books on guerrilla warfare. What kind of guy would be carrying material like that? But it was the tapes of Ajaj's telephone conversations from prison that turned out to be more damaging than the defense could have anticipated.

It is the policy in every federal penitentiary to routinely record prisoners' telephone conversations. Most jails post signs above the pay phones reminding prisoners that their calls are being taped. Cassettes of Ajaj's conversations were stored at prisons where he was housed: Otisville, Lewisburg, and MCC. When Ajaj was arrested as part of the conspiracy, prosecutors wanted to know with whom he had been in contact during the six months of his incarceration. FBI agents, armed with subpoenas, were dispatched to the various prisons, where they found, to their dismay, that too much time had elapsed and that many of the tapes had been used again. The priceless conversations had been recorded over.

Grimly, the agents brought the remaining tapes back to New

York. They sat in an airless room at a long table, with padded green headphones clamped over their ears, trying to pull a few tentative Arabic words from the giant reels of recorded prison conversations. At times it seemed like an impossible task. Perhaps, unable to master English, Ajaj had stayed away from the telephones. Perhaps Palestinian terrorists, like members of the old Mafia, prided themselves on doing their time silently and without complaint.

After weeks of searching, the agents found what they were looking for. In October 1993, lonely and disoriented in a jail full of drug dealers and mobsters, Ajaj had called a friend in Dallas. After a few rounds of salutations and praising Allah, Ajaj had cautioned his friend that prison officials could be listening in.

Then he had described his life in prison, how he could not watch television because of the sexy shows, how he missed his family and his friends. But Ajaj's most urgent request had been for news of his friend Rashed, Ramzi Yousef's alias.

"And tell him please to take care and look after my university papers, may God keep him," Ajaj said.

Later he asked his friend to get in touch with him if anyone called from "the university"—clearly a code name for a larger, unidentified organization.

In December, another friend in Dallas, Abu Omar, used a three-way calling system to patch Ajaj's call through to 40 Pamrapo Road. Ajaj and Yousef spoke in encoded terms about sending the bomb-construction manuals taken from Ajaj at Kennedy Airport to Rashed. They spoke at length about "the university," and argued about minimizing Rashed's exposure to the authorities. "Because you're at work all the time, all busy and that. I don't prefer, in other words, I don't prefer that you go bother yourself . . . to jeopardize your business, a pity."

The calls implied much more than they illuminated, but they might help the government prove that Ajaj had come into the country with Yousef not as an innocent traveling companion but as a fellow conspirator determined to carry out a monumental act of destruction.

But while the prosecutors moved Ayyad, Salameh, and Ajaj incrementally closer to life in prison, the evidence against Abouhalima remained spare.

Childers and DePippo had produced a receipt showing that Abouhalima had purchased black powder, which is sometimes used as a primary explosive. But they had no evidence that the black powder was used in the actual bombing. They showed the jury a receipt for a refrigerator used at Pamrapo to store the bomb's nitroglycerin, but plenty of new immigrants furnish their households by scavenging big-ticket appliances from different places—a washer from a flea market, a small television set from a friend leaving the country, a secondhand refrigerator from a neighbor moving on. The acid-stained shoe was damaging, but not on its own. The telephone records tying Abouhalima to the other conspirators suggested stronger connections than they actually proved. The prosecutors needed other evidence to seal Abouhalima's fate—people who could face the jury and point to the Red.

Childers and DePippo had only two witnesses who could effectively tie Abouhalima to the plot. The first was Carl Butler, a neighbor at Pamrapo who could place Abouhalima at the bomb factory. The second was Willie Hernandez Moosh, the gas-station attendant who had spotted Abouhalima and the others filling their tanks on the way to the Holland Tunnel. Both of them were needed to supply critical eyewitness testimony. Both proved to be disasters on the witness stand.

On November 29, Carl Butler took the stand. He lived, he said, in the top rear apartment at 40 Pamrapo Road with his wife. Every night, at the end of the ten o'clock news, Butler walked his dog around the block. Almost every night he had observed his downstairs neighbors. He had seen the men who lived there, and he'd observed the redheaded man who made frequent visits.

The FBI had visited Butler fifteen times, going over his statement again and again. DePippo was sure the jury would go home that day with the image of Butler extending a long, accusatory finger at Abouhalima.

"Can you tell us what that person looked like?" asked DePippo.

"He was a large man, very well dressed, and he had the weirdest-colored red hair in the world that I ever saw," answered Butler.

"Would you recognize that person if you saw him again?" asked DePippo expectantly.

"To point him out?" Butler replied, suddenly dubious. "The best I could do was tell you that he was a large man and he had strange-colored red hair."

DePippo was reeling. One of his principal identification witnesses, one of the keys to tying Abouhalima to the bomb factory, was balking.

"Do you see anybody here with that color hair?" DePippo said urgently.

"I really didn't look," he answered, then let his eyes swivel around the courtroom. "But no, I don't see anyone with the particular type of hair he had." Sensing DePippo's distress, Butler tried to elaborate. "He had close-cropped curly hair and it was an odd color, the only thing that distinguished him."

Throughout the entire case, the prosecutors had perfected a clipped and colorless style. DePippo fought to maintain it now. Without changing his facial expression, he quickly reassessed the information Butler could supply. What else had he seen? What other detail would help convince the jury that Abouhalima had been there? How could he salvage this witness?

"Describe [him] as best you can," said DePippo, stalling for time.

"Objection!" shouted Abdellah. "He already described it."

"In terms of color," DePippo said evenly.

"He described it," Abdellah complained.

Duffy looked down at the witness, then at DePippo. "If he can go any further, he can go further."

Butler tried. "It was . . . it was an orange reddish color hair. I don't know any better way to describe it."

Bit by bit, DePippo coaxed information from his reluctant witness. The visitor had driven a dark town car with New York Taxi and Limousine Commission license plates. The redheaded man had moved newspapers, clothing, and five-gallon cans from the trunk of his car into the garage.

When he was finished with his direct examination, DePippo sat down, drained.

* * *

In the days that followed Butler's testimony, Childers and DePippo huddled together, wondering whether they should revise their game plan. Their only remaining substantial witness who could implicate Abouhalima was Willie Hernandez Moosh. The idea that their case against the mastermind rode on Moosh's stooped shoulders was more than the prosecution team could bear.

From the days after the explosion, Moosh had proved to be a difficult witness. A sunny, amiable guy with an abiding desire to avoid trouble and to make new friends, when surrounded by federal agents and stern-faced prosecutors, he got nervous. When he was nervous, he sometimes spoke before he really thought about what he was going to say. He didn't want to hurt anybody. He just wanted to pump gas, watch his children grow, and talk about baseball. As a star witness in a federal trial, he struck terror in the hearts of the prosecutors, who had sent a letter to Judge Duffy, asking for permission to bring photographs of the defendants to court that day, just in case Moosh was unable to provide the critical identification.

On December 12, Moosh, a little cricket of a man with an anxious-to-please smile, took the stand. He told the jury how he had worked the twelve-to-eight shift at the Shell station at the mouth of the Holland Tunnel for eleven years. Prompted at each turn by Childers, Moosh told the jurors about the unique group of people, driving a dark livery cab and a yellow van, who had gassed up at three o'clock on the morning of the World Trade Center explosion.

"Mr. Moosh," Childers began, "at this time I'd like to ask you to take a look around the courtroom and tell me if you recognize or see anyone who looks like the person who was driving the yellow van."

Moosh stepped out of the witness box and wandered down to where Childers stood. Perhaps feeling a sense of impending doom, Childers's shoulders stiffened. But Moosh, unfazed, stared out into the press section of the courtroom. He quickly surveyed the defense table, then stared at the spectators. Then he moved over to the jury box.

"A person such as this one," he said, indicating juror number five, a dark-haired man. Salameh burst out laughing. The spectators began to murmur. "It was a person more like that one. A person sort of like that one," Moosh finished lamely as he reseated himself in the witness box.

Childers's ears turned purple. The prosecution's star witness was self-destructing before his eyes. He knew it was about to get worse. He had to ask Moosh to identify Abouhalima.

For the second time, Moosh climbed down from the witness box. With almost exaggerated care, he looked at the spectators, the press, and then, like a heat-seeking missile, walked over to the jury box.

"Look around the courtroom," Childers said, his voice sounding strangled.

Abdellah and Faines, who sat on either side of Abouhalima at the defense table, leaped to their feet, shouting, "Objection!" all but begging Moosh to identify their client. But Moosh, unperturbed, continued surveying the jurors.

"A person like that one," he said finally, picking out juror number six, a redheaded man. "It was a person like that one. Like that one, yeah."

The courtroom erupted. The defense attorneys were grinning as if they had won the lottery. Reporters ran for the telephones. Anita, the forewoman, frowned slightly in confusion. Ajaj, who had become a tense, almost funereal presence at the trial, began to smile.

By the time the prosecution broke for lunch, Ayyad, Salameh, and Ajaj had turned from laughter to tears. They wept as they were led away to the third-floor holding cells, partially out of joy but partially in a religious rapture. They had just witnessed a miracle, they murmured. Just as it was written in the Koran. Allah the All-Powerful had put a veil over the eyes of a liar; Allah the Mighty had confused the star witness so that his messengers would triumph. Moosh's identification was a confirmation of their faith. During these dark days when it seemed their friends had abandoned them, Allah had not forgotten them.

Abouhalima was not crying. He stared at his codefendants, crossed one powerful arm over the other, and allowed himself to smile.

*   *   *

It was as if the prosecutors had called for a tactical air strike, only to find themselves dogging shells. Childers salvaged Moosh's testimony as best he could, asking him to pick the men at the gas station out of a photo lineup, but the damage was done. Moosh had identified two jurors as the bombers of the World Trade Center. Worse, Moosh had opened the very real possibility that Abouhalima could beat the charges.

For the next few days, Childers and DePippo tried to think of ways to regain the advantage. What they needed were witnesses who could tie Abouhalima to the plot, but where could they find them?

The obvious one was Emad Salem. He had hinted to his FBI handlers that he knew about the bombing. But the true weight of what Salem knew about Abouhalima was hard to fathom. Salem managed to create the impression that he knew a lot more than he actually did. It was an effective technique when Salem had wooed lonely American women, but a hard-nosed defense lawyer would destroy him in minutes.

The shock waves from the secret tapes continued to reverberate through the federal law-enforcement establishment. A few days before Moosh took the stand, New York FBI chief James Fox was suddenly suspended—or put on "administrative leave," as the FBI called it—just weeks before he was scheduled to retire. It was a heavy blow to the FBI veteran, who had headed the New York office for six years. Inadvertently, Salem, who had cursed the FBI higher-ups for spurning him, got his revenge.

On December 4, Fox had appeared on a local television news show "11 News Closeup" and was asked to comment on newspaper stories that said Salem had provided the FBI with information about the World Trade Center bombing before the explosion.

Fox responded with barely suppressed annoyance. "He gave us nothing. No one gave us anything. If we had information, we would have prevented the bombing."

It was not the most detailed answer but it was enough to irk Fox's new boss, Louis Freeh, the former Manhattan federal judge who had just been named to replace FBI director William Sessions.

"Director Freeh made the decision to place Assistant Director Fox on administrative leave with pay until his retirement in January," said FBI spokesman John Collingwood. "He did so after carefully reviewing inappropriate public comments Fox made about a pending prosecution."

The federal rumor mill read it in different ways. Without his buddy Sessions to protect him, Fox was vulnerable. Perhaps old enemies were taking the chance to settle an old score. Others saw it as Freeh's very public warning to the loose-lipped FBI agents not to talk about the case.

Sources inside the U.S. Attorney's office said it was a necessity. Federal prosecutors had complained to Freeh that Fox was publicly bashing their star witness; in addition, in their view, what Fox said wasn't exactly the truth.

So the man that oversaw the Trade Center bombing investigation and personally prided himself on overseeing the men who put mob boss John Gotti away for life retired while on leave on January 23 to join the Mutual of America insurance company.

Salem's adjustment to life as a protected witness had not been smooth. After telling reporters he wanted to be remembered as "a man of peace," he was shocked to find himself portrayed with suspicion in newspapers all over the country. He had wanted to be a hero. Now he was having drastic mood swings, and had been prescribed Valium. It was all the prosecutors could do to prepare him for the case against the sheik to be tried the following fall.

Childers and DePippo reviewed the FBI materials on the newest informer in the second conspiracy, Abdo Haggag. The former computer programmer and the sheik's closest confidant had changed sides in October and had spent the last three months being debriefed by the FBI. He had told agents that the sheik had ordered the assassination of Mubarak. He had also told them that Abouhalima, Nosair, and Hampton-El had been leaders of the terrorist cell that shot radical Rabbi Meir Kahane. His information would make him an ideal witness for the second trial. Some of his statements to the FBI directly implicated Abouhalima. He said that after he was arrested on June 24 and thrown into MCC, he had lived temporarily on the secure wing in Nine South. During a conversation with Abouhalima at that time, the Red had admitted his involvement in the bombing.

But there were good reasons not to use Haggag. Jailhouse confessions simply don't play well with jurors. And while Haggag might implicate Abouhalima, it would also expose the computer programmer to rigorous cross-examination. The U.S. Attorney wanted to save Haggag for the second trial.

Lacking a suitable witness, the prosecutors decided to concentrate on DePippo's summation. It was a big risk. The case had relied on the accumulation of forensic evidence: receipts, leases, chemical stains, scraps of metal. But from experience, the prosecutors knew that a witness, one person telling a story to twelve others, impressed jurors far more. Now they had to make the existing evidence sing, make it so dramatic that the jurors were utterly convinced of the defendants' guilt. Childers tried to do this in his opening statement, but that was before the mountain of evidence was presented and then picked apart during soporific cross-examinations. It wouldn't be an easy task. As the final witnesses took the stand, DePippo began drafting his summation yet again. If the government didn't want Abouhalima to beat the case, DePippo had to make his closing statement the hottest story in town.

*   *   *

In the last dark weeks of January 1994, the trial became a test of endurance for the defense team. The financial considerations that had caused Abouhalima's first lawyer, Jesse Berman, to drop out of the case became painfully apparent to Abdellah, Faines, and Ahmed. Without receiving the standard seventy-five dollars an hour as a court-appointed lawyer, Abouhalima's and Ayyad's lawyers were essentially working gratis. Abdellah, Faines, and Ahmed were small-time private practitioners. Without the backing of huge firms or government agencies, they couldn't afford this extended period of largesse. Every Monday, Ahmed traveled by train from Maryland to New York. A few weeks into the trial, those travel expenses started coming out of his own pocket. Every day of the trial, Abdellah calculated that he spent over forty dollars: four dollars for tolls from New Jersey, twenty-five dollars to park his car, as well as money for lunch and for the cost of dry-cleaning his expensive suits. Every penny of the money he spent was his own. Facing financial disaster, Abdellah began moonlighting at municipal court in New Jersey. After putting in a long day in the lavish Manhattan federal court, Abdellah drove back through the Holland Tunnel and defended drunk drivers, petty thieves, and low-level drug dealers across the Hudson.

As their differences divided the defense team, at times the lawyers struggled to remain publicly cordial to each other. Precht and Ahmed seemed utterly vanquished, and opted not to present a defense. Abdellah felt that Moosh's testimony had damaged the prosecution case more than anything he could say or do. He also opted not to present a case. Only Campriello took a chance. He called to the stand a private investigator he had hired, William Natlo. Natlo described how he had purchased bomb-making manuals through *Soldier of Fortune,* a magazine whose audience was made up primarily of survivalists, right-wing extremists, and would-be mercenaries. Campriello had his witness point out that this magazine, from which the bombers had learned much of their craft, was printed in the American heartland, in Racine, Wisconsin. He tried valiantly to demystify the contents of Ajaj's luggage. But mostly he had to wait and see what DePippo would say about Ajaj in his summation.

On the morning of February 15, 1994, Henry DePippo, looking like a pale young Jesuit with his dark suit and stern expression, stood to face the jury. As soon as he opened his mouth, the tenor of the trial changed. For months the prosecutors had presented evidence without supplying interpretation, without tying up loose ends. Now DePippo addressed the jury like a master storyteller. As he spoke, the heavy formality of federal court fell away. DePippo's moment had arrived. He could finally tell the jury at least some of what the government knew about these evil men. He could share at least part of the story that had obsessed him for almost a year.

"No one witness in this case could tell the whole story," he said. "You have to now put all of the evidence that you've heard before you together to hear the story . . . [of] how these defendants bombed the World Trade Center."

As DePippo spoke, the case came together with heart-pounding intensity.

As he described them, the defendants looked less and less like fanatics and bunglers and more like devious and sophisticated players in an international spy thriller. Yousef, DePippo said, was the "evil genius" behind the operation. Salameh and Ayyad were his willing apprentices. DePippo ticked off the evidence against them: the van, the storage shed, the chemicals, the letters. Then he moved on to Abouhalima. The Red had supplied the munitions expertise he had picked up in Afghanistan, and advised them during his nightly visits to Pamrapo. Just visiting the bomb factory was enough to convict any of these men of conspiracy, DePippo insisted.

"You know that Abouhalima is there all the time. And to put Mohammad Salameh and Ramzi Yousef at Pamrapo is to convict them in this case. . . . There was no other reason to go to 40 Pamrapo except to help make the bomb."

In fact, none of the witnesses had conclusively put Abouhalima at the bomb factory, but DePippo wisely glossed over that point. Instead, he emphasized what the prosecution had been able to prove. He held out the telephone record from Abouhalima's phone card, which showed calls among the defendants, the chemical companies, the rental van, and the factory at Pamrapo. During his summation, DePippo began to refer to the phone card as "the conspirators' calling card." He was using every rhetorical trick he could muster. "That card links him to the conspiracy." DePippo paused for emphasis and then shouted, "He's caught!"

The jurors, who had at one time resorted to counting the slats on the window blinds in order to stay awake, reacted with pleasure to this dramatic turn. Anita, the forewoman, smiled and nodded. The other jurors straightened and leaned forward.

He explored every inch of the case against Abouhalima, calling each thread—the shoe, the refrigerator receipt, the purchase of black powder—"absolutely devastating evidence."

The case against Ajaj came next. The skinny Palestinian was a trained explosives and munitions expert who had left friends and family in Houston and traveled to Peshawar, Pakistan, to be instructed on his role in the plot. He described how Ajaj had traveled to the United States with Yousef and then carried out an elaborate ruse to get Yousef into the country. Even getting caught by immigration, DePippo suggested, was evidence that Ajaj was taking part in the conspiracy.

"He made sure that Ramzi Yousef got through. That was part of his plan," said DePippo. "[Ajaj] sacrificed himself and when he got caught, he was carrying the terrorist kit."

Actually, the basis of DePippo's argument made no sense. Ajaj and Yousef had pretended not to know each other at immigration; no one knew they were connected in any way. INS agents had testified that Ajaj's being caught and Yousef's getting through was a matter of chance. Besides, if Ajaj was prepared to "sacrifice himself" so Yousef could get in and bomb the Trade Center, why would the sacrificial lamb be carrying the bomb-making manuals they needed for the operation? But DePippo was counting on the beauty of a strong narrative to obscure the boundaries of logic. People, and especially bored jurors, want to hear a good story. Facts, as former President Ronald Reagan once said, are stupid things.

"Using that good common sense, sift through the evidence," he continued, "because it's through the evidence and the evidence alone that you will find the facts of this case. If you sift through the evidence, you will see that these defendants are the ones that planned and carried out the bombing at the World Trade Center that killed six people, that injured over a thousand, that caused hundreds of millions of dollars in destruction. They did it to send a terrorist message, and they told you exactly what that message was. If you sift through the evidence and apply your good common sense, you're going to conclude that these are the World Trade Center bombers before you. You will conclude that they are guilty of each and every count of the indictment."

DePippo's forceful words faded and he closed his notebook. For a moment the spectators and the jury sat quietly, absorbing the aftershocks of the riveting scenario he had presented. DePippo had made his case.

*   *   *

Wounded, the defense lawyers turned on each other like sharks in bloodied water. Salameh's lawyer, Precht, saw that his client was being crushed under a mountain of evidence. He felt he had no choice but to acknowledge the plot and Salameh's limited participation in it. His strategy was to argue that Salameh was an unwitting dupe of those who were smarter and more devious. He needed someone else to take the blame, and the fugitive defendant Yousef was as good a villain as anyone. Precht could have said that Yousef had come into the country and then enlisted Salameh's help in carrying out his newly hatched plan to blow up the Trade Center. None of the defense lawyers could have anticipated what Precht would do instead. Taking a cue from DePippo, he argued that Yousef had come into the country with Ajaj for the sole purpose of bombing the Trade Center, then had enlisted the aid of Salameh. The argument made Ramzi Yousef look more like the devil, but it would effectively convict Ajaj.

As Precht was about to begin his summations, Ajaj's lawyer, Campriello, noticed bank letterheads and bombing manuals taken from Ajaj's suitcase placed in front of Precht as props.

Campriello walked over to Precht and pointed to the manuals. He dispensed with his usual familiarities. "Are you going to say Ramzi came into the country with the idea?" he demanded. Precht didn't give him a clear answer. Campriello's head began to spin. It was one of the thousand little lulls in the courtroom. The jury had not been seated. The judge was settling himself on the bench. The prosecutors were milling around, slightly out of earshot. It was the last moment when Ajaj had a chance of beating the charges.

"You gotta say that Ramzi got the idea when he arrived here," Campriello hissed.

But Precht just threw up his hands. It was a question of survival. The choice was between Salameh, the man who had been involved in almost every phase of the bombing, and Ajaj, who had been serving a six-month jail sentence at the time. And Salameh's lawyer got to sum up first.

Precht admitted that Salameh had rented a van, and that his client's fingerprints were found on bottles in the storage shed. But Salameh, Precht explained, thought he was starting a small business. He was being "terribly manipulated" by an "evil genius" who had flown here from overseas with the sole purpose of blowing up the Trade Center.

"Ramzi Yousef did get Mr. Salameh to help him, but kept Mr. Salameh in the dark," said Precht.

At the end of his summation, in which he all but sentenced Ajaj to a life term in prison, Campriello demanded a mistrial. "In my view, Mr. Precht did more damage to Mr. Ajaj in the first six minutes or so of his summation than Mr. DePippo did in the six hours of his summation. . . . Mr. Precht has bought into what I think is Mr. DePippo's view of the case, namely that Ramzi Yousef came to this country with a plan already in mind, to blow up the World Trade Center."

But Duffy, who had sat through six laborious months of testimony, was not about to sit through six more. Campriello's request for a mistrial was denied.

Campriello was not the only one who was disturbed by Precht's summation. That night, Salameh telephoned a friend and told him to alert the news media that a miscarriage of justice was taking place. "I was shocked to hear what the lawyer was saying," said Salameh. "I object to everything that came in the summation. The things that Mr. Precht said do not represent me. Mr. Precht is only representing himself. . . . I couldn't believe my ears. I thought the interpreter was just misunderstanding or made a mistake interpreting what my lawyer was saying. How can you make up a story like that which the government could itself not prove?" He sent a letter to Duffy, complaining about his representation, but the judge was not moved.

Next Ayyad's lawyer, Ahmed, stood behind the podium, facing the jurors. He opened his mouth and prayed: *"Bismillah-Ar-Rahman-Ar-Raheem,"* he said, then translated. "In the name of God, most compassionate, most merciful."

Ahmed needed help from God. His awkward cross-examinations had provoked the public ire of Judge Duffy and, privately, the anger of some members of the defense team as well. More than once, out of earshot of the jury, Duffy had had to instruct him on basic courtroom techniques. He had shocked the defense during his cross-examination of Patrick Galasso, who had rented the Ryder van to Salameh, by implicating Ayyad in that phase of the scheme. During direct examination, Galasso testified that Salameh had been accompanied by another man when he rented the van. Galasso gave a rough physical description of the other man, recalling that he had dark hair and wore glasses. DePippo never asked Galasso if he could identify him further. For reasons understood best by himself, Ahmed picked up on that line of questioning. With a theatrical flourish, he asked both Salameh and Ayyad to stand next to their seats.

"You indicated there was a two-inch difference between the two gentlemen who walked into your office. Right?" Ahmed asked.

"Yes, sir."

"Would you say there is a two-inch difference between these gentlemen, or is the difference more like one foot?" demanded Ahmed, indicating Salameh and Ayyad.

"It's more than two inches, sir," replied Galasso.

"Thank you," said Ahmed, bowing slightly to the jury. Anita, the jury forewoman, lifted an eyebrow.

"Now, the gentleman who was standing next to me," he said, indicating Ayyad, "the one who is about a foot taller than me, have you seen him before?"

"I think so, sir," said Galasso.

"And where did you see him, sir?" Ahmed asked.

"In my office, sir," Galasso answered politely.

Members of the press stared at each other in wide-eyed amazement. Campriello dropped his gaze and began shuffling papers on the defense table. But Ahmed was not put off.

"So, would it be your testimony that he was the gentleman that accompanied Mr. Salameh to your office?"

"I think so, sir," replied Galasso.

It was an almost insurmountable piece of evidence against Ayyad, made more persuasive by the fact that his own lawyer had elicited it.

Ahmed's summation was a hodgepodge of feeble attacks on the FBI and a civics lesson that touched upon John F. Kennedy, Thomas Jefferson, and Dr. Martin Luther King. Unfortunately for Ayyad, none of these great men was on trial. After presenting no defense case to back up his statements, Ahmed delivered a full-blown alibi to the jury, suggesting that Ayyad was on his honeymoon or on a business trip during the time phone records indicated calls between the conspirators. If he did make telephone calls, Ahmed suggested, he was calling on behalf of friends who were starting a new business called Kamal & Co. It was Ayyad's "kindness and gentleness," Ahmed told the jury, that had led him to "simply help a friend."

It was too much for Judge Duffy. "You suggested you would prove certain things and you didn't," he told Ahmed when the jury had left the courtroom for a short break. "And yet you have summed up as though they are in the record."

Ahmed bristled. "Your Honor, I am drawing certain inferences and that's what I am trying to tell—"

"Yes, but you can't make it up," Duffy interrupted him. "And what you have done is come up with things which have absolutely no basis whatsoever in the record."

Shortly afterward, Ahmed rested.

A pugilist to the last, Abdellah came out swinging. By conceding that Salameh had participated in a bombing conspiracy, Precht had short-circuited Abdellah's underlying strategy: to refuse to concede that there was a bomb, that there was a conspiracy, and that Abouhalima was involved. But Abdellah was not ready to give up the fight.

"The decision you make that day when you leave is going to have an impact. It's going to have an historical impact. Look around the courtroom. Doesn't it remind you of the time of Moses when the people gathered, and you had to deal with truth and falsehood?"

Using the Old Testament, the Koran, and a sprinkling of street logic for good measure, Abdellah warmed up the jurors like an old-time preacher.

"Your patriotism is not just to sit here and rubber-stamp something that Mr. DePippo would tell you is right," Abdellah told them. "He tried to recreate a certain type of story. But was it based on facts? Was it even based on testimony? See, I know they writing [sic], but they can't write that fast. Get the transcript." Like an enthusiastic congregation, supporters of the defendants softly began to call out words of encouragement.

"Go, brother."

"That's right."

For the next few hours, Abdellah did the best he could to distance Abouhalima from his fellow defendants, to remind the jury that no witness had implicated the Red as part of the plot.

Last came Campriello. He had been robbed of just about every logical defense strategy. He couldn't very well persuade the jury that Ajaj was another in a long line of dupes. He couldn't convincingly argue that Yousef was simply Ajaj's traveling companion. His fellow lawyers, in their desperation, had left Ajaj and his attorney nothing. Campriello decided to play on human fallibility.

"I wanted to just walk through with you some, not all, some of the mistakes made during this trial so you can get comfortable with the concept that my guess is that most of you weren't comfortable [with] when you walked in here, mainly that the government could have made a mistake by bringing Ajaj here."

Without dropping his avuncular style, Campriello launched into his attack. The FBI had made a mistake in letting Abdul Yasin, one of the fugitive defendants, flee, he pointed out. The Bureau of Prisons had made a mistake in erasing the tapes of Ajaj's telephone calls, he reminded them. Maybe, just maybe, they got the wrong guy when they charged Ajaj with the bombing.

He talked for eight hours, nicking and slicing at the version of events painted by both the prosecutors and the defense. Campriello hoped that the jury would mistake the tiny rivulets of blood for a fatal hemorrhage.

*　　*　　*

Now it was up to the jury. They set aside the games, such as Uno and Scattergories, that they had played in the jury room, and prepared to get down to work. After explaining the laws they had to consider, Duffy gave them a road map, suggesting a way to logically debate the indictment. Consider whether you believe there was an explosion and whether the explosion was caused by a bomb, Duffy said. Then review the facts of the case and determine who was responsible for building and planting the bomb. With Duffy's words ringing in their ears, the jurors faced each other across a highly buffed table and deliberated.

For six months they had met every morning in midtown at Grand Central Terminal and been driven to the lower Manhattan courthouse in a van with tinted windows. They sat through every minute of testimony, ate lunch together, and once a week were escorted by federal marshals to a local restaurant. They addressed each other by their first names and, sensing the security surrounding the case, didn't pry too much into one another's personal lives. Despite record-breaking cold and snow, epidemics of flu and family crises, their attendance throughout the trial was nearly perfect.

Now they had to begin debating the evidence, evaluate the credibility of 206 witnesses, and make sense of more than ten thousand pages of testimony.

Although they had been under specific instructions not to discuss the case before the testimony was completed, they found, now that they were allowed to talk about it, that they had formed similar impressions about the two sides.

"The prosecutor presented enormous amounts of evidence," one of the jurors said later. "The defense presented nothing. It was almost overwhelming."

They reheard early testimony describing the blast, and quickly decided that there had been an explosion caused by a bomb. Then they had to decide who was behind that blast. After reviewing the evidence, they quickly voted to convict Salameh and Ayyad of the bombing conspiracy. They were, the juror said, "probably the easiest." After so many weeks of passive listening, they were eager to press forward. Patiently and courteously they began to debate the charges on the other two. Abouhalima was harder. But in a discussion that would have delighted the prosecution and sickened the defense, none of the jurors seemed prepared to dismiss Moosh's flawed testimony.

"After ten months, if you saw these guys at three in the morning, [you] might not be able to recognize them either," the juror said later. The jurors once again asked to rehear testimony linking Abouhalima to the plot. Satisfied, they moved on.

By the third day, when the jury was considering whether to convict Ajaj, Childers began compiling a list of the home telephone numbers of people who had lost family members in the blast: Eddie Smith, the husband of Monica Smith; the family of Steve Knapp; Bill Macko's wife and kids; the mother of John DiGiovanni, the driver of the silver Taurus that had preceded Timothy Lang into the parking garage; Bob Kirkpatrick's wife; and Mrs. Wilfredo Mercado. Even if some of the defendants were acquitted, Childers wanted the people who had lost loved ones to hear it directly from him. The defense lawyers began checking into upcoming cases, reminding themselves that whatever the outcome for the clients, they would take the verdict like professionals.

Mohammad Salameh called home and told his parents that the trial was almost over, and predicted he would be flying home at the end of the weekend to see them. Then he asked God to bless them and hung up.

Ajaj could barely eat or sleep. During the trial, anxiety and near-constant headaches made it almost impossible for him to swallow the unappetizing prison food. But now, with the jury out, he was almost paralyzed by fear. Abouhalima remained impassive. On the chance he was convicted, he was already making plans to have the famed lawyer William Kunstler represent him on appeal. After all, it was the legend, Kunstler, who had succeeded in nearly rescuing his friend Nosair.

*　　*　　*

Anita, the jury forewoman, answered the court clerk. The jury had reached a verdict.

"How do you find the defendant Mohammad Salameh on the first count of the indictment?" That count was conspiracy to blow up the World Trade Center, a crime that carried a mandatory life sentence. It would hold him responsible for the bloody day when he had killed six people and tried to kill tens of thousands.

"Guilty," answered Anita, her voice clear.

Salameh slumped in his seat.

"How do you find Nidal Ayyad?" The evidence against Ayyad was as strong as the case against Salameh. Maybe even stronger. Ayyad pulled his red prayer rug out of a legal folder and gripped it.

"Guilty."

Ayyad's face turned red and his eyes filled with tears.

"Against defendant Mahmud Abouhalima?" The evidence linking Abouhalima to Salameh was strong. The evidence linking him to the bombing was nonexistent.

"Guilty."

Abouhalima remained expressionless. Then a wry grin began playing around his mouth. Childers and DePippo looked stunned, then happy. They fought back their grins.

Only Ajaj remained.

"Guilty."

Thirty-eight times, on all charges, Anita uttered the world *guilty*. Conspiracy, explosive destruction of property, interstate transportation of explosives, and assault on a federal officer. Anita never looked at the defendants.

As soon as the clerk finished his official statements, Salameh rose out of his green leather chair.

"It is injustice!" he screamed, his face contorted with rage. "An unjust!'" He pointed a finger at the jury, at the twelve faces regarding him in shock.

Ayyad rose from his chair, his lanky body unfolding like a lion springing upon his prey. He opened his mouth. *"Allah!"* he roared, drawing out the word like a curse or maybe a prayer.

"Allah Akhbar," answered Salameh. God is great.

Salameh bent over and pounded on the table. "This is no. Cheap government. Cheap people." He prepared to lunge for the jurors, but the marshals moved up swiftly behind him.

Ayyad's younger brother, who had been sitting in the last row, stood up and began screaming. "Allah watch over you!" The marshals were upon him too, hurling their bodies into his in an effort to move him out the door.

But Ayyad's brother would not be moved. "You are fucking liars! Liars!" he screamed. Then he was overpowered and dragged away.

But by then Ajaj had taken up the chant. *"Il-ya!"*

The sound ricocheted around the courtroom. The defendants screamed out for their God. A God, they seemed to say by their chanting, that had given them reason to kill five men and a woman and her unborn child. A God who asked for a sacrifice of fifty thousand more.

"Il-ya Islam!" howled Ayyad. Islam will be victorious. A God that spoke to them, and them only, and gave them the undeniable moral authority to take a life.

"Allah be praised," answered another.

Islam will be victorious.

Only Abouhalima was silent. He sat calmly, his arms folded, his face arranged in a bemused smile. The marshals interrupted the chanting by handcuffing the prisoners and dragging them out of the courtroom. In the holding cells, where they could not be seen, the marshals trampled a copy of the Koran that had fallen on the floor in the tussle.

"Where is your God now?" they asked the bombers, who cursed them in Arabic.

Back in the courtroom, the howls of the defendants slowly grew fainter. Then one of the jurors began to cry.

EPILOGUE

The translator came through all the clearances, boarded the elevator, and rode to the high security floor at the Metropolitan Correctional Center, the federal jailhouse in New York City. He stopped at the vending machines and bought a Snickers bar. He had another set of quarters ready and played the machine for a second bar. Then he walked into the conference room and sat down with Sheik Omar Abdel-Rahman.

The sheik barely grunted hello before he reached across the table and grabbed the candy bar. He tore the wrapper from the chocolate and wolfed down the sweet in a few awesome bites. *New York Newsday* reporter Kevin McCoy watched in wonder. Here was the man who had frightened America with his sunglasses and wild beard and extravagant hatred of a government in Egypt that few people in the United States had ever given much thought to—and he was putting all business aside until he scarfed down a Snickers bar.

Munching on snacks, the sheik prepares to go on trial. He was planning to represent himself, and even the old adage about having a fool for a client may not help the government win its prosecution of Abdel-Rahman on charges of seditious conspiracy.

Simply put, the case against him is weak. Its defects arise not for a want of evidence that the blind sheik has spoken of insurrection against various governments, or from any ambivalence about his desire to see Egyptian president Hosni Mubarak six feet under. Indeed, many of those kinds of speeches would seem to fit the textbook definition of sedition: advocacy of the overthrow of the government. But the case's flaw is fundamental: all sedition crimes are political, and virtually all sedition prosecutions, including this one, are politically motivated. American juries traditionally have little tolerance for armed crimes; but they also have shown little interest in finding a person guilty of a felony for political beliefs, no matter how foreign or abhorrent.

Of course, it would be impossible to predict how a jury would rule in this case. The evidence includes video and audio tapes, which typically are very potent weapons in a courtroom. But most of that won't go against the sheik; for him, the prosecutors will be relying on the testimony of insiders who became government witnesses only after their own involvement was preserved forever on digital tape. This makes it a distinct possibility that Abdel-Rahman will emerge from the trial acquitted, then deported. If his shaky health does not deteriorate—he is a diabetic and has a blood pressure problem—he would be even more of a hero in the fundamentalist world for having defeated the great Satan.

The World Trade Center bombers bought hydrogen tanks, rented a van, stirred chemicals, and killed six people. The sheik has done nothing like that. The bombers were nailed by a brilliant, meticulous prosecution and investigators who pulled out all the stops to correct the gigantic error they made in letting the bombers slip through their fingers before the explosion.

Contrary to the vague understandings of the general public, no one has charged Abdel-Rahman with ordering the bombing or planning attacks on American landmarks. He is accused of ordering the assassination of the Egyptian president. Was this a serious threat, or was it like a fan in the baseball park shouting out, "Kill the umpire"?

The sheik is due to stand trial in the fall of 1994 on a charge that could put him away for life: sedition. It is a crime most people have never heard of, and even fewer understand.

A man rents a van and drives a bomb into a garage: that is simple. Another group rents a house in a quiet neighborhood and mixes a bomb to blow up a tunnel: that, too, is simple—particularly if the entire cooking session has been caught on videotape.

Yet the charges against Sheik Omar Abdel-Rahman arise not from anything he did, but from his words—and even those appear to be laced with ambiguity about his intentions. When the government informant Emad Salem tried to lure the sheik into blessing a plan to blow up the United Nations, Abdel-Rahman demurred.

"We shall prepare a big thing," Salem said. "A big thing, God willing, and let her have its fate. Is this action permitted by the Islamic faith we believe in or is it *haram* [forbidden]?"

"It would not be *haram* but it will muddy the waters for Muslims," the sheik replied.

"Do we do it or—"

"No," the sheik said flatly.

"We don't?"

"Find a pl—find a plan," the sheik began.

"Ah," Salem acknowledged.

"To inflict damage on the army, the American army, because the United Nations would harm Muslims, harm them tremendously."

"Then we don't do the United Nations?" Salem repeated.

"No."

"Something to the military?" Salem asked.

"Yes," said the sheik. "Let it, let it—think of something else, because the United Nations will be considered as a center for peace."

"What about 26 Federal Plaza?"

"Well, a little bit later. We'll talk about this."

Salem told him the plans to strike FBI headquarters were already under way.

"It doesn't matter," said the sheik. "Slow down. Slow down a little bit. The one who killed Kennedy was trained for three years. We don't want to do anything in haste."

Are these the words of a man ordering the overthrow of the United States government? Or are they the verbal wet rags of a man trying to cool the fevers he had raised in the young fundamentalists who flocked to him for religious guidance?

The basis of the charges is not that the blind man handled chemical nitroglycerin, but that he was a master detonator of passions and emotions. The sheik therefore is charged for his great influence over these men. Yet when he orders them not to blow up the United Nations, they continue with their plotting anyway.

The government has at least three informants—Salem, Haggag, and Siddig Ali—who will say that the sheik ordered the assassination plot against Mubarak. By the time the sheik goes on trial, most likely others in the plot will have cut deals, and those with the most to say about him will have the strongest hand to play in their negotiations. Siddig Ali was particularly close to the sheik. He also was heavily implicated in the plot as its mastermind. Still, Ali will have to go beyond the obvious to prove a devastating witness. It was no secret that the sheik wished Mubarak ill—and the assassination plot never developed as far as the aborted bomb factory in the Queens garage. In fact, Abdel-Rahman often had hoped aloud for Mubarak's death—even to news reporters, saying that the Egyptian president should end up like his predecessor, Anwar Sadat: assassinated. Did he ever tell anyone to go out and shoot Mubarak?

The main informants can't connect him to the World Trade Center bombing. They can't connect him to the Kahane assassination. They can't connect him to the United Nations plot: as the tape excerpt on page 295 shows, Abdel-Rahman tells them *not* to bomb the place because it would be terrible public relations for Muslims everywhere.

The government does have many tapes of Sheik Omar advising the accused conspirators—people who the government says were filmed mixing the bomb, buying the weapons, casing out targets. The prosecutors also have tapes of his sermons, some of which were seized from the home of a paralegal working on the case, and so might not be admissible in court. In them, the sheik says all Muslims must be "terrorists." But will the jury find the sheik's role to be seditious, an act of belligerent rebellion against the existence of the United States government? Or was he acting as a spiritual adviser?

The sedition conspiracy law always has raised the specter of political persecution whenever it has been used. It was created in the nineteenth century to prosecute Confederate organizers. It was used again briefly in the early 1900s to prosecute socialists and then basically fell into public and legal disfavor.

The advantage to prosecutors is that it is very vague. Also, it is the only conspiracy statute that really fits these wide-ranging allegations. The government couldn't use the Racketeering Influenced Corrupt Organizations Act—the other broad federal conspiracy statute—because it requires that some economic incentive be involved in the conspiracy.

Unlike the racketeering laws, the sedition act doesn't make the prosecutors prove that a defendant committed any overt act to further the conspiracy. The feds don't even have to prove that a defendant even *knew* about the acts others in the conspiracy committed. Guilt is measured by how much plotting goes on, not by whatever actually occurs.

It simply makes it a crime to "conspire to overthrow, or put down, or destroy by force the Government of the United States." While this sounds like a prosecutor's dream, the disadvantage is that it almost always comes down to putting politics on trial. And that can be risky with a jury.

In the 1980s, the government dusted off the sedition charge for the Ohio Seven case. In trials in 1982 and 1984, several of them were convicted of other charges but all seven were acquitted of sedition. In 1985, the feds won sedition convictions against four Puerto Rican nationalists. But in the next two cases to use it—the 1986 trial of fifteen white supremacists in Arkansas and the 1989 bombing trial of three people in Massachusetts—everyone was acquitted.

People who are privy to the group defense sessions for the sedition trial say that the sheik is a funny, ironic, and probing man who is well aware of the weaknesses and strengths of the case against him. The blind cleric, working through the massive American legal system, could be more of a sympathetic figure than a terrorist devil, the head of a "Sheik Omar Crime Family." His followers are based in mosques in New Jersey and New York, in Michigan, California, and "elsewhere," the government says in court papers. It may well be that a small army of religious fanatics is waiting for a word from one holy man or another to attack the United States. The World Trade Center bombing proved that the United States was not immune to terrorist impulses. But the Justice Department has yet to produce evidence—or even suggest—that Abdel-Rahman ever gave the command for that bombing.

In the days after the bombing, when the people accused of the act were known to be followers of the sheik, intense political pressure arose to implicate him. The government tried to solve a political problem with a legal solution. It might have been far simpler to deport him, as he no longer had legal status in the United States. But American allies in the Middle East—particularly Hosni Mubarak of Egypt—were in no hurry to see Abdel-Rahman back home raising hell on their streets.

Now Abdel-Rahman and the government are tied together in a legal knot that one side is bound to let slip.

At home in Egypt, people who listen to the sheik's sermons continue to attack tourists. In the spring of 1994, the Mubarak government brought a case that led to a sentence of hanging for a large group of Abdel-Rahman-ites. To the north, in Israel, the circle of violence continues: a peace pact was worked out with the PLO, to the dismay of hard-line Jewish settlers. Near the end of the bombers' trial, a Jewish doctor named Baruch Goldstein walked into a mosque in the Occupied Territories and killed dozens of Muslims at prayer. Goldstein, one of his friends said, had attended the trial in New York of El Sayyid Nosair, the man accused of murdering Kahane. He sat with the Kahane followers, who railed at the fundamentalists and who argued that a broader conspiracy was afoot than a single act of violence by the Prozac-popping Nosair. Goldstein would have sat across the aisle in the Manhattan courtroom from, among others, Mohammad Salameh and Mahmud Abouhalima, the World Trade Center bombers.

The great hatred in the little room of the Mideast endures.

ABOVE THE CONTINENTAL UNITED STATES
MAY 19, 1994
2:00 A.M.

"Sir," whispered the stewardess. "Are you all right?"

The flight from New York to Los Angeles was about halfway across the country when the stewardess noticed tears running down the clean-shaven cheeks of the big man with the sandy hair. He was holding a pen in his fist and was bent over a pad of legal-size paper.

"Oh," said Ed Smith, startled. He recovered quickly. "My allergies are terrible. They always act up in the springtime."

"Let me see if I can find something for you," she said.

"Please, don't go to any trouble," said Smith.

"No trouble."

On his lap, the legal pad was filling up fast. In a few days, he would be returning to New York for the sentencing of the four bombers. He planned to speak. The bombers would go away to jail for some incredibly long sentence, he was sure. But they could not be allowed to go away without thinking about what they had done. What they had stolen. He would tell them.

The damages had been unbelievable: at the end, the Port Authority estimated the explosion cost $300 million for repairs to the basement, and another $225 million for cleaning the soot from all 110 stories of both towers. Men and women who had worked on the original construction of the towers, now peacefully retired, just showed up in the work areas and put on hard hats to pitch in. The Port staff worked sixteen-hour days for a month. By the end of

March, Governor Mario Cuomo led a line of tenants into the building. By and large, the tenants stayed with the building—in fact, the lease renewal rate was up. The structural engineer, Leslie Robertson, had a contractor pick up the 14,000-pound brace that had been torn away by the bomb. He had it carted up to his weekend home in Connecticut and mounted it on a concrete pedestal. He planned to install a sculpture bench beneath it. He was proud of his building.

The police and fire departments awarded thousands of medals and commendations to their members. A made-for-television movie celebrated the heroics of the investigators. The immigration status of the bombers was noted often and loudly; few mentioned that two of the people killed, Monica Rodriguez Smith and Wilfredo Mercado, were hard-working immigrants living in the palm of the American dream. Muslims protested that they were being tarred by the acts of a few. Arab countries blamed Israel for the explosion. No one would forget the World Trade Center bombing, but few people thought about it very much.

Ed Smith had put the house in Seaford, Long Island, on the market, and it sold very quickly. People walked into the house and were thrilled by the high gloss of the floor that he and Monica had varnished seven times, painting and laughing their ways out the door in the morning.

Smith had been asked by the lead prosecutor, Gil Childers, if he'd like to make a statement when the bombers were sentenced. Crime victims rarely speak in the federal courts. Smith said he'd be glad to—in fact, he had a number of things he wanted to say. Childers told him to hang on, that it was up to Judge Kevin Duffy, and a petition had to be filed, which Duffy promptly granted.

In his work, Smith smiled fast, laughed easily, a salesman born with an agreeable manner. He also spent hours in airplanes, flying across the country. Alone, seven miles up, he brooded. That night, Smith sat in the business class section of a Continental flight from New York to Los Angeles and wrote the five-page speech he would deliver in court.

One night, in the autumn of 1992, I was at school and called home as I did every night between classes. But this call would be different from any other I had ever made. My wife, Monica Smith, told me to hurry home after class. She had purchased a pregnancy test and wouldn't take the test until I got home. The anticipation grew and I left class fifteen minutes early and raced home. . . .

"Excuse me, sir."

It was the stewardess again. She had found an antihistamine somewhere on the plane and handed it to Ed with a cup of water.

"You shouldn't have done that," said Ed, smiling.

"We don't want people to think you're sitting here crying your heart out," she said.

"You're so right," he said.

A salesman, but a gentleman: he did not want to dump his own pain onto strangers. That was something for the television shows that specialized in public therapy sessions. He thanked the stewardess and stared out into the black night sky over America.

U.S. DISTRICT COURT
FOLEY SQUARE, MANHATTAN
MAY 24, 1994
11:00 A.M.

"We took the test and it came back positive. Our lives and marriage would now have everything we wanted. A new baby was on the way, and I can remember that night as if it were yesterday, because I never felt so close to another human being. We slept in each other's arms as if we were one person."

Ed Smith stood at a podium in the courtroom, six feet from Mohammad Salameh, eight feet from Nidal Ayyad, ten from Mahmud Abouhalima, fourteen from Ahmad Ajaj. Smith's mother sat in the first row, and next to her were Monica's brothers, Ernie, Patrick, Vito, and Jay.

The bombers wore headsets, listening to a simultaneous translation of Smith's words. Their faces were expressionless. Salameh dug a finger into his nose, then wiped his hand on his pants.

"Through testing, we learned we would have a boy. We named our son Eddie. From then on I would come home at night and sing to our baby, as Monica, Eddie, and myself lay in bed too excited about life to sleep. We had fixed our house from top to bottom. We visited the doctor together and listened to the baby's heart beating contentedly inside his mom. Near the end of February, with just a few months to go before Eddie was due, we went shopping for baby furniture."

The defendants each had protested that they were unable to be represented by a new counsel for the sentencing. Each had fired his trial attorney and chosen William Kunstler for the sentencing.

Judge Duffy said Kunstler couldn't represent them all because he would have divided loyalties: what if one of his clients wanted to cooperate with the government at the expense of another? The defendants gnashed their teeth at the judge's ruling. But when Smith spoke, they seemed bored and distant.

"Then came February 26, 1993. The day started out exciting and happy as I was coming home from a business trip to be with Monica and Eddie.

"I can remember it better than yesterday. A fellow employee walked into a meeting and said there was a fire at the World Trade Center. A few minutes later the employee came back in and told me that it was not a fire, but an explosion. I immediately called Monica's office. There was no answer. And there would never be an answer. I raced in my car for New York, calling everyone, anyone, to see if they had heard from Monica. They had not. At 11 P.M., Monica's best friend's mom called the New York City morgue, and the worst part of my life started. I was told that I should come right away.

"I asked the man on the phone: 'What about my son?'

" 'Sir,' he said, 'do you know how bad it was?'

"Nobody could have ever prepared me for the feelings I was experiencing. I had lost my wife, my best friend, my idol, and my son. I would never get the chance to tell Monica how much I loved her. I would never get to tell her what an inspiration she had been. I would never get to tell her what a best friend meant to me. We would never get the opportunity to hold baby Eddie in our arms. We would never get to hear Eddie say his first word, to say 'mommy,' 'daddy,' 'love.' We would never get the opportunity to see Eddie walk or go to school. We would never see Eddie grow up and experience all the love, respect, friendship that parents share with a child."

Once again, the entrance to the courthouse was heavily barricaded. The sentencing day seemed another likely moment for a terrorist attack. Indeed, Salameh had sent greetings around the world to fundamentalist Muslims.

"We lost all this because the four men you are to sentence today wanted to terrorize the people of the United States. I always ask myself what type of person shows no regard for human life and would bomb the most populated buildings in the world.

"What God would want people to die in his name?"

Alone of the families of the dead, Smith had come to the trial and the sentencing. The day before, he had received a call from Louise Knapp, the widow of Steve Knapp. The Knapps had been at Ed and Monica's wedding. Louise had baked eggplant parmigiana for Monica as a treat during her pregnancy, sending it to work with Steve. But she had avoided the trial and the prosecutions, as had her two children. She read in the newspaper that Ed would be speaking in court. "Are you going to be there in court by yourself?" asked Louise, anxiously. Ed assured her that he would have his mother and Monica's brothers alongside him.

John DiGiovanni's eighty-year-old mother had sent a letter to the judge, describing the horrible death of her son, and calling for justice. As she explained to a friend at the Port Authority: "I would like to split them open like chickens." However closely Ed Smith agreed with her, he carefully measured his words as he spoke that day.

"I have two final remarks. First, to Judge Duffy: On behalf of our nation of laws, Your Honor conducted a trial here that focused on a long, difficult, and perhaps abstract body of evidence.

"Judge Duffy, we ask that you remember the crimes committed just a few blocks away from this courtroom were not abstractions. As you deliver sentence, we ask that you remember that these crimes are not, in the end, about a VIN number found in rubble; or chemical swabs taken from a storage locker; or any of the volumes of evidence that have brought us to this day. The crime is not the sum of concrete destroyed, pipes smashed, or millions spent.

"We who have buried our dead without a chance to lay a comforting hand on their heads ask that you remember this bombing was an act of multiple murder."

Ed's mother dabbed her eyes. She had fixed his hair just before he walked into the well of the court. The killers did not look at him.

"Lastly, to those who committed this act, those here in this courtroom, and those around the world: Remember this day.

"And whether you live out your days in a federal penitentiary or on the run, remember these names.

"They will follow you always.

"Robert Kirkpatrick, husband, uncle, friend, born 1933, died February 26, 1993.

"William Macko, husband, father, born 1946, died February 26, 1993.

"Stephen Knapp, husband, father, born 1946, died February 26, 1993.

"John DiGiovanni, son, uncle, friend, born 1948, died February 26, 1993.

"Wilfredo Mercado, son, father, husband, born 1956, died February 26, 1993.

"Monica Rodriguez Smith, daughter, wife, expectant mother, best friend, born 1958, died February 26, 1993.

"Our son, Edward, died February 26, 1993, never born, except in our hearts."

Judge Duffy calculated how many years each of the victims could have expected to live and sentenced each bomber to a year in prison for each year of life they deprived their victims. The sentencing went on for hours, as each defendant made lengthy speeches. Ahmad Ajaj spoke for three hours about the history of Zionism. Mohammad Salameh complained that he had not been allowed to take a shower before the sentencing. Nidal Ayyad promised that the only constitution was the Koran. Mahmud Abouhalima complained that a piece of Express Mail had not gotten to him in timely fashion. They said virtually nothing about the evidence against them, and only Ajaj spoke directly of the crime, calling the bombing a "horrible" crime.

About halfway through, the judge called a lunch break. Ed Smith walked out of the courtroom with his family. They decided to go for a beer on Queens Boulevard. They sped off in a Port Authority van, past the window of J&R Music where Mahmud Abouhalima had stood waiting for the towers to fall. The window was empty.

On Wednesday, the morning after the sentencing, Smith went to a law office in Long Island, signed some papers, and handed over the keys to the house in Seaford that he and Monica had rebuilt from scratch. With their home sold, he boarded a plane for the southwestern United States and left New York behind, escaping the skyline dominated by the Twin Towers that are, to him, giant tombstones.

The plume that trails Ed Smith, brooding in the air, smiling on the ground, is a love story, a tale that dangles in tatters from the New World Order, shredded by the ancient dementia of the fanatic heart.

NOTES

1   **No one would remember seeing the tall, muscular, red-headed Egyptian in J&R Music:** Abouhalima told of some of his activities, worries, and thoughts on the day of the bombing to his federal cellmate Theodore Williams, and the Egyptian military authorities, who submitted a report to American law-enforcement authorities. Williams was interviewed by one of the co-authors. The contents of the report were described to a co-author by a confidential informant.

9   **The World Trade Center sways in the breeze:** Description of the history and activities in the World Trade Center on the day of the bombing come from official records of the Port Authority of New York and New Jersey and from interviews with Robert DiChiara, Mark Marchese, Charles Maikish, and Stanley Brezenoff of the Port Authority, and Leslie E. Robertson, consulting engineer.

14   **"I need some of that good eggplant":** Interview with Louise Knapp, March 2, 1994.

15   **Ed Monteverde stood up:** Interview with Monteverde, February 27, 1994, by *New York Newsday* reporter Ray Sanchez.

17   **Sitting across from Steve:** Interview with Bill Lavin, March 1994.

18   **A purchasing agent:** Interview with Vito DeLea, March 1994.

19   **He went to sleep:** Interview with Port Authority Detective Sam Nordmark, March 23, 1994.

20   **At eleven-thirty, one of his friends:** Testimony of Joaquin Fernando Villafuerta, *U.S.* vs. *Salameh et al.*

21   **This van was not the largest:** Interview with Ryder Truck personnel, Jersey City, N.J., March 1994.

21   **This, in turn, would detonate:** Interview with bomb experts of the FBI, ATF, and NYPD.

22   **Timothy Lang sat:** Interview with Timothy Lang, March 23, 1994.

27   **Each kilogram of explosive:** Interview with Pers Anders Persson, March 1994.

28   **A "mirror" effect:** Interview with Leslie E. Robertson.

29   **was hit with the concussive blast:** Interview with EMS Chief Paul Maniscalco and Chief Medical Examiner Charles Hirsch, March 1994, and trial testimony of Dr. Jacqueline Lee, *U.S.* vs. *Salameh et al.*

31   **Lieutenant Matt Donachie stood on Liberty Street:** Interview with Donachie, February 26, 1993.

33   **New York City's 911 system:** Interview with NYPD spokesman. Tapes made available by confidential source.

40   **After ten minutes by himself:** Written recollection and letter of Carl Selinger made available by Selinger.

41   **He was agitated:** Testimony of secretary at trial of *U.S.* vs. *Salameh et al.*

44   **Sal Ciniglia, a Port Authority electrician:** Interview with Ciniglia, March 1994.

44   **Another man saw Secret Service agents:** Testimony of James Reilly at *U.S.* vs. *Salameh et al.*

44   **Him again:** Testimony of Pat Galasso, *U.S.* vs. *Salameh et al.,* and interview with *New York Newsday* staff.

48   **"to a window on hell":** Interview with Yasyuka Shibata, February 26, 1993, and interviews with Brezenoff, Maniscalco, and others.

48   **Ed Smith shook his head:** Interviews with Edward Smith, March, April, and May 1994.

49   **Robertson had first come to New York:** Interview with Robertson, March 1994, and trial testimony, *U.S.* vs. *Salameh et al.*

58   **The big redheaded man:** Trial testimony of Wahed Moharam, *U.S.* vs. *Salameh et al.*

60   **"Mark, you have to help me":** Interview with Mark Marchese, March 1994, and Charles Maikish, March 1994.

62   **A good thing for "Abdul:** Confidential law-enforcement source.

65   **"They should have gone to lunch":** Pamela Newkirk, *New York Newsday,* February 28, 1993.

65   **"How could you have let this happen?":** Interview with Maikish.

66   **Moharam could not understand:** Trial testimony of Wahed Moharam, *U.S.* vs. *Salameh et al.,* U.S. District Court, Manhattan, S4 93 Cr 180.

67   **The governor was there:** Details of law-enforcement organizational meetings were provided by confidential sources in attendance.

70   **twenty-seven callers:** Review of NYPD 911 log.

71   **Salem . . . was watching television, too:** Interview with Salem.

73   **Malcolm Brady would have been surprised:** Material describing the investigative methods employed at the bomb scene was gathered through interviews with Malcolm Brady, other members of the ATF team, members of the NYPD bomb squad, and other explosives experts.

76   **Donald Sadowy completely forgot:** Interview with confidential source in NYPD, May 10, 1994.

77   **Hanlin was what investigators called a "bomb guy":** Interview with Jack Hanlin, March 18, 1994, and testimony by Hanlin in *U.S.* vs. *Salameh et al.,* U.S. District Court, Manhattan, S4 93 Cr 180.

78   **the explosion had been caused by dynamite:** *New York Newsday,* February 29, 1993.

78   **the prime suspects were Bosnians:** Ibid.

78   **in the rubble-strewn ballroom:** Interview with confidential law enforcement source who participated in the search and attended the meeting.

80   THIS IS A PEACEFUL PROTEST: *New York Newsday,* April 20, 1992.

81   **Boser had been seated:** Interview with retired NYPD Lieutenant Walter Boser, January 28, 1994.

81   **scattering evidence over 845 square miles:** *The Fall of Pan Am Flight 103: Inside the Lockerbie Investigation,* by Steven Emerson and Brian Duffy (New York: G. P. Putnam's Sons, 1990), page 43.

82   **a radio cassette player:** Ibid., page 175.

86   **a piece of a Rockmaster blasting cap:** Incident report on the bombing, prepared by the Federal Bureau of Alcohol, Tobacco and Firearms.

87   **some crude timing device:** Ibid.

89   **A microphone was taped to his body:** Atkinson's dialogue and statements are drawn from his testimony in *U.S.* vs. *Salameh et al.,* U.S. District Court, Manhattan, S4 93 Cr 180.

92   **"This has got to be him":** All dialogue from the rental agency office was taken from a transcript of the FBI's secret tape recordings of the conversation between Salameh and the undercover FBI agents. The transcript was admitted as evidence in *U.S.* vs. *Salameh et al.,* U.S. District Court, Manhattan, S4 93 Cr 180.

101   **had grown suspicious:** Interview with Melvin, March 4, 1994, and Melvin's testimony in *U.S.* vs. *Salameh et al.,* U.S. District Court, Manhattan, S4 93 Cr 180.

103   **"What's going?":** Confidential law-enforcement source.

103   **"These people we had under surveillance six months ago . . .":** Ibid.

113   **In the driver's seat:** Description of Kahane murder scene taken from *New York Newsday* account, testimony at the trial of El Sayyid Nosair, and statements made by Abouhalima to Egyptian authorities.

114 **Like Nosair:** Kahane biographical details from Robert I. Friedman's *The False Prophet.*

116 **The chief medical examiner:** Interview with Charles Hirsch, March 23, 1994.

116 **"I, Rabbi David B. Kahane:** New York State Supreme Court file, *People of the State of New York* vs. *El Sayyid Nosair.*

118 **On this street:** Interviews with spectators and mourners at Kahane funeral, November 7, 1990, in Jerusalem.

119 **Barbara Ginsburg, director of Kahane's Museum:** Susan Sachs in *New York Newsday,* November 8, 1990.

121 **The suspect, El Sayyid Nosair, was arrested:** Transcript, *People of the State of New York* vs. *El Sayyid Nosair.*

121 **"At this point it looks like he was a lone gunman":** *New York Newsday,* November 6, 1990.

122 **Ronald Kuby had an uncomfortable secret:** Interview with Ronald Kuby, February 24, 1994, and interview with Michael Warren, April 6, 1994.

124 **"I am innocent":** Note was submitted as evidence in *People of the State of New York* vs. *Sayyid Nosair.*

126 **In all, the cops seized forty-nine boxes of evidence:** Confidential source, NYPD Detective Bureau.

126 **plus a suspected "hit list":** *People of the State of New York* vs. *Sayyid Nosair.*

127 **even did a little detective work of their own:** Robert I. Friedman, *Village Voice,* November 5, 1991.

130 **what it lacked: a motive:** Interview with William Kunstler, February 24, 1994.

136 **During jury selection:** Ibid.

137 **there was something fishy about the case:** *Washington Post,* December 23, 1991.

137   **"If they want somebody to blame:** Ibid.

137   **Bernice McClease, later seemed to be under the mistaken impression that the jury had actually convicted Nosair:** Interview with Bernice McClease, April 12, 1993.

138   **Kunstler had represented inmates during the riot of 1971:** *A Time to Die,* by Tom Wicker (New York: Times Books, 1975), page 78.

138   **He admitted that he had indeed killed Kahane:** Nosair's admissions about his role in the Kahane killing were reported to the FBI by Emad Salem. Transcripts of Salem's conversation with agents are included in *U.S.* vs. *Abdel-Rahman et al.,* U.S. District Court, Manhattan, S3 93 Cr 181.

138   **a virtual terrorist starter kit:** Interview with confidential law-enforcement source familiar with the FBI's inventory of the raid.

140   **Tears streaked down:** Interviews with Ezzat El Sheemy, June 22, 1993, and Abdukalder Kallash, March 16, 1994.

140   **"In the name of Allah:** Ibid.

142   **"Islam is the solution":** Interview with confidential source, Abu Bakr mosque, February 12, 1994.

144   **She was a lonely, sickly woman of thirty-three:** Interview with Renate Soika.

145   **"This mighty, decadent infidel:** Ibid.

149   **armed conflict was only the last resort:** *The Islamic Threat: Myth or Reality?* by John L. Esposito (New York: Oxford University Press, 1992), pages 32–33.

149   **If Islam was attacked:** *Covering Islam,* by Edward W. Said (New York: Random House, 1981), pages 107–8.

150   **Afghani veterans began feuding:** Interview with confidential law-enforcement source.

150   **it was receiving more than $100,000 per month:** Ibid.

151   **They circulated their own flyers:** Interview with Abdukalder Kallash.

151   **a single red hair:** Interview with confidential law-enforcement source.

152   **Abouhalima had driven his cab:** Abouhalima's admissions about his role in the Kahane killing were first made to Egyptian authorities, then relayed to the FBI. Details of these were given by confidential sources familiar with the Egyptian report and the NYPD investigation. Abouhalima's role in the Kahane assassination was also detailed in sworn statements made by Abdo Haggag, who is a cooperating witness in *U.S.* vs. *Abdel-Rahman et al.*, U.S. District Court, Manhattan, S4 93 Cr 181.

152   **Twenty-six Egyptians were given subpoenas:** Interview with Ahmed Sattar, March 4, 1993.

155   **"Dr. Omar says Mubarak should be overthrown":** *New York Newsday,* June 8, 1993.

158   **The bomb makers had a fit:** Material in this chapter describing the bomb plot is based on interviews with confidential sources, reviews of investigative files, and trial testimony, *U.S.* vs. *Salameh et al.*, U.S. District Court, Manhattan, S4 93 Cr 180.

158   **"What do you guys do for a living?":** Dialogue in this chapter is based on witnesses' testimony at trial, *U.S.* vs. *Salameh et al.*

160   **Salameh had always operated in Mahmud's shadow:** Descriptions of the organization inside the terrorist cell are based on information from confidential law-enforcement sources and sources close to the four suspects.

161   **Back home in Jordan:** Interview with Salameh's family in Jordan by Susan Sachs in *New York Newsday,* March 8, 1993.

162   **Salameh taped this aphorism:** Interview with Ashref Moneeb by Russell Ben-Ali, *New York Newsday,* June 16, 1993.

164   **began reading the Koran:** Interview with Ahmed Sattar.

164   **Their collaboration had ended bitterly:** Material that describes Salem's activities as an FBI informant is based on interviews with confidential sources, a review of tape recordings Salem secretly made of himself and his FBI handlers, and two memorandums filed by the U.S. Attorney's Office for the Southern District of New

York, *U.S.* vs. *Abdel-Rahman et al.*, U.S. District Court, Manhattan, S3 93 Cr 181.

165   **"They suspected me:** Interview with Abouhalima by Ralph Blumenthal, in *The New York Times,* May 7, 1993.

167   **Ayyad was from a strict family:** Interview with Ayyad's father and uncle.

167   **The original source:** Based on interviews with confidential law-enforcement and State Department sources.

170   **One of them was approached:** Based on information from confidential law-enforcement sources.

171   **Abouhalima was furious:** Wahed Moharam's statement to FBI.

173   **the yellow van emerged:** Details and dialogue at the gas station are based on the testimony of Willie Hernandez Moosh.

174   **a work in progress for more than two months:** The description of the actual World Trade Center bomb is based on interviews with confidential sources, NYPD squad sources, explosives experts, and testimony at trial.

177   **"What they are doing is:** Conversations involving Salem and his FBI handlers are based on transcripts of Salem's secretly recorded tapes. Dialogue is taken from those transcripts (*U.S.* vs. *Abdel-Rahman et al.*).

179   **Last time around:** Confidential sources and transcripts of Salem's tapes have described the circumstances of Salem's activities with and departure from the FBI.

183   **The newlyweds didn't have much money:** Interview with Barbara Rogers by Kevin McCoy in *New York Newsday,* October 3, 1993.

184   **Salem reported what sounded like a wild tale:** Details of Salem's allegations are contained in a confidential memorandum filed by the U.S. Attorney's Office and are listed as overt acts in the indictment for *U.S.* vs. *Abdel-Rahman et al.,* filed August 25, 1993.

193   **asked Salem to kill him:** Ibid.

198 **"In other words:** All dialogue between Salem and his FBI handlers appears in transcripts of Salem's secretly recorded tapes.

199 **sweep it for bugs:** Details of the second conspiracy plot have been provided by interviews with confidential law-enforcement sources and a review of court documents. Specific acts are alleged in the indictment for *U.S.* vs. *Abdel-Rahman et al.*, filed August 25, 1993.

203 **bankroll a massive grassroots campaign:** *The New Yorker*, April 13, 1994.

206 **When Shawki was killed:** Ibid.

209 **He had gone to the Egyptian consulate:** Confidential investigative sources.

209 **"It works by batteries":** Dialogue and description of meetings are contained in transcripts of Salem's tape recordings made as an undercover agent for the FBI in *U.S.* vs. *Abdel-Rahman et al.*

217 **A shaken Salem:** Interview with Barbara Rogers by Kevin McCoy in *New York Newsday*, October 3, 1993.

220 **Now Salem was reporting:** *U.S.* vs. *Abdel-Rahman et al.*, U.S. District Court, Manhattan, S4 93 Cr 181.

222 **This time they didn't hesitate:** Interview with confidential FBI source.

223 **Salem grew indignant:** All dialogue is culled from a transcript of taped conversations between Salem and FBI agents, *U.S.* vs. *Abdel-Rahman et al.*, U.S. District Court, Manhattan, S4 93 Cr 181.

228 **nearly a dozen TV crews:** *New York Newsday*, July 3, 1994.

229 **Before the van could pull away:** Ibid.

229 **a more tangible sacrifice:** Interview with Michael Warren, April 4, 1994.

229 **"If they come in, we must fight:** Ibid.

239 **At dawn on March 14, Abouhalima had been sleeping:** Details of Abouhalima's torture were provided by his attorneys, Jesse Berman and Hassen Ibn Abdellah, and by Abouhalima's statements to

Judge Kevin Duffy during and after the trial, and were confirmed by an independent physician who examined Abouhalima once he arrived in the United States.

242 **"You want a cigarette?":** Testimony of Louis Napoli, *U.S.* vs *Salameh et al.,* U.S. District Court, Manhattan, S4 93 Cr 180, January 1994.

243 **In the last year and a half:** various articles by Susan Sachs in *New York Newsday,* 1992–94.

245 **"I'll talk":** Testimony of Linda Traficanti, *U.S.* vs. *Salameh et al.,* U.S. District Court, Manhattan, S4 93 Cr 180, November 1993.

246 **Hosni Nagdi, risked his life and came out of hiding to give an interview:** Interview with Hosni Nagdi by Zina Hemady for the Associated Press, March 25, 1993.

248 **For the first month behind the tan walls of MCC:** Material describing Abouhalima's pretrial incarceration was compiled from confidential FBI sources, written statements by Abouhalima and Salameh to Judge Kevin Duffy, and interviews with Theodore Williams, a cellmate who attempted to mediate Abouhalima's negotiation with federal prosecutors.

248 **He made friends with an overweight killer named Theodore Williams:** Interview with Theodore Williams, spring 1993, Valhalla, New York.

250 **"He pressured me out of the case":** Interview in *New York Law Journal,* "District Judge Duffy Takes Tough Stance with Attorneys," September 14, 1993.

251 **Duffy left Abouhalima without an active lawyer:** Ralph Blumenthal in *New York Times,* June 4, 1993.

259 **it was already clear that the lawyers were not going to be acting as a team:** Details about the relationship among the defense lawyers and the relationship between the lawyers and their clients were taken from interviews with defense lawyers and the presentencing statements issued by all four defendants.

279 **"They wept as they were led away":** Details of the prisoners' reactions are taken from the prisoners' presentencing statements, a se-

ries of confidential interviews, and interviews with members of the defense team.

280   **"Director Freeh made the decision to place:** William K. Rashbaum, *New York Newsday,* December 21, 1993.

281   **He had wanted to be a hero:** Interview with Barbara Rogers by Kevin McCoy in *New York Newsday,* October 30, 1994, and confidential FBI sources.

281   **He told agents that the sheik had ordered the assassination:** Haggag's statements to the FBI were provided by confidential FBI sources.

292   **In the holding cells, where they could not be seen:** The description of the verdict was taken from presentencing statements of all four defendants.

INDEX